WHAT YOUR COLLEAGUES ARE

"This book is for any secondary content teacher, ELD specialist, or administrator seeking to create a lasting impact and improve the likelihood for long-term success for experienced multilingual students."

—**Crystal Reid**
English Language Development Program Specialist
Littleton Public Schools
Littleton, CO

"Every learner has a right to see themselves as capable, independent learners. This text certainly provides teachers with practical strategies, scaffolds, and structures to create perfect conditions for experienced multilinguals' long-term success."

—**Renee Nealon**
Teacher
McDowell Elementary at Petaluma City Schools
Petaluma, CA

"The explanation of the uphill battle experienced multilinguals face, even compared to single language/native English speakers, brings into sharp focus how much more critical our role is in students' success. Each subsequent chapter gives teachers an exhaustive toolkit in the strategy described to do just that."

—**Deanna McClung**
NBCT Biology Teacher, HS PLTW Coordinator
Elkhorn Area High School
Elkhorn, WI

"*Long-Term Success for Experienced Multilinguals* is a treasure of strategies designed to address inequities in ESL education, yet as a bonus, these strategies are ideal for struggling students as well. These strategies can be combined in numerous ways for a variety of lesson plans that can easily be changed as the students' skill levels increase so that all students can be successful."

—**Toni Ramey**
Biology and Chemistry Special Education Teacher
Gwinnet County Public Schools
Atlanta, GA

"Tan Huynh and Beth Skelton have created a resource that will increase academic success for experienced multilinguals. The book is timely and desperately needed in the field of education. It reflects the reality of language services for multilinguals as well as the professional learning needs of general education teachers. The 'From the Field' features are incredibly realistic and should assist teachers in moving away from a negative mindset toward multilinguals."

—Alice Collins
ELD Consultant
Denver, CO

"I think that this may be the only practical guide written to truly help the teacher of experienced multilinguals and provide resources that support and help experienced multilinguals progress and flourish. The authors guide teachers through planning, through collaborating, through revising lessons, and through resources."

—Patricia Payne
ESL Teacher
Evanston Township High School
Evanston, IL

"The book *Long-Term Success for Experienced Multilinguals* will make a great addition to schools' professional development libraries. Considering the growth in student population that now fall under the category of LTEL [long-term English learner], the book makes a great case for changing to an asset-based name and definition, while explaining clearly how to implement a new framework for instruction and assessment planning. The ideas presented in the framework are clear and structured in an easy way to follow and implement."

—Altagracia H. Delgado
Executive Director of Multilingual Services
Aldine ISD
Houston, TX

"From the first few sentences, readers can see that the authors know our students and their needs. They understand characteristics of today's students, their strengths, and what they truly struggle with. The vignettes could be my students, my schools, and my teachers. The authors understand how schools are structured and provide realistic next steps for teachers to put recent impactful language development research into effective practice."

—Jessica Martinez
Director of Multilingual Education
Eagle County School District
Eagle, CO

"This is a book I would recommend to my colleagues, administration, and anyone in the field ready to make that shift or strengthen their approach to a more asset-based mindset when working with multilingual populations."

—Michelle Kotwica
ESL/ML Instructional Coach
SD83
Melrose Park, IL

"The book is full of so many valuable resources and plans for how to improve teaching and learning. I wish all teachers I work with would read it and implement the strategies."

—Erika Chapman
ESL Teacher/Coordinator
CAISL
Lisbon, Portugal

"This book clearly addresses supporting former ELLs [English language learners] who are still not proficient and successful in academics due to a less than mature understanding of English. More importantly, this book systematically teaches a teacher how to explicitly support these students. The authors state their desired outcome is to help teachers support what used to be called long-term English users that they want renamed to be experienced multilinguals, and this book practically and usefully does this."

—Karen Kozy-Landress
Speech/Language Pathologist
Brevard Public Schools
Merritt Island, FL

LONG-TERM SUCCESS FOR **EXPERIENCED MULTILINGUALS**

LONG-TERM SUCCESS FOR **EXPERIENCED MULTILINGUALS**

TAN HUYNH • BETH SKELTON

Illustrations by Jen Giffen

Foreword by Jim Cummins

FOR INFORMATION:

Corwin
A SAGE Company
2455 Teller Road
Thousand Oaks, California 91320
(800) 233-9936
www.corwin.com

SAGE Publications Ltd.
1 Oliver's Yard
55 City Road
London EC1Y 1SP
United Kingdom

SAGE Publications India Pvt. Ltd.
Unit No 323-333, Third Floor, F-Block
International Trade Tower Nehru Place
New Delhi 110 019
India

SAGE Publications Asia-Pacific Pte. Ltd.
18 Cross Street #10-10/11/12
China Square Central
Singapore 048423

President: Mike Soules
Vice President and
Editorial Director: Monica Eckman
Program Director
and Publisher: Dan Alpert
Acquisitions Editor II: Megan Bedell
Content Development
Editor: Mia Rodriguez
Senior Editorial Assistant: Natalie Delpino
Project Editor: Amy Schroller
Copy Editor: Colleen Brennan
Typesetter: C&M Digitals (P) Ltd.
Cover Designer: Gail Buschman
Marketing Manager: Melissa Duclos

Printed in Canada

ISBN 9781071891278

This book is printed on acid-free paper.

23 24 25 26 27 10 9 8 7 6 5 4 3 2 1

CONTENTS

For additional resources related to *Long-Term Success for Experienced Multilinguals*, visit the companion website at **resources.corwin.com/Long-termSuccessforExperiencedMLs**

FOREWORD

Jim Cummins
University of Toronto

Over the past 50 years, many books have been written that review the research and recommend instructional strategies for students who are learning English as an additional language, typically labeled "English language learners." More recently, a handful of books and articles have addressed the challenges of supporting students who have been labeled "long-term English learners." This label refers to the fact that some multilingual learners of English progress through elementary school without attaining the (largely arbitrary) levels of English proficiency deemed necessary for them to understand instruction and thrive academically in a "mainstream" classroom.

As Tan Huynh and Beth Skelton point out, these labels are deficit-oriented because they define students exclusively by what they are perceived as lacking, namely, proficiency in English, and ignore the multilingual abilities and rich life experiences that students bring to the classroom. Despite the best efforts of educators, many of these students become trapped in a cocoon of questionable administrative regulations enforced by standardized tests that prevent them from engaging academically to their full potential. Inevitably some teachers are likely to perceive these students as less capable academically (and intellectually), and some students themselves may internalize these perceptions. The administrative and regulatory structures that have generated the construct of "long-term English learners" have resulted in low graduation rates, curtailment of students' life opportunities, and perpetuation of an education system that contributes to social inequality.

How can we extricate ourselves from this self-inflicted administrative quagmire? *Long-Term Success for Experienced Multilinguals* provides the most comprehensive, insightful, and lucid answers to this question that I have read (and I have been reading books and articles on teaching English for much of the past 50 years!). The authors adopt a radically different, and much more evidence-based, approach to supporting multilingual students than many of the approaches that have been implemented in jurisdictions across the United States and elsewhere.

They signal their orientation initially with the term *experienced multilinguals,* which highlights the linguistic, cultural, and experiential assets that students bring to their schools and communities. Throughout the book, they model the instructional approaches they recommend by scaffolding the content through crystal-clear language, transparent organization, engaging visuals, tables that summarize and synthesize information and lesson plans, personal accounts of their own practice, insightful observations and experiences of successful teachers, and narratives that express students' experiences, frustrations, academic breakthroughs, and identity challenges. Unlike many academic volumes (including some that I have written), engagement with this book is painless, invigorating, and inspirational. Furthermore, clarity of communication is achieved without any dilution in the accuracy of the research and theory that form the foundation of the instructional directions proposed by the authors. In a fundamental way, this volume illustrates the observation of 1960s communication theorist (or media "guru") Marshall McLuhan (1964) that "the medium is the message."

How should educators use this book? It would be ideal if policymakers at state and district levels were inspired by the book to revisit administrative regulations and guidelines that have been instrumental in creating the category of "long-term English learners" (experienced multilinguals). This would involve re-evaluating the assumption, operating at both elementary and secondary levels, that students in the process of learning English are not capable of succeeding academically in "mainstream" classes. This assumption holds true only in the situation where teachers in these classes are not prepared (in both senses of the term) to teach a student body that is characterized by all kinds of diversity (linguistic, cultural, socioeconomic, religious, racialized, etc.). Certainly, additional support from specialist language teachers can play a significant role in helping schools respond to linguistic diversity, but classroom teachers must also have the knowledge base and be familiar with instructional strategies that have proven effective in enabling students from linguistically diverse, low-income, and socially marginalized backgrounds to succeed academically.

Much as we might appreciate rapid action from policymakers to dismantle the disabling educational structures that produce so-called long-term English learners, we probably should not hold our breath that rapid action is imminent. However, even in the context of problematic policy mandates, educators within schools have the power to implement powerful evidence-based and inclusive instructional strategies that respond to the opportunity gaps experienced by linguistically diverse, low-income, and marginalized group students. The instructional framework I proposed (Cummins, 2021), which overlaps significantly with the framework elaborated in this book, specified six major instructional directions to address these opportunity gaps:

- Scaffold comprehension and production of language across the curriculum.
- Engage students' multilingual repertories.
- Reinforce academic language across the curriculum.
- Maximize print access and literacy engagement.
- Connect instruction to students' lives.
- Affirm student identities in association with academic engagement.

The development and implementation of evidence-based whole-school policies that pursue these instructional directions, and those elaborated in much more detail by Tan Huynh and Beth Skelton in this book, can produce dramatic improvements in students' academic performance (e.g., Isola & Cummins, 2020). I can think of no better starting point for schools that aspire to maximize the academic and intellectual potential of all their students than to read this book collectively and to develop school-specific policies and instructional directions that, over the medium term, may dispense with the perceived need for exclusionary labels such as "long-term English learners."

ACKNOWLEDGMENTS

If this book is the fruit of our labor, then we must acknowledge the many gardeners who lovingly nurtured it alongside us. We would like to thank Dr. Diane Staehr Fenner, who planted the first seed by enthusiastically introducing us to our loving Corwin team. We had a specific dream and vision for our book. When we met with Dan Alpert, our gifted editor, he could see the harvest we wanted to produce. Dan encouraged us from the initial meeting and even suggested we write the final chapter for school leaders to inspire schoolwide implementation of the framework. This was not originally in our plan, but it is essential for creating a culture of success for experienced multilinguals. Our supportive and talented editors, Megan Bedell and Mia Rodriguez, provided timely, specific, and helpful feedback throughout the writing process. We did not feel like they were a publisher but caring co-authors guiding us on the way. We also want to recognize Dr. Maneka Brooks for gifting us the term *experienced multilinguals* to capture the assets-based approach of this book. Lastly, we want to thank our illustrator, Jen Giffen, for patiently bringing to life the message through her careful and thoughtful drawings.

From Tan:

I would like to thank Tim Hodgeden who I have learned so much from. Much of what I have shared with you has been inspired through my collaboration and mentorship with Tim when we co-taught social studies. Our two years of collaboration continues to shape my practice and guide this book. Lastly, I would like to thank Beth for co-writing this book. I leaned on your many strengths, and your wealth of experiences elevated this book. I could not have asked for a better traveling buddy on this journey through the valley and hills. You cheered us all the way to the top, and when we arrived, we became family.

From Beth:

To my colleagues, Mia Allen, Mimi Allen, Erika Chapman, Alice Collins, Kira Cunningham, Sarah Davis, Amber Gonzalez-Cortes, Jen Hanson, Dr. Piedad Kaye, Michelle Kotwica, Jessica Martinez, Patty Payne,

Crystal Reid, and Ana Weiser, thank you! You and so many others are leading the work to make secondary education more equitable for experienced multilinguals. Thank you for encouraging me, reading drafts of the book, and sharing your insights and ideas with us. To my former middle and high school experienced multilingual students, thank you for sharing your many assets with me. You have enriched my life and inspired me with your stories, your cultures, your humor, and your grit. This book was written with you in mind. To my supportive husband, Peter, thank you for keeping me well-fed and the house clean while I worked on this project. To my brilliant daughter, Mari, thank you for reading and commenting on every chapter through your lens as an educator, linguist, and writer. To Tan, thank you for inviting me to co-write this book with you. You have enriched my life and my practice. It's been a joy.

PUBLISHER'S ACKNOWLEDGMENTS

Corwin gratefully acknowledges the contributions of the following reviewers:

Patricia Baker
Retired Educator/ Present School Board Chair
Culpeper County Public Schools
Culpeper, VA

Erika Chapman
ESL Teacher/Coordinator
CAISL
Lisbon, Portugal

Alice Collins
ELD Teacher
Denver, CO

Altagracia H. Delgado
Executive Director of Multilingual Services
Aldine ISD
Houston, TX

Dr. Ronda Gray
Clinical Associate Professor
University of Illinois at Springfield
Springfield, IL

Melanie S. Hedges
Art Teacher, NBCT
West Gate Elementary School
West Palm Beach, FL

Dr. Kemen Holley
K-12 Director of World Languages and English Language Learners
New Canaan Public Schools
New Canaan, CT

Michelle Kotwica
ESL/ML Instructional Coach
Mannheim SD83
Melrose Park, IL

Karen Kozy-Landress
Speech/Language Pathologist
Brevard Public Schools
Merritt Island, FL

Dr. Charles L. Lowery
Associate Professor of Educational Studies
(Educational Leadership)
Ohio University
Athens, OH

Jessica Martinez
Director of Multilingual Education
Eagle County School District
Eagle, CO

Deanna McClung
NBCT Biology Teacher, HS PLTW Coordinator
Elkhorn Area High School
Elkhorn, WI

Renee Nealon
Teacher
McDowell Elementary at Petaluma City Schools
Petaluma, CA

Patricia Payne
ESL Teacher
Evanston Township High School
Evanston, IL

Toni Ramey
Biology and Chemistry Special Education Teacher
Gwinnet County Public Schools
Atlanta, GA

Crystal Reid
English Language Development Program Specialist
Littleton Public Schools
Littleton, CO

Rachel Skinkis
Sixth Grade Math Teacher/ Former District
EL Teacher
New Holstein Middle School
New Holstein, WI

Jameelah R. Wright
Teacher/Doctoral Candidate, Teacher Education/Teacher Development
Montclair State University
West Orange, NJ

ABOUT THE AUTHORS

Tan Huynh (he/him) (tankhuynh.com) is a career international school teacher, consultant, and author specializing in secondary multilinguals and teacher collaboration. Coming to America as a refugee at the age of five, Tan vividly remembers the difficulties of acquiring a new language and integrating in American society while nurturing his Asian roots. This experience is the main engine that drives his work today. At school, he spends most of his time collaborating with teachers and in content-area classes to make content accessible. The rest of the time is spent teaching English language and literacy skills. Outside of school, Tan often presents internationally to schools and districts to support their work with multilingual students. Tan also hosts a blog, online courses, and a podcast about teaching multilinguals. With whatever time is left, Tan likes to work out, play badminton, and get lost in nature with his dog child. You can collaborate with Tan at Tan@tankhuynh.com and @TanKHuynh on Twitter.

Beth Skelton (she/her) (www.bethskelton.com) is an independent consultant focused on creating equitable educational experiences for multilingual learners. She has been working in the field for over three decades teaching elementary, middle, high school, and adult language learners in urban, suburban, rural, and international settings. As a university exchange student to Germany, Beth experienced first-hand the challenges that experienced multilinguals face when studying new content in their non-heritage language. She could communicate with peers but still needed additional scaffolds to successfully write formal papers, read academic texts, and comprehend dense lectures. This influential experience still informs her work with students, teachers, schools, and districts around the world. Through workshops, coaching, and consulting, she advocates for all multilingual learners, especially those who have years of experience. Beth also enjoys hiking, skiing, yoga, playing marimba, gardening, and spending time with her family. You can connect with Beth by email at ellbeth@bethskelton.com or on Twitter at @easkelton.

ABOUT THE ILLUSTRATOR

Jen Giffen is a Canadian teacher, librarian, and EdTech consultant. She has a master's degree in education from the University of Toronto and a specialist in education technology. She is a Google Innovator, sketchnoter, podcaster, and dad-joke aficionado. Jen seeks to ensure learning is authentic and relevant, especially for struggling students.

Tan: To my sister, who lovingly holds our family together.

Beth: To my truly special daughter, Mari.
You are a gift that keeps on giving.

INTRODUCTION

A note from Tan: My connection to experienced multilinguals started in my sixth-grade English language arts class. I remember my lovely English teacher asking students to read a short story from our district-issued textbook. My classmates each read an entire column of text and I eagerly volunteered to read as well. As I started to read aloud, I sounded like a beginning piano player trying to find the right keys and the correct combination, yet there was no music. I struggled to pronounce the words, read with intonation, and even decode some of the words. As I heard myself stumble over the words, I started turning red around my ears. I felt the judging eyes of my classmates, and when I reached the end of the first paragraph, my teacher rescued me from the drowning embarrassment and said, "OK. Thanks for reading, Tan. Who would like to read the rest of the column?"

I wasn't a recent arrival to America. Actually, I had been in American public schools for the past five years and even repeated kindergarten. My only formal schooling was in America. Yet, I still read below grade level. That was the first time I realized that I wasn't as academically capable as others. Like many experienced multilinguals we teach, I powered through, overcompensating by using my fluent social language skills to mask my underdeveloped academic English.

That experience is why I have teamed up with the incomparable Beth Skelton to write this book. Everything that I do now—from posting blogs, writing books, hosting a podcast, and consulting internationally—is to support teachers who teach multilinguals like me. I did not give up on school despite reading and writing significantly below grade level all the way through graduation, but many experienced multilinguals do end their education before graduation and many are not able to pass college entrance exams. I do not know what that sixth-grade teacher felt as she heard me painfully read aloud; she might have wanted to help me but did not know the best approach. I hope that this book offers a framework so that teachers feel confident in instructing their experienced multilinguals. With this book, I hope experienced multilinguals feel more capable at school and their competence blossoms into confidence. This is only possible through the dedication of teachers, like yourself, who invested time in reading this book to add to your already polished craft.

A note from Beth: *I consider myself an experienced multilingual in my second language, German. I began learning this language in high school and studied it in college. By my junior year of college, I had gained enough German proficiency to qualify for a year of study at a German university. When I arrived at the university, I felt confident chatting with Germans in the dorms and cafeteria, but when I went to my first class, a health psychology course, I felt like the professor was speaking in a different language. I struggled to understand the highly technical vocabulary and long, convoluted sentences used in the lecture. I became quickly fatigued while reading articles for homework, and I had difficulty writing the required reports. I regularly made embarrassing mistakes when discussing class content, like calling an escalator a wheelchair. I just did not have the academic German skills I needed to express myself or comprehend college-level content. I began to question my intelligence and lost confidence in my ability to succeed. However, with the encouragement and support from patient German friends and classmates, who revised my papers and helped me understand the readings, I eventually passed my courses.*

This experience gives me great respect for experienced multilinguals, who have to work exceptionally hard just to make sense of content classes and complete required work. I know they too can succeed in their academic courses, when educators provide supportive scaffolds. Now in my workshops, coaching, and consulting, I share ideas for supporting these multilingual learners across the curriculum. I am honored to have partnered with Tan Huynh to co-write this book for secondary teachers who serve experienced multilinguals. In this book, we share a framework and scaffolds that would have helped me succeed and feel more confident from the very first day in each of my classes.

CHAPTERS OVERVIEW

CHAPTER 1: AN AFFIRMING SHIFT

This first chapter will address the term currently used to describe this subgroup of students (*long-term English learners* [LTELs]) and the rationale for addressing them as *experienced multilinguals* instead. With this new term, we make a shift from a deficit mindset regarding these students and focus instead on their linguistic, cultural, and experiential assets. The chapter provides an overview of how the strategies in the book can provide experienced multilinguals the support and challenge they need to reach higher levels of academic English proficiency.

The chapter also offers two portraits of experienced multilinguals who are part of this diverse subgroup of multilingual learners. Tan and Beth encourage educators to teach experienced multilinguals grade-level content while developing their academic skills and literacy.

CHAPTER 2: INSTRUCTIONAL FRAMEWORK FOR EXPERIENCED MULTILINGUALS

This chapter provides the framework for planning instruction and assessments with a focus on academic English development through content classes. It explains the need for content teachers to teach academic language and the importance of teaching students learning strategies explicitly. Because many experienced multilinguals no longer receive direct English language development services in their schools, the only way they can continue to develop academic English is through their core content and elective courses.

CHAPTER 3: ENGINEERING SUMMATIVE ASSESSMENTS

Chapter 3 introduces the first stage of the instructional framework. We provide guidance on how to create the conditions that enable experienced multilinguals to be successful on final unit assessments. This chapter focuses on strategies for engineering the end-of-unit exams and project-based assessments.

CHAPTER 4: WRITING INTEGRATED OBJECTIVES

Writing integrated objectives for lessons with a focus on academic language development is the main concept in Chapter 4. We explain the why and how of integrated objectives across the curriculum. We share clear examples of these objectives from different content areas and the impact they have on learning outcomes. The "Try It Out" sections throughout the chapter break down the process of writing an integrated objective.

CHAPTER 5: ESTABLISHING COMPREHENSIBLE INPUT

This chapter introduces five essential ways content teachers can scaffold content instruction to make it comprehensible for experienced multilinguals. Each section of this chapter provides concrete examples from different content classrooms of each of the five types of scaffolds.

CHAPTER 6: STRUCTURING ACADEMIC OUTPUT

The penultimate chapter addresses ways teachers can extend experienced multilinguals' oral and written output in the classroom. We present scaffolds for vocabulary, complex sentence structures, and academic discourse patterns that encourage secondary multilinguals to express, both verbally and in writing, their understanding of increasingly complex content.

CHAPTER 7: COLLABORATING FOR LONG-TERM SUCCESS

The closing chapter provides school leaders (principals, coaches, coordinators, department leads, etc.) with a suggested sequence of actions to methodically implement the instructional framework in this book schoolwide. This chapter shows how teachers can collaborate to amplify the linguistic, cultural, and experiential assets of experienced multilinguals. Through collaborative analysis of student work, coplanning instruction, and lesson study, school leaders can create conditions for experienced multilinguals to thrive in every content area.

MEET THE TEACHERS

Throughout the chapters we discuss how secondary content teachers use strategies to support and challenge experienced multilingual students. In order to protect the identity of the teachers in each vignette, we have changed names and backgrounds, and, in some cases, we have combined experiences of several teachers we have worked with. However, the scenarios we describe remain authentic.

Mrs. Rivera (Chapter 1 and 7): Mrs. Rivera was born in the United States to Spanish-speaking parents from Mexico. As the English language development specialist at Graciela's diverse high school in the United States, she knows how to support experienced multilinguals. She identifies with experienced multilinguals like Graciela because she was also classified as an English language learner until she was in high school. Unfortunately, she does not have enough time in her schedule to directly teach students who are no longer beginning-level English learners. Additionally, she only sees Graciela in passing, at school-related events, or when she has to give her the annual English language proficiency assessment.

Mr. Nguyen (Chapter 2): Mr. Nguyen was born in Vietnam and educated in the United States. He has been a math teacher at an international school in several different countries in Southeast Asia for fifteen years. He understands the academic language needs of multilingual students because Mr. Nguyen also studied in English, which was not his heritage language. In this chapter, Mr. Nguyen follows our instructional framework to help all students become successful mathematicians who can clearly express their thinking and explain their processes.

Mrs. Maple (Chapter 3): Mrs. Maple, who hails from the Midwest, is an experienced international school teacher who is certified to teach science. She received little coursework on instructing multilinguals during her teacher college preparations. However, over her years of collaborating with English language specialists in her various international schools, she has acquired several strategies and approaches to scaffolding learning for multilingual students, especially at the assessment level.

Ms. Maita (Chapter 4): This Afro-Brazilian educator teaches art at a public high school in the United States. As a multilingual learner herself, she empathizes with her students and firmly believes in their potential to succeed in her class. She is certified as an art teacher and is working on her endorsement in working with multilingual learners as well. In Chapter 4, Ms. Maita uses a lesson planning approach that integrates both content and academic language.

Mx. Delgado (Chapter 5): Mx. Delgado is another Spanish-speaking teacher born in the United States. They teach design and have attended several workshops focusing on sheltered instruction for multilinguals. They share ways to make design concepts and its language comprehensible. Their experience shows that everyone is responsible for teaching academic language in order for students to be successful.

Mr. Ichiro (Chapter 6): Born to a Japanese-American family, Mr. Ichiro now spends his time teaching social studies at international schools. Before transitioning over to social studies, he spent many years as an English language specialist, so working with multilinguals is a passion of his. As a social studies teacher, he wants students to think like historians. So that his students can communicate like historians, Mr. Ichiro structures opportunities for them to speak and write using academic language. In this chapter, he shares strategies that structure academic language output.

Ms. Valladares (Chapter 7): Mrs. Valladares teaches high-school business. She was born in the United States, but her parents emigrated from Cuba and she grew up bilingual. She is passionate about working with experienced multilinguals and has seen their growth in her business classes. She actively seeks ways to support these students and challenge them to continue their education beyond high school, including leading the Latinos in Action club. In this chapter, Ms. Valladares shows the benefits of collaborating with the school's English language specialist and participating in lesson study as meaningful, relevant forms of professional learning.

FEATURES OF THE BOOK

The following special features in each chapter of the book are intended to make the concepts and strategies presented in the book more concrete and comprehensible. These features are just some of the ways we intentionally model the numerous teaching strategies for experienced multilinguals. They invite readers to write reflections and make notes directly in the text and encourage educators to frequently reference it when planning a new unit or lessons. These features are intended to create the best conditions for implementing the instructional framework to support experienced multilinguals. We hope that through this book, experienced multilinguals and the passionate teachers that serve them will experience *long-term* success.

Chapter Sketchnotes

Every chapter begins with a colorful sketchnote hand drawn by our graphic artist, the talented Jen Giffen. These sketchnotes capture the key ideas in the chapter, serve as a visual summary of the information in the chapter, and model one way teachers and students can use sketchnotes to make content more comprehensible.

Student Portraits

Each chapter begins and ends with a short story of a secondary multilingual student and their successes and challenges in a grade-level content class. We follow two different students, Min Woo (Korean) and Graciela (born in the United States to parents from Mexico), through a middle school or high school day as they meet the integrated objectives of different classes.

Image source: iStock.com/gigavector

We have developed charts, tables, and graphics that summarize and illustrate key points. These figures also serve as models for summarizing.

From the Field

These stories come from our and other teachers' experiences in schools and share another perspective on the topics in the chapter.

Try It Out

These boxes ask questions that encourage teachers to try the strategies discussed and apply them to their own classes.

Reflections

These reflection questions at the end of each chapter encourage teachers and leaders to reflect on their own practice. These questions could be stimuli for department meetings, professional learning communities, or a book study.

Templates

These templates can be downloaded and customized. (Visit **resources.corwin.com/Long-termSuccessforExperiencedMLs.**) They are designed as a resource for educators as they work with experienced multilinguals across the curriculum.

Appendices

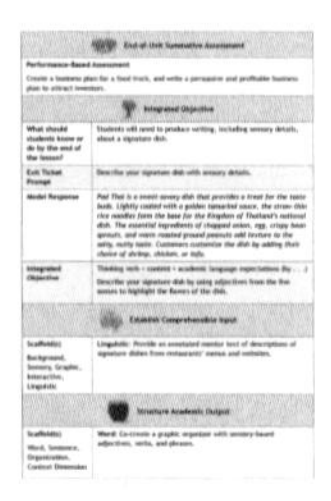

These additional resources consist of

- a chart with verbs, definitions, and some related sentence frames; and
- completed lesson plans from seven different content areas that follow the instructional framework presented in the book.

1

AN AFFIRMING SHIFT

A high school English language development teacher walks into the Grade 10 English Language Arts class. Graciela sinks into her chair upon seeing the teacher, Mrs. Rivera. The teacher gently taps Graciela on the shoulder. "Hola, Graciela. It's time for the annual English language proficiency test. Please follow me." Graciela sighs and grudgingly puts away her class work, hurriedly packs up her school bag, and ducks self-consciously out of class, trying to draw as little attention to herself as possible. She always feels a bit embarrassed about taking the test every year, especially since some of her multilingual classmates no longer have to. She had just begun to understand figurative language in poetry and did not want to miss the rest of the discussion with her table group. Now she will have to do extra work to figure out what she missed. Every year during the state English language proficiency test, Graciela feels the same frustration. In the hall, she asks with some irritation, "Why do I have to take that test *again*? I speak English already, and I was born in America!"

Graciela was first identified as an English language learner (ELL) when she started kindergarten, because her mother noted at registration that she only spoke Spanish at home and an English language test indicated she was not yet proficient in English. In elementary and middle school, Graciela experienced a variety of programs designed to help her develop English, including two years of bilingual education and a few years of pull-out English classes. Now in high school, she feels comfortable speaking English in class and works hard to complete all her assignments. Although writing essays, presenting reports, and reading textbooks are still a challenge for her, she is proud that she is passing her classes. She thought she had also "passed" the English proficiency test last year, but her scores in reading and writing did not meet the state requirements.

Like all students in the United States who are classified as an English language learner, Graciela has to take an English proficiency test every year until she meets certain criteria. Yet, her peers and teachers would not know that she is still considered an English learner as her spoken and social English is on par with her classmates. Until she is **"reclassified"** as English proficient, she will be required to take the yearly test to assess her English language proficiency in listening, speaking, reading, and writing.

Reclassified: When students classified as English language learners (ELLs) achieve a state-required level of English proficiency and receive the status "fully English proficient (FEP)." This process is also known as "redesignation" or "exit" in some states.

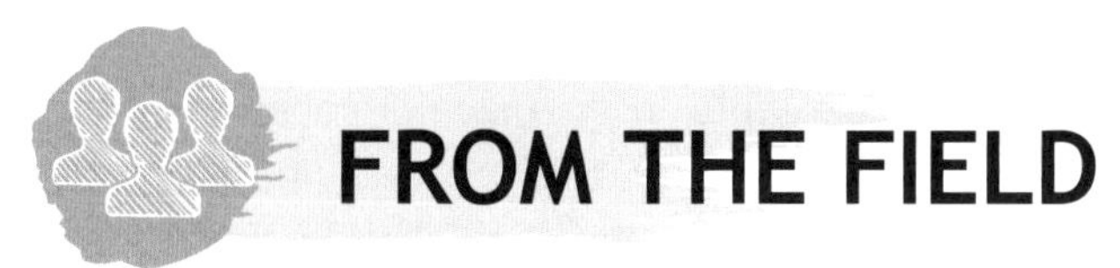

English Language Proficiency Testing

Jackie Doner-Campbell teaches experienced multilinguals in the United States. She recently posted on Facebook the following note about her experience during the annual English language proficiency testing period.

"I had such a hard day at school today. It started with one of my LTEL students expressing their frustration about still being in the program and then saying it's because he is dumb. I tried my best to help him reframe that, but it's so hard. This student is truly smart and has a lot of knowledge and vocabulary, but has not done well on tests."

In this chapter, we describe a specific group of multilingual learners in Grades 6 through 12 who are currently classified as long-term English learners (LTELs). These multilingual learners have been studying in English for six or more years but are still classified as "English language learners" (Every Student Succeeds Act, 2015, p. 163). In the United States, these students still have the right to language assistance programs (U.S. Department of Justice & U.S. Department of Education [USDOJ & USDOE], 2015). When schools fail to provide students with appropriate services, this can be seen as a violation of students' civil rights to equitable learning (Calderón et al., 2020). While continuing to offer direct English language development classes for these secondary multilinguals is one way to provide appropriate services, this book focuses on the scaffolds and appropriate grade-level expectations all content teachers across the curriculum can provide. We believe all teachers need to understand this diverse group of students so they can serve their needs.

We have designed this chapter to build background knowledge about these secondary multilingual learners so their math, science, social studies, language arts, and other content area teachers can meet their needs. First, we situate this group of English language learners within the bigger picture of multilingual learners. Then, we provide some insights into the state and federal requirements that these students need to meet in order to be considered as English proficient. We ask educators to consider how these requirements impact their own students and their perception of their students, who are labeled as LTELs. Later, we address the research about how long it takes to develop grade-level academic language skills and the issue of the overrepresentation of these students in special education. Finally, we propose a new, asset-based term for this growing population of students: *experienced multilinguals*. We highlight the linguistic, cultural, and experiential assets these students bring to their schools and communities. We will close by introducing two experienced multilingual students who will be featured throughout the book.

As you read, consider this series of guiding questions:

- Who are multilingual learners?
- Who are long-term English learners, and how are they classified?
- What are the impacts of the LTEL label?
- How long does it take to develop proficiency in English?
- How did the COVID-19 pandemic impact secondary multilinguals?
- Who are experienced multilinguals?
- Why and how should teachers get to know the experienced multilinguals in their classes?

WHO ARE MULTILINGUAL LEARNERS?

Multilingual learners comprise a growing population of students in classrooms across the United States and around the world. In fact, people who speak more than one language make up the majority of the world's population (Gration, 2021).

> Around the world, being multilingual is the norm, not the exception.

The umbrella term **multilingual learner** (ML) includes all students who speak more than one language. In this book, we apply this term to students learning in schools where English is the primary language of instruction and "whose parent or guardian reports speaking one or more languages other than English at home" (Snyder & Staehr Fenner, 2021, p. 2).

Some of these multilinguals may already be considered English proficient, but many are still developing the English proficiency necessary

---

Multilingual learners: Students who speak more than one language

to succeed in schools where English is the primary language of instruction, also known as English-medium schools. Multilingual learners who are still developing English proficiency now represent over 10 percent of total school enrollment in the United States (National Center for Education Statistics, 2021). As shown in Figure 1.1, the term *multilingual learner* comprises a veritable alphabet soup of labels for different groups of students, each with unique backgrounds, assets, and educational needs. With this book, we hope to share the central message that multilingual learners are diverse and dynamic; they bring tremendous assets to the classroom and enrich the educational experience for all learners.

1.1 Categories of Multilingual Learners With Some Terms Used by States, Organizations, and Countries

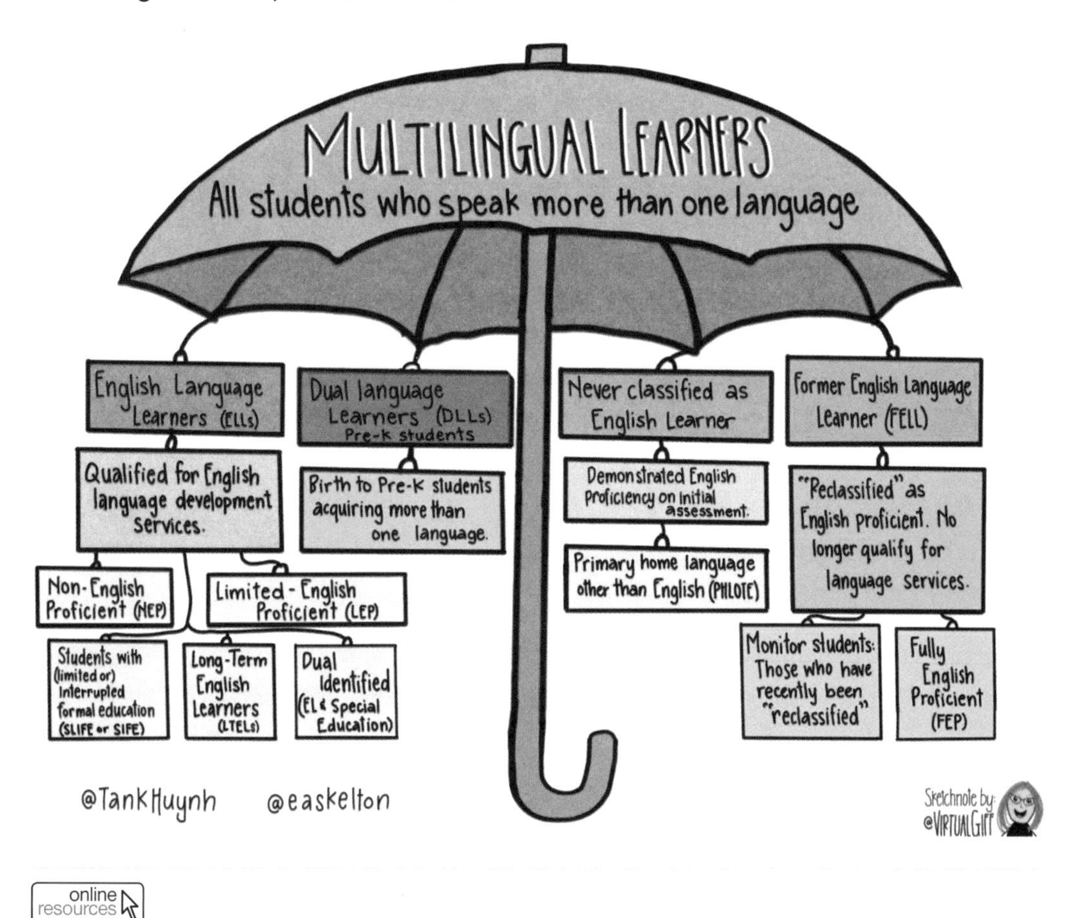

online resources

English-medium schools: Schools where English is the primary language of instruction

WHO ARE LONG-TERM ENGLISH LEARNERS, AND HOW ARE THEY CLASSIFIED?

The term *long-term English learner (LTEL)* has been used in the United States for over two decades to distinguish between newcomers, refugees, and other beginning-level English language learners and students like Graciela who have attended school in English for many years. They no longer need the type of support provided in newcomer English language classes, but they still do need appropriate scaffolds and grade-level challenges in order to continue developing their academic English skills and content knowledge. Because these secondary multilinguals have experience in English and understand the culture of their schools, they possess different strengths and needs than students at more beginning levels of English language acquisition. They are often quite fluent when interacting socially with their peers and teachers, which may lead some educators to misinterpret their ability to comprehend class content and follow instruction without additional support. However, when their strengths are not recognized and their needs are not addressed, these students may not experience success in school.

In the United States, multilingual learners are classified as long-term English learners if they "have not attained English language proficiency within 5 years of initial classification as an English learner and first enrollment in the local educational agency" (Every Student Succeeds Act, 2015, p. 163). Determining exactly what constitutes English language proficiency, however, has been left up to individual states.

There is no nationwide, consistent definition of English language proficiency or federal-level data about students classified as LTELs.

Sources from regional and state agencies reveal that students with the classification LTEL make up between 25 and 75 percent of all middle and high school English learners in many cities and states across the country (Buenrostro & Maxwell-Jolly, 2021; Menken et al., 2012; Uro & Lai, 2019). Because each state, agency, and international school sets its own requirements for determining if a student has reached English proficiency, the numbers of students with this classification vary widely.

In addition to requiring a certain language proficiency level on a standardized English assessment, some states and international schools also require students to prove their proficiency through a body of evidence that may include standardized academic tests, passing grades in core content classes, and teacher recommendations (Okhremtchouk et al., 2018). It is possible that a student like Graciela living in California may still be classified as an LTEL, but if she were in Colorado with those same scores and body of evidence, she would be considered English proficient and no longer carry the LTEL label. In international schools, the determination of which students qualify for additional English language support services is made at the school level and varies widely from school to school, even within the same country. Some of the different ways states and international schools determine English proficiency are shown in Figure 1.2.

The various requirements for demonstrating proficiency in English indicate that the construct of English proficiency is neither static nor standard. It is no wonder that Graciela questioned why she had to take the English language proficiency assessment. Some students currently classified as LTEL may have scored at a proficient level on their state's English language proficiency test one year but unfortunately have not yet met the required score on a state academic achievement test. In other equally upsetting cases, they may have scored well on the state academic achievement test *and* the English proficiency test but received low grades in a core content class. Although many monolingual English-speaking students also score unsatisfactorily on standardized achievement tests and receive low grades in core content classes, they are not therefore labeled as English Learners. Students who are currently classified as LTELs clearly have a significant, inequitable burden of proof to be reclassified as fully English proficient (FEP). As Dr. Maneka Brooks states,

> "It cannot be assumed that the primary reason that [a student] remains classified as an [English Learner] is because of her English proficiency" (Brooks, 2016).

1.2 Requirements for Reclassification to English Proficient

Criterion	Explanation	Examples
English Language Proficiency Assessment	There are many different English Language Proficiency assessments used across the United States and internationally. Each has a different definition of *proficiency* based on different criteria such as accuracy, fluency, use of discipline-specific language, etc. Some tests weigh each language domain (listening, speaking, reading, writing) differently.	WIDA ACCESS or MODEL test, ELPA 21, ELPAC, LASLinks, EILTS, Oxford English, IDAT, Woodcock-Muñoz, TELPAS
Grades	Some states and schools require students to achieve a certain score or grade in core content classes. Individual teachers vary in how they grade, and the criteria for a passing grade can vary from teacher to teacher, even within the same department at the same school.	Course grades may include criteria not related to English language proficiency such as attendance, bringing materials, homework completion, and participation.
Standardized Achievement Tests	Some states and schools require students to achieve at a certain level on a standardized test in reading, math, and other content areas.	SAT, ACT, ISA, NAEP, PARCC, IGCSE, iREADY, MAP, and various state-developed tests
Other Requirements	Some states and schools also require an additional body of evidence to show English proficiency. In some places, a student may not be reclassified unless they meet all of the criteria in one academic year.	Writing sample, teacher recommendation, classwork, additional reading assessment

With the need to meet so many requirements for reclassification as English proficient, it is no surprise that these students comprise such a high percentage of middle and high school students. The tremendous variation in requirements students need to meet in order to shed the label of LTEL also means that students in this subgroup of multilingual learners are highly diverse.

REFLECTION

How has your understanding of students labeled as LTELs shifted based on the information presented in this section?

____

____

____

____

WHY IS THE LTEL LABEL PROBLEMATIC?

Unfortunately, students classified as LTEL are often viewed as a homogenous group of struggling learners; we know they are diverse and dynamic individuals.

Because the label itself indicates these students are taking longer than their peers to achieve English proficiency, a series of undeserving, deficit-based characteristics such as "unmotivated," "struggling reader," and "disengaged" often come attached to the label. The LTEL label itself is therefore problematic because it is deficit-based, and that perception can detrimentally impact students' educational experience.

The problematic classification of LTEL is not neutral and can "have life-impacting consequences for individuals" (Kibler & Valdés, 2016). If secondary content teachers perceive that students with the LTEL label are struggling, they may hold lower expectations or even over-scaffold lessons. As author and educator Dr. Doug Fisher says,

> "Teachers' perceptions become students' realities" (Fisher, 2021).

That reality for many students classified as LTEL is all too often classes focused on basic skills rather than challenging and engaging content. While the intention may be to support these students and "fill gaps," the result is too often unmotivating skill drills, knowledge-level questions, and less engaging content that leaves students further behind. When Soto (2021) shadowed high school students classified as LTEL throughout their school day, she discovered that they mostly completed worksheets in classes and rarely had the opportunity or expectation to discuss rigorous topics with their peers. Additionally, if content teachers believe these students are struggling readers, they may not require them to read the grade-level text but instead provide oral summaries or simply bullet points of the main ideas (Brooks, 2020). These well-intentioned supports are actually examples of over-scaffolding that reduces the rigor of the lesson so significantly that students are no longer challenged. Certainly, students who frequently experience these kinds of lessons and scaffolds may appear unmotivated or disengaged. When teachers think that secondary multilinguals cannot learn grade-level content, students may not be held to the same expectations. The lack of consistently high expectations and challenging content across the school day may also cause students to stagnate in their development of both academic English and content-specific skills.

When teachers think that secondary multilinguals cannot learn grade-level content, students may not be held to the same expectations.

REFLECTION

- How has the LTEL label impacted the way you instruct these learners in your classes?

- To what extent are LTELs held to the same grade-level expectations, or do they receive simplified assignments and assessments?

- How does your school collect data for this subgroup of students?

Students' educational programming may also be affected by the LTEL label. In some schools, students classified as LTEL are required to take an English language development class or enroll in specialized content courses designed for English learners, which unfortunately may restrict their access to Advanced Placement, International Baccalaureate, elective courses focused on a blossoming area of interest, or other challenging, upper-level courses. These specialized language development courses may also negatively influence how students perceive themselves. When one student who was classified as an LTEL was asked why they were in an English language development class, the student simply said, "Because we are dumb" (Thompson, 2015, p. 35). Additionally, some schools and districts require students at lower English language proficiency levels to take lower-level content courses as well, which can negatively impact their entire high school career. If students do not have access to higher-level courses, they may not meet necessary graduation requirements or college entrance expectations. An opportunity withheld is a door closed on a new world full of potential. One recent study of graduation rates across four different subgroups of multilingual learners found that students classified as LTEL had a lower graduation rate than even newcomers (Haas et al., 2014). Statistics like this confirm that many students classified as LTEL "have not been well-served by their schools" (Calderón et al., 2020, p. 23). In this book, we hope to shift the deficit-based narrative around these students, provide administrators with practical approaches for schoolwide supports, and set these students up for a more equitable educational experience in secondary schools.

> An opportunity withheld is a door closed
> on a new world full of potential.

FROM THE FIELD

Educational Programming

Beth shares an experience with an experienced multilingual who advocated for participating in grade-level English classes.

historia de ejemplo

When I was a high school English language development (ELD) teacher, one of my ninth-grade students approached me at the end of the first week of school. He respectfully requested a change in his schedule from my ELD class to the ninth-grade English Language Arts (ELA) class. I hesitated because his scores on the English proficiency test suggested he would struggle in the ninth-grade ELA class without additional support. I asked him why he wanted to switch classes and his thoughtful response moved me. He argued that he wanted to graduate and study at a university. He knew that the ELD class did not give him the necessary credits for graduation. He did not want to take both the ELD class and the ninth-grade ELA class, because he wanted to explore an elective during the ELD class instead. After I explained the situation to the ninth-grade ELA teacher and got her approval, I changed the student's schedule. I told him he could come to me for extra help at any time. He gleefully changed classes, and I never saw him for extra support. He passed the ninth-grade ELA class with a B. When he stopped by to thank me at the end of the year, I had to thank *him* for helping me see beyond a test score.

When identified English learners struggle with academics or seem to underperform relative to their peers and grade-level expectations, schools may begin the process of providing appropriate interventions and eventually identify a learning disability. While "timely and accurate identification of disabilities for ELs can be extremely challenging" (Sahakyan & Poole, 2022, p. 4), many schools around the world do follow a careful, multitiered process for identifying learning disabilities in multilingual learners. Despite these processes, many studies have shown that students classified as LTEL are overrepresented in special education compared with other groups of students (Thompson, 2015; Uro & Lai, 2019). In fact, a recent longitudinal study of over a half a million multilingual learners in a U.S. state revealed that up to 80 percent of students identified with a learning disability in elementary school later became classified as LTEL (Sahakyan & Poole, 2022). This overrepresentation may be due to the initial identification process or the later reclassification process.

The process of identifying and reclassifying multilingual learners with learning differences and disabilities is not the intention of this book; providing general educators with a framework and strategies for serving the needs of all students classified as LTEL, even those who have been dual-identified with special learning needs, is the intent. This book focuses on secondary content classes because "even if a student is found eligible for special education services, their academic progress will be influenced by the quality of instruction they receive in their *general* education classes" (Haas & Brown, 2019, p. 29). The framework and strategies in this book are designed to help teachers provide high-quality instruction in general education classes for all students classified as LTEL.

HOW LONG DOES IT TAKE TO DEVELOP PROFICIENCY IN ENGLISH?

Since one of the ways students are classified as LTEL is the length of time they take to achieve English proficiency, it is important to review the research in this area. The time multilingual learners need to develop grade-level English proficiency varies widely depending on many factors, including the following:

- Prior schooling
- Socioeconomic status
- Access to bilingual education
- The student's heritage language
- Quality and language of instruction
- Age of entry into an English-medium school
- Literacy development in the student's heritage language

Regardless of all these variables, research indicates that students require between four and ten years to develop a level of proficiency in English that approaches grade-level peers, if they receive comprehensible instruction and supported opportunities to speak and write across the curriculum (Collier & Thomas, 2002; Cummins, 1981; Takanishi et al., 2017). Based on this research, we contend that students who are classified as LTELs after just five years may actually be on an *expected* English development trajectory. Developing grade-level academic English is a long process just like mastering any complex skill. Although our society expects students to take years to master a complex skill like playing an instrument, when it comes to academic English development, we expect full proficiency after just a few years. These unreasonable expectations are then expressed in the deficit-based LTEL label. By stating these students are taking a long time to develop English,

the LTEL label indicates they have a problem.
We believe they have potential.

Of all the factors listed previously, the one teachers have the most control over is the quality of instruction. This book provides a framework so that secondary multilinguals can receive quality content and academic language instruction across the curriculum.

HOW DID THE COVID-19 PANDEMIC IMPACT SECONDARY MULTILINGUAL LEARNERS?

An additional factor that has impacted the time students need to develop academic English is the COVID-19 pandemic. The unexpected pandemic interrupted the formal educational experience of all students around the world for many months. Online and hybrid instruction, social distancing, masking requirements, and frequent quarantines made it especially challenging for multilingual learners to learn new content in English and forge meaningful relationships with their peers and teachers. Although schools did their best to provide students with the necessary technology to connect to online classes, many students, including multilingual learners, sadly lacked a consistent high-speed internet connection. Even when the technology worked, most teachers (we included) had little to no experience prior to the pandemic in providing engaging, comprehensible lessons with adequate academic language scaffolds in a virtual environment. Most students also never experienced virtual instruction. Teachers, schools, students, and their families were all in uncharted, unfamiliar waters. In addition, some multilingual learners also experienced food and housing insecurities (Lazarín, 2020), which impacted their ability to focus during online and hybrid classes.

The long-term impacts of school closures, online instruction, and lack of consistent face-to-face interaction with teachers and peers on school-age multilingual learners is not yet known. However, we can predict that two years of interrupted in-person education means that many students may not have received the consistent academic English support they needed during the pandemic. Students may experience the repercussions of these two years of crisis teaching for the next decade. For example, students who were beginning-level language learners during the spring of 2020 may not have received the necessary comprehensible input and support required to develop academic English at the expected rate during those first years as teachers were understandably careening from the whiplash of the transition to online teaching. Students who were already at intermediate levels of English proficiency at the beginning of the pandemic may not have had regular opportunities for interactions with English-proficient peers. Once schools went back to consistent face-to-face instruction, students could again more easily develop academic English and content skills, but those years during the pandemic will still count toward a possible future classification as LTEL. These interrupted school experiences will likely result in even more middle and high school students being classified as LTEL in the coming years.

Despite the challenges of learning during the pandemic, experienced multilinguals showed remarkable resilience as they participated in virtual classes while caring for younger siblings, cooking meals for their family, or sitting in a car outside a public library to access the internet. They may not have made expected gains in academic English, but we believe that these students gained tremendous life experience that teachers can now build on. Additionally, many multilingual learners supported their families financially and took on more adult roles in the household when their guardians had to work frontline jobs. This is the perfect time to reconsider the limitations of the LTEL label and shift our focus instead to the assets these students have.

FROM THE FIELD

Learning During the COVID-19 Pandemic

One of Beth's students illustrates the resilience and growth many students experienced during the height of the pandemic.

I had the privilege of tutoring several highly resilient students classified as LTEL during the pandemic. One of the eighth-grade students, Josue, decided to move back to Mexico to live with his grandfather because the school offered a fully online option for the fall of 2020. Josue continued to Zoom into school in the United States for all of his classes and signed up for extra virtual tutoring hours with me after school twice a week. Due to the time difference between Mexico and his school in the United States, he had to log in very early in the morning every day. During our tutoring sessions, he showed me how to navigate various websites, and I provided him with additional scaffolds for completing assignments in his core content classes.

After school, he helped his grandfather around the ranch. He fed the animals every day, cooked meals, and repaired the chicken coop. He played on a local baseball team and learned how to waltz for a friend's quinceañera celebration.

When he decided to return to face-to-face instruction in his U.S. school for the second semester, he successfully reintegrated into grade-level classes. He had improved his Spanish language skills, regained his connection to his Mexican culture, and passed his academic courses in English. The life experiences this student gained during his virtual schooling are irreplaceable and will certainly support his continued education.

- What … our students make …

- What have your students learned during school closures and virtual instruction that you could tap into during your content lessons?

____

____

____

____

WHO ARE EXPERIENCED MULTILINGUALS?

In order to focus on these students' assets, we are choosing to refer to students currently classified as long-term English learners as *experienced multilinguals* (EMs) (Brooks, personal communication, July 30, 2021). This assets-based term highlights the fact that these middle and high school students have gained valuable experience and that they already speak at least one other language. We hope to shift teachers' perceptions and focus the attention on the assets these students bring to the classroom rather than focusing on perceived deficits.

Labels matter. As Brooks (2020) wrote, "Labels impact the way in which educators engage with students and understand their needs and abilities" (p. 7). Therefore, we have chosen a label that aims to *positively* shape the way educators view these students. Experienced multilinguals bring many positive life experiences, linguistic assets, and cultural funds of knowledge to their learning (Moll, 2019). They know how to navigate multilingual, multicultural spaces fluidly. Teachers can value the experiences these students, their families, and their communities possess as important instructional treasures that play a central role in teaching and learning (Zacarian et al., 2021). The assets that experienced multilinguals, families, and communities offer include such things as

- having lived through specific historical events,
- a rich tradition of oral and written literature,
- personal experience living in different regions, and
- knowledge of various cultural practices, traditions, and beliefs.

Throughout the book, we will focus on what experienced multilinguals *can* do. We understand that they continue to need support across the curriculum, but we take an asset-based perspective on what these students can achieve and how to best provide that support. We believe their heritage languages, cultures, and lived experiences are valuable resources that enhance and facilitate learning (González et al., 2005; Little et al., 2017; Moll, 2019). Developing an assets-based mindset as shown in Figure 1.3 is one essential way to create long-term success for experienced multilinguals.

1.3 Differences Between a Deficit-Based and an Asset-Based Mindset

Deficit-Based Mindset	Asset-Based Mindset
• Experienced multilinguals (EMs) are not capable of learning grade-level content. • EMs' heritage languages hinder their ability to learn English. • EMs lack the experiences needed to learn this content. • EMs are reading below grade level so they won't be able to access the text.	• EMs are capable of learning and excelling in grade-level content. • EMs' cultures provide rich opportunities for curricular connections. • EMs' languages enhance learning. • EMs' lived experiences provide context for learning. • EMs who are less proficient in English can learn grade-level content with intentional support and graduate from high school.

We encourage educators to begin using the more assets-based term *experienced multilinguals* when referring to their students who have been learning in an English environment for five or more years. We hope this book goes a long way in achieving the wish Claravall expressed on his podcast, "Maybe ten years from now the word LTEL is gone" (EdPod, 2018). In its place, we hope that more experienced multilinguals will find the long-term success they are capable of.

REFLECTION

- How does the term *experienced multilingual* shift how you perceive students who have been learning English for five or more years?

___

___

___

___

- What would happen if the term *experienced multilingual* were used more often at your school?

___

___

___

___

- How would you explain the purpose and benefits of shifting to the term *experienced multilingual* to a colleague?

___

___

___

___

WHY AND HOW SHOULD SECONDARY CONTENT TEACHERS GET TO KNOW THE EXPERIENCED MULTILINGUALS IN THEIR CLASSES?

We recognize that this group of multilingual learners is as diverse as any other group of students. Understanding the complex identities of experienced multilinguals is an essential first step in successfully and equitably educating them. If secondary content teachers understand their students' rich backgrounds—including their vast experiences in and out of school, their heritage languages, and their cultural values—they can meaningfully connect their lessons to these funds of knowledge (Moll, 2019; Paris & Alim, 2017; Snyder & Staehr Fenner, 2021). Throughout the book, we will share concrete ways to make these connections to enrich the education of all students.

Therefore, we encourage teachers to spend some time getting to know their experienced multilinguals. There are many ways to listen to students' stories and learn about their educational experiences, including the following:

- Surveys
- Journal entries
- One-on-one interviews
- After-school or lunchtime chats

Surveys may seem like the most efficient way to gain this information, but we caution teachers to build rapport with their students first and only ask a few questions at a time. It is often more effective to ask questions about students' backgrounds that directly connect to the current unit rather than asking students to complete a long survey at the beginning of the year. Figure 1.4 provides some topics and questions teachers might ask students as journal prompts, in informal interviews, in small focus groups, or on written surveys. Although we include a variety of open and closed questions in several different categories, we advise teachers to be cautious asking questions about students' educational background and family. While this information can be valuable in informing instruction, it may also cause students some anxiety, especially if they are undocumented or have interrupted formal education. Sometimes asking the more open-ended questions like "Please tell me something about your education before you came to this school" or "Please tell me something about the adults in your home" allows students to share within their comfort zone and open the communication channels for follow-up questions later. We suggest teachers ask just a few of these questions at a time and continue building connections to their students throughout the school year through a variety of interactions. These interactions not only build relationships with the students but also help teachers design lessons to connect with their students.

1.4 Possible Questions for Interviews, Surveys, Focus Groups, or Informal Chats

Topic	Possible Questions or Prompts
Educational Background	• Where were you born? • What countries have you lived in? • Tell me about your schooling before you started at this middle school/high school. • When you were in elementary school, how did your teachers help you learn English? • Did you go to a special English language development class? What did you do in that class? • Have you ever had bilingual classes or instruction in your heritage language(s)? What was that like for you? • Did any of your teachers ever use your heritage language(s) in class? What was that like for you? • Did you change schools during your elementary education? How often? Did you change schools during your middle school education?
Linguistic Background	• Which language(s) do you speak with adults in your home? • Which language(s) do you speak with siblings in your home? • When you speak with bilingual friends, which language(s) do you use? • In which language(s) do you prefer to read for fun outside of school (texts, chats, games, books, websites, articles, etc.)? • In which language(s) do you prefer to write outside of school when texting, writing lists, sending emails, and so forth? • Which language(s) do you consider your most proficient or "best" language(s)? Why? • If you have a choice to read or write in any language in a class in school, which language would you choose? Why?
Current Academic Experience at School	• When do you feel most successful at school? Why? • Do you feel motivated to succeed at school? Why or why not? • What do you like about school? • What is challenging or frustrating for you at school? What kind of assignments are most difficult for you (essays, readings, extended projects, etc.)? • What is your favorite subject at school? Why? • How do your teachers support you? • What could your teachers do to support or challenge you? • What do you do when you are having difficulty in a class, with homework, or with a project? • Which classes do you think will be most useful for you in the future? Why?

(Continued)

(Continued)

Topic	Possible Questions or Prompts
Sense of Belonging	• What activities are you involved with at school (clubs, sports, volunteer activities, etc.)? • How do you feel about your peers? Do you feel respected by other students in your classes? • Do you have a group of friends at school? • Is there a teacher, coach, or other adult at school that you feel close to? What do you like about that person? • What is something you wish your teachers knew about you? • How do you perceive yourself as a student at this school?
Family	• Tell me about the adults who live in your home. • Who do you feel closest to in your family? Why? • How do you help your family or around the house (chores, work, child care, etc.)? • Do you have any siblings? Tell me about them. • What do you like to do at home or with your family members?
Other Experiences	• What do you like to do outside of school or school-related activities? • Are you involved in community organizations (church, youth groups, community sports, music groups, etc.)? • What brings you joy? • What are your hobbies or personal interests outside of school?
Future Plans	• What would you like to do after high school? • What goals are you most excited to achieve by the end of middle school/high school? • How have your experiences and education influenced your interests for the future? • How could this school best support your plans for the future?

Adapted from Dr. Maneka Brooks, Patty Payne, and the CUNY-NYSIEB Framework.
Available at **resources.corwin.com/Long-Term SuccessforExperiencedMLs**

Teachers in the United States may be surprised to learn that the majority of experienced multilinguals in their classrooms were born in the United States and have attended U.S. schools since kindergarten (Batalova et al., 2007). They may discover that some students no longer speak their heritage languages well and others consider English as their most proficient language. Most likely, these interviews and interactions will reveal students who are motivated to succeed and have high aspirations for their future (Kim & García, 2014). Through these personal connections, we can get to know the individuals behind the labels and counter the negative stereotypes.

TRY IT OUT

Student Interview or Survey

1. Create a set of interview questions for your experienced multilinguals that includes at least one question from each topic in Figure1.4.
2. Use an online survey platform like Survey Monkey or Google Forms to collect the information. Use the information you gather to inform your instruction and interactions with the students.

STUDENT PORTRAITS

There is no one "typical" experienced multilingual. The students highlighted in the following portraits are composites of many students we have worked with over the years. The following students provide a sense of the diversity and variety of assets experienced multilinguals bring to school. These student portraits provide a focus for our work and the strategies we present. Although we focus on just two experienced multilinguals, their educational experiences mirror many of these students. We acknowledge that the educational programming we describe for both of these multilinguals for many reasons may be considered out of compliance with federal requirements, but these portraits share the reality of many experienced multilinguals.

We will follow the students in these portraits, Graciela and Min Woo, through their school day and use them as examples of how teachers can support and challenge their experienced multilinguals. We believe all students will benefit by building on the assets of experienced multilinguals and offering appropriate scaffolds in challenging secondary content courses.

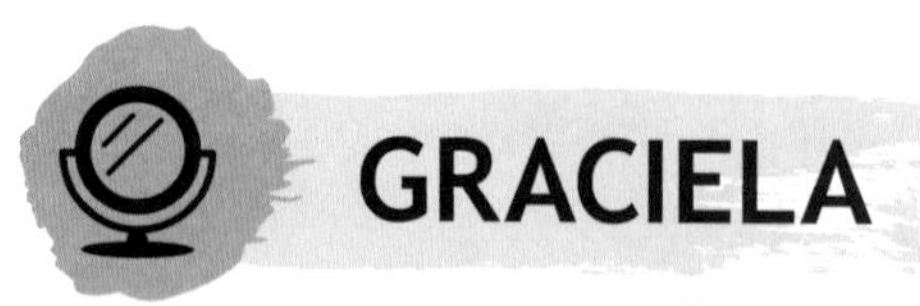

GRACIELA

Portrait of an Experienced Multilingual

Graciela is a hard-working tenth-grade student. Her parents are from Mexico, but she was born in the United States. She went to a bilingual school from kindergarten to second grade. However, when her parents moved to a new school district, she received pull-out English language development classes instead of bilingual education. As a middle school student, she received academic language support in the sheltered English language arts class but took all other content classes without additional academic language support. Now in tenth grade, she has no direct English language support classes.

Graciela speaks Spanish with her parents, bilingual friends, and community members. She reads shopping lists, menus, and headlines in Spanish but prefers to read books and magazines in English. She uses her complete linguistic repertoire (Spanish and English) when interacting socially between classes, at lunch, and at recess. On the weekends, she helps her father in their family store and interacts with customers in Spanish and English. At this point, she is interested in marketing and graphic design and is planning to study at a university in the United States.

In school, Graciela is motivated to do well but is often disappointed when her grades on projects and report cards do not reflect her hard work. She tries to complete all the assignments, so she wonders why her grades are not better. Occasionally she asks for extra help, but she is fearful of being ridiculed by her classmates, so she often slips under the radar as she tries to figure it out on her own or with her friends.

Talking with her friends is the best part of each school day. Graciela appreciates the opportunity to talk to her bilingual classmates about class topics, because it helps her understand content texts. When she has to read independently, she depends on visuals, headings, and key words to comprehend the main ideas.

Graciela would rather give an oral report in class than labor to write an essay. She knows how to write full, comprehensible sentences, but she needs more coaching and explicit instruction to write more like a scientist, mathematician, and historian. When teachers give her specific feedback on writing, she gladly makes changes.

Although Graciela is still classified as an English learner, she does not receive any extra support classes or work with an English language development teacher anymore. After ten years of education in the United States, she sees herself as English proficient.

MIN WOO

Portrait of an Experienced Multilingual

Min Woo is a bouncy, positive, and helpful seventh grader born in Korea to adoring Korean parents. Min Woo's dad works for a Korean technology company that has manufacturing plants throughout Southeast Asia. Min Woo went to Korean-speaking schools in Korea up to first grade when he followed his father as he worked on multiyear projects outside of Korea. In each place, he enrolled in international schools where English is the language of instruction. Fortunately, at these schools, Min Woo continued to learn Korean formally through after-school tutors and at international schools that offered opportunities to learn Korean. Understandably, his reading and writing level in Korean is not on grade level compared with other seventh graders in Korea. Not surprisingly, Min Woo has a more proficient command of English than Korean.

At home, Min Woo's family speaks Korean but everyone in the household is literate in English as well. Min Woo is highly literate in Korean for a person who only spent his first school year in Korea as a result of his parents painstakingly investing time and financial resources to grow his Korean language skills.

During free-voluntary reading time at school, he switches between Korean and English books. When speaking to Min Woo, one would see he is a fluent, confident user of English without any issues following his teachers' spoken instructions. Min Woo can decode and pronounce all words found in a grade-level text but needs support to comprehend the text. He can write in grammatically correct sentences and paragraphs but needs support in producing writing that meets discipline-specific expectations and to use evidence drawn from texts and video resources.

Though Min Woo does not qualify for English language development services at his international school, he still needs additional support to be successful in his content classes.

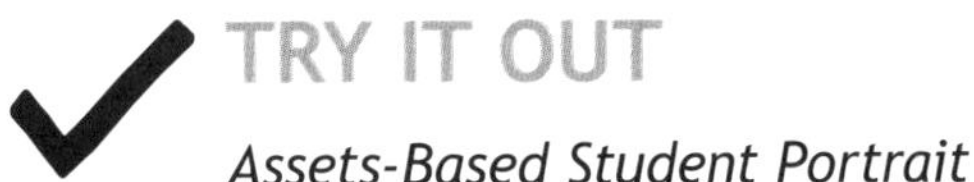

TRY IT OUT

Assets-Based Student Portrait

1. Use the information you gathered in the student survey or interview to create a student portrait that highlights the student's assets.
2. Share the portrait with your colleagues and encourage them to build on the student's assets in their lessons.

CLOSING REMARKS

This book serves as a guide for all secondary content teachers who are fortunate enough to work with experienced multilinguals. In the following chapters, we share a framework for planning and teaching so that all students receive appropriate support for both academic English and content learning. We stand by the belief that through the collective efforts of all teachers in the school, experienced multilinguals will have long-term success.

As Robinson (2010) explains, "Farmers and gardeners know you can't make a plant grow. . . . The plant grows itself. What you do is provide the conditions for growth." In Chapter 7, we offer some suggestions for programming that will create the conditions for more equitable educational experiences across the curriculum. We offer a systematic approach to collaboration that raises awareness, capitalizes on teachers' expertise during co-planning, and provides differentiated support for experienced multilinguals. We are convinced that if more teachers implement the equity-based framework in this book, they will create the conditions for growth so their experienced multilinguals can reach their fullest potential.

CHAPTER SUMMARY

- *Experienced multilingual* is an assets-based term that highlights the valuable resources these secondary learners possess.
- In many middle schools and high schools, experienced multilinguals make up a large and growing percentage of students identified as English learners.
- Experienced multilinguals have the right to equitable education that includes meaningful access to grade-level content courses.
- Content teachers have the responsibility to learn about the linguistic, experiential, and cultural assets of their experienced multilinguals.
- Experienced multilinguals are a diverse group of individuals with rich backgrounds.

2

INSTRUCTIONAL FRAMEWORK FOR EXPERIENCED MULTILINGUALS

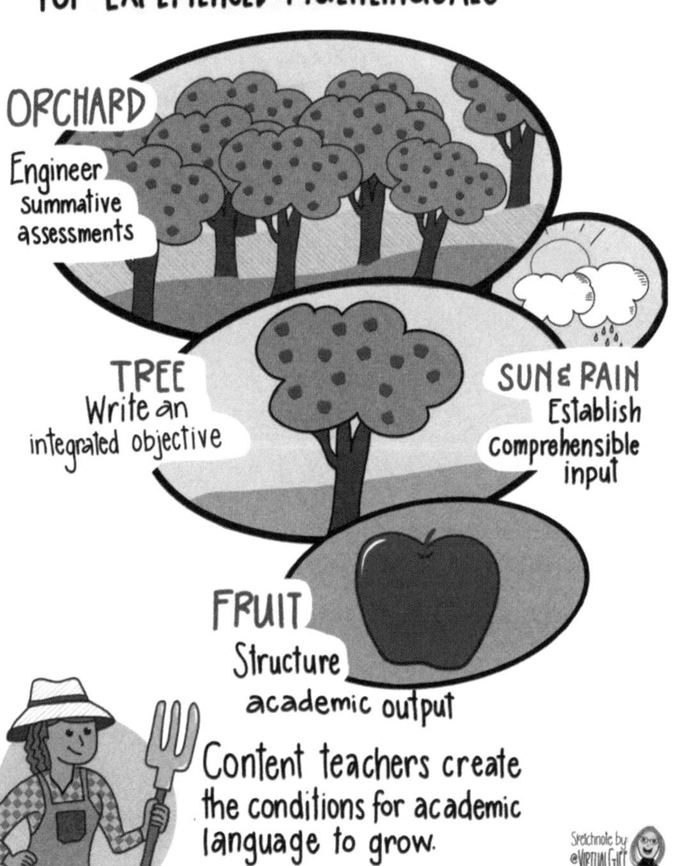

Min Woo walks into his favorite class, math, sits down next to his partner, and reaches into his backpack for the folder with the papers for their current project. They are learning to think like city planners by using angles and lines to plan out the roads and buildings for a new city. Mr. Nguyen, the seventh-grade math teacher, greets each student by name at the door. When the bell rings, he gestures to the board where the next step for the project is posted. To get the class started with the next step in their city planning project, he tells them to read the prompt with their partners, making sure to restate the directions in their own words or ask each other questions about the prompt. Min Woo reads aloud, "*Draw at least two parallel streets and two transversal streets to form acute and obtuse angles.*" Puzzled, he asks his partner, "What does *transversal* mean?" His partner points up to the poster on the wall with labeled angles and lines. They study the poster and then start talking about how they want to draw the parallel and transversal lines for their city streets. When Mr. Nguyen calls the class back from their discussion, Min Woo and his partner are ready for the next step.

Mr. Nguyen knows that several of the students in his math class are still classified as English learners, even though they have been in the school district for many years. Because he wants all students to experience success in his math classes, he thoughtfully provides content instruction with scaffolds for academic language development.

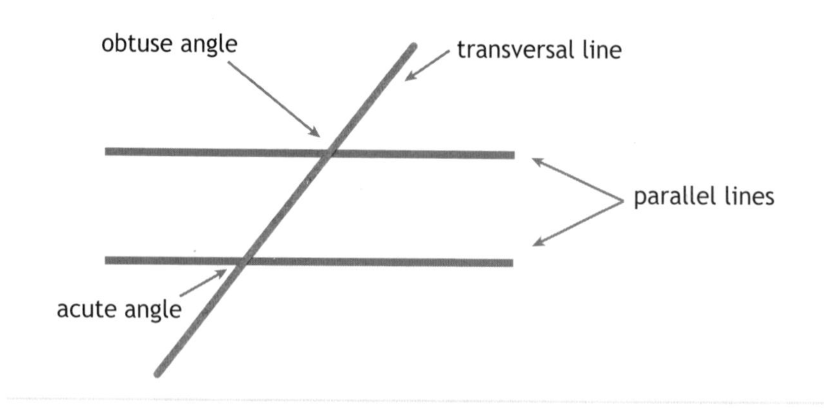

Scaffold: Anything that temporarily supports students in engaging in tasks that they would not be able to do independently (Gibbons, 2015)

In the lesson described in the previous paragraph, Mr. Nguyen used the following scaffolds:

- Labeled visuals
- Time for partner discussions
- Step-by-step instructions for solving problems
- Chunking the final performance assessment project into shorter daily tasks

For Mr. Nguyen's lesson plans on lines and angles, see Appendix B.

None of these scaffolds "water down" the grade-level expectations of the lesson but rather provide the necessary support so that experienced multilinguals can meet these high expectations. In fact,

> providing the right scaffolds at the right time exemplifies equitable learning.

In the hands of a skillful teacher, scaffolds stretch students' skills, proficiency, and confidence.

Since most of the experienced multilinguals in his class no longer receive any direct, specialized English instruction, Mr. Nguyen knows he not only has to teach the math curriculum but also the academic English skills required to process and communicate the math-specific ideas.

If teachers provide appropriate scaffolds, experienced multilinguals like Min Woo are capable of learning new content in English in grade-level content classes.

> As experienced multilinguals reach higher levels of English proficiency, their English development needs become less obvious, but the academic language demands continue to increase.

For many learners, these increasingly challenging academic language demands make them feel like they have finally reached an apparent summit on the mountain only to discover another higher peak ahead. Scaffolds give them support to reach the highest peak, even as the trail gets more difficult.

Some experienced multilingual students like Min Woo have greater proficiency in spoken English than in reading and writing in English. Therefore, when they answer questions and participate in class discussions, teachers may assume they will also be successful on the written exam. However, when these students do not perform as expected, some teachers may be tempted to label them as "lazy," "unmotivated," or "unfocused." We offer a different way of thinking about these responses and provide a framework that will address the academic language needs of these students in every content class.

In this chapter, we introduce the concept of **academic language** and advocate for teaching this type of language meaningfully within the context of the content classroom. Experienced multilinguals need high grade-level expectations coupled with high support to engage in content classes. In addition to teaching complex content and the academic language of each discipline, we suggest that experienced multilinguals benefit from explicit instruction in effective learning strategies. These strategies help students learn, transfer skills to other content areas, and become more independent learners. We share several of these learning strategies, which are anything a student does to boost their understanding of new content and use of academic language. Finally, we provide an overview of our framework for designing equitable content instruction that supports and stretches experienced multilinguals as they develop academic language proficiency across the curriculum. This framework serves as the outline for the rest of the book.

ACADEMIC LANGUAGE

Academic language is more than just vocabulary words. It includes complex sentence structures, transition phrases, and organizational patterns used for different purposes like writing lab reports, arguing a claim, or analyzing a poem. Each of these purposes requires students to use academic language differently (WIDA, 2020). When students learn the language to justify their choices of lines and angles in math class, they can transfer that language to justify choices in science or language arts class. Teaching this cross-disciplinary academic language helps students succeed in the long-term.

Honigsfeld (2019) explains that academic language is "not something students *have* or *do not have;* it is something all students *use* daily to

---

Academic language: Discipline-specific and transferable vocabulary, sentence structures, and discourse patterns needed to comprehend and communicate ideas in content areas

learn" (p. 49). While experienced multilinguals have generally acquired the ability to communicate clearly in most social situations, they are still developing the ability to use academic English. Developing this

> "academic language proficiency helps students achieve long-term success at school" (Dutro & Moran, 2002, p. 231).

Experienced multilinguals may also have different linguistic abilities in different fields and content areas (Walqui & van Lier, 2010). One experienced multilingual student may find the most success in a math class, while others triumph in social studies, sciences, or the arts.

The various dimensions of academic language are often described through an architectural metaphor as shown in Figure 2.1 (Dutro & Moran, 2002; Zwiers, 2008). The first dimension—vocabulary words and phrases—is like the bricks that form the foundation of the structure or text. Next, the sentence structures are like the mortar that connects the bricks to form the walls of that building or academic work. In the next dimension, the organizational features such as transition phrases and paragraphing conventions are like the roof, windows, doors, and interior design. As economics teacher David Carney says,

> "If students don't write with academic phrases and organization, their essays read like a pile of bricks; there is no cohesion" (D. Carney, personal communication, February 2022).
>
> David Carney

Finally, the context for the written or spoken project is like the neighborhood or community, in which the structure is located. Students need explicit instruction in each dimension of discipline-specific language in order to succeed on classroom assignments and assessments.

The bricks in Min Woo's math lesson are the words and phrases used to describe the angles and lines. The walls of this lesson are formed with the sentences that explain the relationships between the lines and angles. Finally, the entire house structure will be completed when he organizes his presentation. The purpose of the presentation will be to explain the location of each line. He will have to justify the

---

Discipline-specific language: Words and phrases specific to each content area

2.1 Dimensions of Discipline-Specific Language

Dimension	Description	Examples From Mr. Nguyen's Math Class
Word	• Technical vocabulary words and phrases specific to the content	Parallel to, adjacent to, opposite side of, intersected by, transversal, obtuse angle, acute angle, interior angle, exterior angle, corresponding angles
Sentence	• Sentence structures for different purposes (compare, contrast, explain, argue, describe, etc.) • Complex, compound, and simple sentence structures needed for an academic purpose	I drew ___ streets in the city center, because ___. I created an ___ angle in this corner, because ___.
Organization	• Organizational structures of discipline-specific texts such as lab reports, arguments, persuasive essays, etc. • Transitional phrases and cohesive devices that link one idea to another	• Present the city map. • Describe the position of lines (streets) and angles on their city map. • Justify why they drew the map with those angles with at least three different reasons and explanations.
Context	• Purpose for the project, report, essay, etc. • Students' role in the project	• Present to town council using formal language and style • Propose a street map to council members for a city expansion project

Adapted from Dutro & Moran (2002); WIDA (2012); Zwiers (2014).

Image sources: istock.com/da-vooda, istock.com/Antti Hekkinen, istock.com/Nadiinko, istock.com/yugoro

layout of his street map to the audience. The context or audience for this project is the presentation to the town council. As apprentice city planners in the math class, Min Woo and his classmates will develop mathematical reasoning as well as the mathematical-specific language needed to share their developing understanding. When Mr. Nguyen asks students to justify their choices for placing the lines and angles on the city map, the sentence structures and organization they use must justify their decisions, not just describe the lines and angles. As math teacher and author Molina (2012) writes, "the phrase *'the problem with math is English'* applies to *all* students, not just those whose native language is not English" (p. 1). Therefore, all students in the class will benefit from explicit instruction in using math-specific academic language to be successful engaging with this project.

TRY IT OUT

Discipline-Specific Language

Review an upcoming lesson or unit for two dimensions of discipline-specific language.

1. Words and phrases related to the unit
2. Sentence structures for the purpose students will use academic language (describe, explain, argue, compare, etc.)
3. Expected organization and any transition phrases students should use between ideas
4. Context for using academic language (Who is the audience? What is the students' role?)

REFLECTION

- In which academic disciplines are your content knowledge and skills most developed?
  - When you discuss topics in these content areas, do you use academic language? What academic language do you use that colleagues from other fields may not be familiar with? Think in terms of
    - discipline-specific vocabulary, — Level Power words
    - sentence structures, and
    - organizational patterns.

____

____

____

____

(Continued)

(Continued)

- Which disciplines challenge you the most?
    - Why?
    - How is the academic language associated with that field a part of the challenge?

CONTENT TEACHERS AS ACADEMIC LANGUAGE TEACHERS

2.2 Unpacking Academic Language and Content

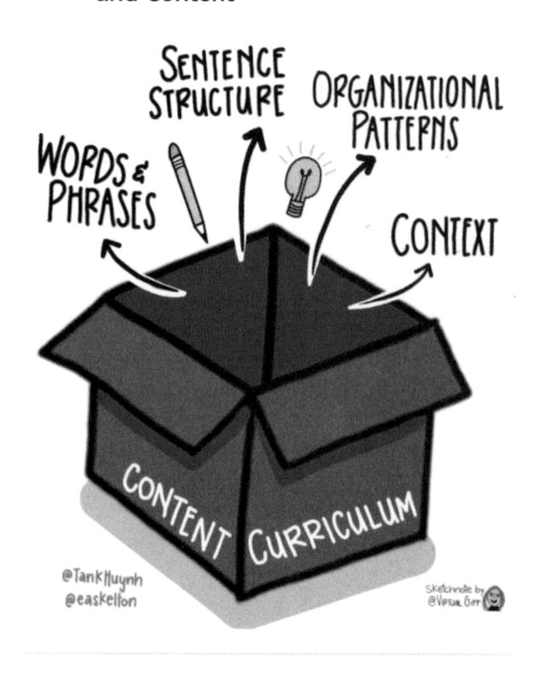

> We believe the most equitable place for experienced multilinguals is in content classes because they provide the fertile soil for both content and academic language to grow.

The visual of the box in Figure 2.2 illustrates the content curriculum educators are charged with teaching. Inside that box is the academic language of that curriculum. We value secondary teachers for their expertise in the field and deep knowledge of the content and mastery of specific skills. Secondary content teachers are well versed in the standards that guide their content instruction such as Common Core State Standards, International Baccalaureate

Standards, or the Next Generation Science Standards. However, they may need additional professional learning to unpack the academic language hidden in these content standards or "boxes" that hold their units and lessons and teach that language to their students. We wrote this book to be a part of that professional learning.

We know that many secondary teachers have taken at least one workshop or course focused on meeting the needs of English learners. In fact, at least 39 states in the United States require educators to complete professional development hours focused on the needs of multilingual learners in order to maintain their teaching license (Rafa et al., 2020). International school teachers are often encouraged or required by their school to take a course called Teaching English in Multilingual Classrooms (Dare & Polias, 2020). Typically, these professional learning courses provide an overview of academic English and general strategies for students at all levels of English language development, or they share strategies for newcomers and students with limited or interrupted formal education (SLIFE). This book focuses on the often-overlooked group of experienced multilinguals who have been learning in English for at least five years.

Experienced multilinguals develop increasingly complex academic language through their content classes with the careful attention and support of their secondary content teachers (Echevarría et al., 2017). If educators serving in middle and high school settings explicitly teach the academic language expected in written and oral responses, students will find more success. Linguist Schleppegrell (2004) suggests that students may understand the concept, but just do not know the academic words and structures to express that understanding like experts in the field. Explicit instruction in academic language will support experienced multilinguals in achieving across the curriculum as it develops their ability to express what they know with greatly clarity.

> Learning new content is inseparable from learning the language for that content (Gottlieb & Ernst-Slavit, 2014; Halliday, 1993; Schleppegrell, 2004; Walqui & van Lier, 2010; Zwiers, 2014).

Unpack academic language: Analyze academic language used in the curriculum to make it explicit to students

Mr. Nguyen understands that fact, so he designs his lessons with academic English development in mind. Even though Mr. Nguyen did not study linguistics or major in English, he can still teach both the concept of angle relationships and the mathematical language students need to successfully express their growing understanding of the mathematical concepts. This focus on academic language serves all learners. Since academic language is rarely used outside of school and professional settings, all students are academic language learners (Gottlieb, 2016; Ottow, 2019). Given the complexities of math-specific language, Mr. Nguyen knows that *all* his students, regardless of the other languages they speak, will benefit from the scaffolds in his lessons. He knows that they will need support describing how they got an answer, so the scaffolds guide students to communicate using math-appropriate language.

Mr. Nguyen does not assume his students have the academic language they need to explain their thinking or justify their choices on the city plan. He has heard Min Woo and other students speaking quite fluently about their weekend activities in the local community, so he plans to connect their background knowledge of the layout of the town streets to the new unit. Then, he will introduce the new words and phrases, sentence structures, and the desired organization of the final presentation as shown earlier in Figure 2.1. He plans to model how to speak like a city planner and give time to practice before they present their proposals to the town council. Mr. Nguyen's careful planning unpacks both the content and academic language students need to succeed in the lesson. In this way, academic language in his math class "becomes a vehicle, rather than a barrier, to learning" (Dutro & Moran, 2002, p. 236). Explicitly teaching the language for his math lessons makes his instruction more equitable for his experienced multilinguals. Chapters 3 through 6 will guide content teachers through the steps to planning assessments and lessons with a focus on academic language development.

Since we are focusing on developing academic language skills, some teachers may wonder about the role of the dedicated English language development (ELD) specialist. As highly skilled educators, ELD teachers have many opportunities to serve experienced multilinguals across the curriculum, including teaching specialized English classes, co-planning and co-teaching with content teachers, and coaching. Even if the ELD educator teaches a specialized English class for experienced multilinguals, these students should not miss the rich opportunity to learn content *in* content classes with guidance *from* discipline-specific experts. As Walqui said, "Nobody uses the language of history better than a history teacher" (OELA Podcast Series, 2021). Content teachers are experts regarding concepts, skills, thinking, and the academic language used in their disciplines. Therefore, we urge all teachers to develop academic English across the curriculum rather than relying only on the English language development specialist, who may not have the same level of expertise to teach the academic language for every discipline. Chapters 3 through 6 present each part of our instructional framework that is designed to scaffold and teach both academic language and content for experienced multilinguals. In Chapter 7, we share specific ideas for implementing the framework and scaffolds schoolwide with the support of the ELD specialist.

FROM THE FIELD

Developing Academic Language in Social Studies

Beth shares how one teacher made instructional changes to explicitly teach academic language in his social studies class.

For two years, I have been supporting one middle school with a high percentage of experienced multilinguals. The social studies teacher, Mr. Kruger, was interested in how the experienced multilinguals were using academic English during structured interactions in the class. Because he could not listen to every group of students during each interaction, he asked the school's English language development coach and me to transcribe student responses during class discussions and small group cooperative learning activities. In one activity, students had to work together to place tokens on a chart and justify how much they thought the government should spend on different categories like education, military, and infrastructure. As students talked collaboratively, we transcribed some of the following responses:

"Environment. To help the planet."

"More for foreign aid."

"We should spend money on the educational system."

When we showed these transcribed responses to Mr. Kruger, he noticed that the students were discussing the topic and participating in the activity, even though they were not fully justifying their choices. He could tell they understood the concept, but needed support for using more academic English to justify the amount they wanted to spend. He decided to model a desired response and provide some sentence frames to extend their academic language. This type of coaching feedback can support all learners in the class by clearly communicating academic expectations and providing equitable scaffolds for students to achieve success.

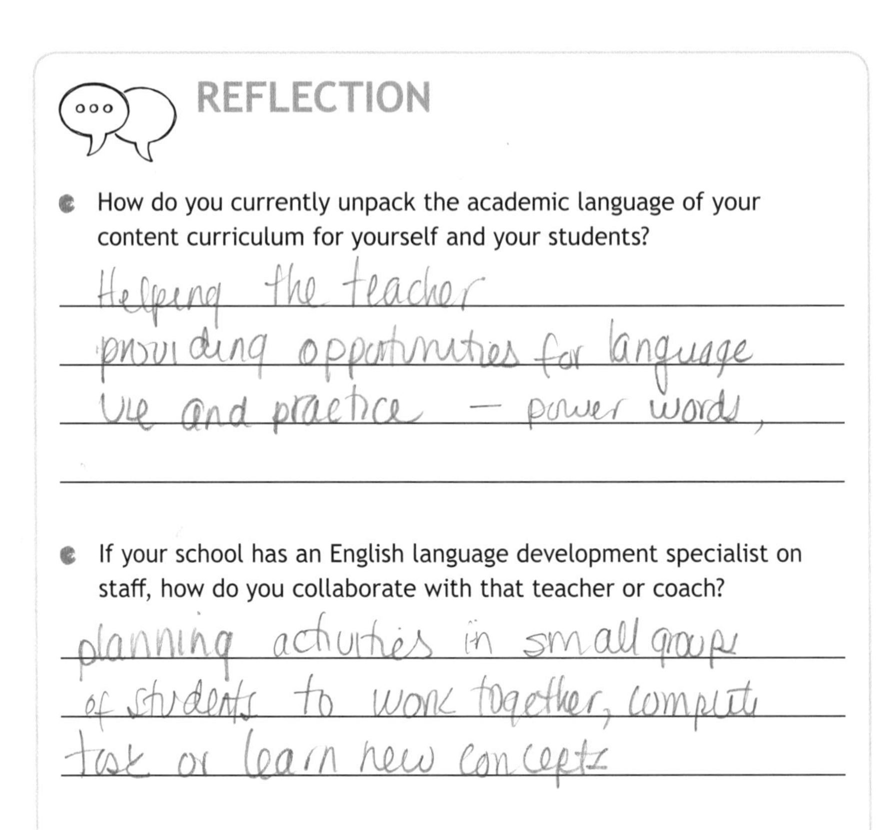

REFLECTION

- How do you currently unpack the academic language of your content curriculum for yourself and your students?

Helping the teacher
providing opportunities for language
use and practice — power words,

- If your school has an English language development specialist on staff, how do you collaborate with that teacher or coach?

planning activities in small groups
of students to work together, complete
task or learn new concepts

BALANCING GRADE-LEVEL EXPECTATIONS AND EQUITABLE SUPPORT

Finding the balance between grade-level appropriate challenges and supports for experienced multilinguals can be a tricky task. Some secondary teachers may believe experienced multilinguals can manage in content classes without any extra support, especially with such fluent speaking skills. Others may believe that experienced multilinguals who have not yet experienced much success in grade-level content courses just need a simplified text or a reduced curriculum until their English improves. Some educators may argue that explicitly teaching academic English and providing scaffolds will lower grade-level expectations or water down the curriculum for the English fluent students in the class. We believe equitable learning for experienced multilinguals happens when high expectations are met with intentional scaffolding.

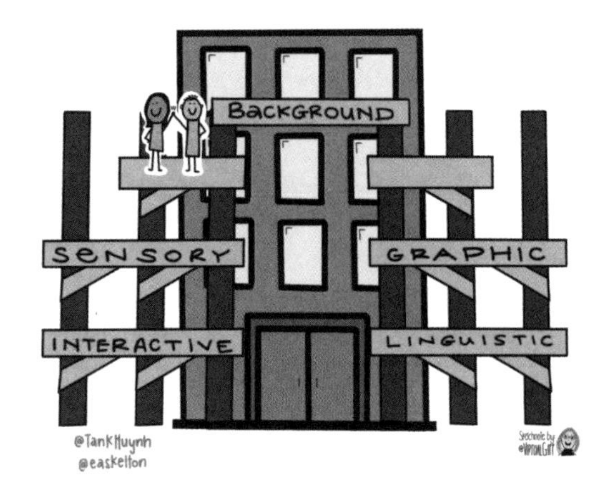

The physical scaffold used in construction serves as a metaphor for the kinds of scaffolds that balance high academic expectations and support. Just as the scaffold on the outside of an edifice supports construction workers to safely access parts of a building they otherwise could not reach on their own, instructional scaffolds for experienced multilinguals support them in successfully reaching new heights academically. Once the construction of the building is completed, the scaffolds are removed. If the scaffolds are kept in place after the construction has been completed, they will obstruct the function of the building. Once students can complete assignments and assessments independently, scaffolds are removed or else they will hinder autonomy. Knowing when to remove the scaffolds from a physical building may be obvious, but knowing when to remove scaffolds so students can work independently requires careful observation and experimentation. It can be helpful to collaborate with an ELD specialist through co-planning, co-teaching, or coaching to find the most appropriate time to intentionally remove scaffolds.

Removing scaffolds prematurely leads to disengagement and frustration, while leaving them in place when they are no longer necessary breeds dependence.

In their book *Scaffolding the Academic Success of Adolescent English Language Learners,* Walqui and van Lier (2010) argue that "for the scaffolding process to work, the teacher's role is not to control the learner but to support and encourage the learner's emergent autonomy" (p. 25). When Mr. Nguyen models and labels lines on an example street map, he is providing an essential scaffold, what Krashen (1982) refers to as comprehensible input. This comprehensible input creates the conditions for students to independently discuss and analyze the angles and lines on their own map. When he asks students to compare and contrast the lines on their street maps with several actual city plans, he is apprenticing them into using math in real-world situations, which is his ultimate goal. By reflecting on the desired outcome

Comprehensible input: Making ideas understandable

for the content unit, teachers can identify the required scaffold that builds autonomy and maintains a high challenge. The framework and scaffolds in this book are meant to provide teachers ways to challenge while supporting experienced multilinguals, so they can successfully meet and exceed grade-level expectations.

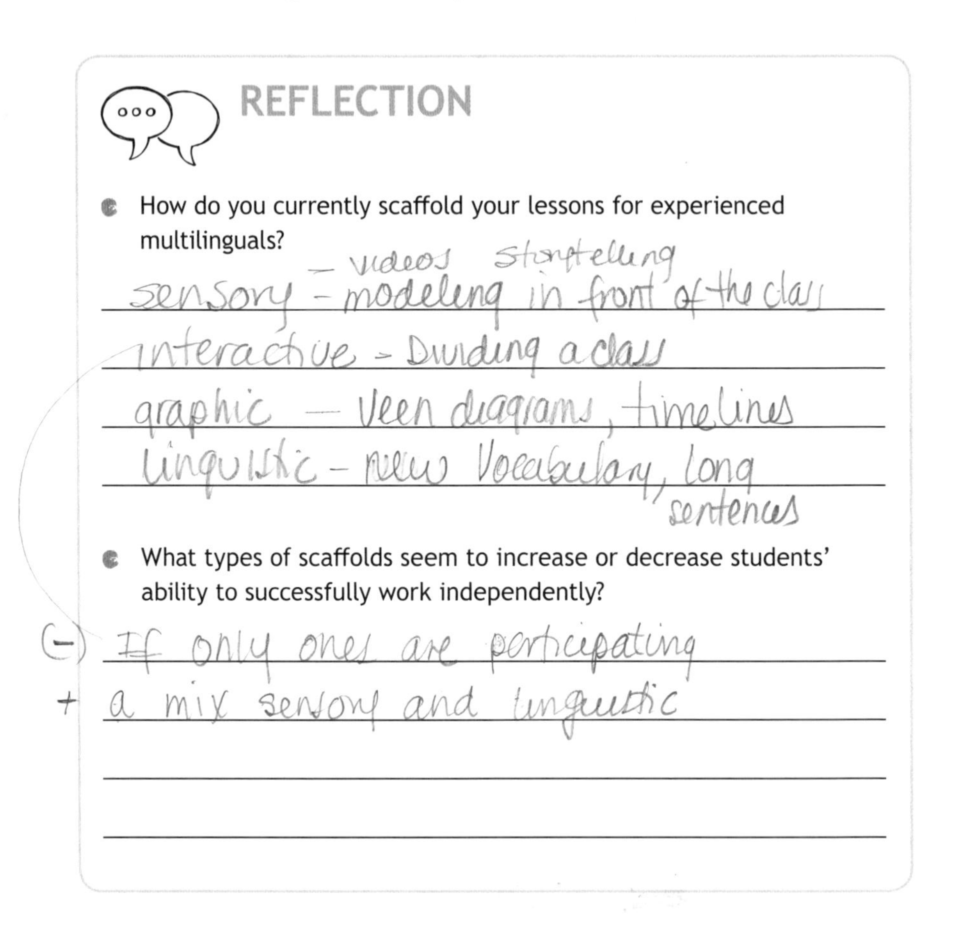

REFLECTION

- How do you currently scaffold your lessons for experienced multilinguals?
- What types of scaffolds seem to increase or decrease students' ability to successfully work independently?

LEARNING STRATEGIES FOR LONG-TERM SUCCESS

When teachers unpack and teach the academic language of their curriculum, experienced multilinguals can meet success in content classrooms. The teacher's role in this process is essential, and so is the student's role. While students may rely on teachers for comprehensible input at initial stages, we also want students to become more independent learners by relying on strategies we model. Teaching students how to apply appropriate learning strategies

Learning strategies: Any action a student does to boost their understanding of new content and use of discipline-specific language

serves them by developing the skills they need to learn in any content area. For long-term success, experienced multilinguals can learn to rely on effective learning strategies whenever they face academic challenges.

Learning strategies include activities like those shown in Figure 2.3. When students know *when* and *how* to use these learning strategies—such as activating their background knowledge, using mental imagery, monitoring their comprehension, or cooperating with others—they become more independent learners. Teachers can make learning strategies explicit throughout the lesson and encourage students to try these strategies in different contexts. The teachers mentioned by Marcus and Carolina in the following feature "From the Field" directly taught learning strategies, which helped these experienced multilinguals become more successful and positive about the class.

FROM THE FIELD

Learning Strategies Lead to Success

Beth interviewed several ninth-grade experienced multilinguals who had been students in a school in Colorado for seven to ten years already. Their responses to questions about their favorite classes reveal insights into the benefits of teaching of learning strategies. It is clear that they like the class because they feel successful due to the teachers' careful use of scaffolds and explicit focus on learning strategies.

Interview question: Tell me about your favorite class and why you like it.

Marcus	Carolina
I like math class the most. I've always liked following the clear steps to solve problems. My teacher showed me how to find important words in word problems, which helps me understand the problem. He also writes notes on the board with numbered steps that help me solve complicated problems.	*Biology is my favorite class because I love learning about science. I want to study medicine after high school. The teacher gives step-by-step directions for every project so I know exactly how to complete it. She also labels pictures and explains the concepts clearly.*

2.3 Learning Strategies

Strategy Name	Description	Examples
Visualize	Use images (real or mental) to learn new information, solve a problem, or remember key concepts.	• Make a mental movie while reading a story. • Draw a math problem. • Google an image of a new vocabulary word. • Add pictures to a graphic organizer.
Cooperate	Talk with a peer to synthesize new content, solve a problem, understand a text, or practice a skill.	• Read a text with a partner, and discuss each section. • Work with a team to complete a task. • Ask a peer questions about the content, text, vocabulary, or grammar. • Read a peer's example work.
Use Resources	Use dictionaries in any language, videos, images, calculators, and other tools to comprehend new information, problems, or texts.	• Watch a YouTube video to build background on a new concept. • Use a calculator to check math solutions. • Look up unknown words in an online dictionary.
Take Notes	Write or draw ideas and concepts while listening, reading, or working in teams.	• Complete a Venn diagram to compare and contrast ideas. • Write notes and questions in the margins of the text. • Use Cornell Notes to study for a test. • Draw sketchnotes during or after a lesson with key ideas.
Summarize	Make a mental, oral, or written summary of main ideas during a pause in listening or reading.	• Tell a partner what you understood in the lesson so far. • Write a one-sentence summary of the paragraph or page. • Draw a sketch to summarize key ideas of the lesson.

Strategy Name	Description	Examples
Activate Prior Knowledge	Think about what you know about the topic. Connect the new information to something from background knowledge.	• Make an analogy, metaphor, or simile to describe new learning. • Link the task, text, or information to something you've done before. • Make a personal connection to the new information.
Monitor Comprehension	Notice what you do or do not understand when listening or reading. Notice when comprehension breaks down and what causes it.	• Make notes about what you do and do not understand. • Highlight specific words or phrases you do not understand. • Ask clarifying questions.

Adapted from Chamot & O'Malley (2001).

Image sources:istock.com/Rakdee, istock.com/Alexander Ryabintsev, istock.com/bananajazz, istock.com/Hiranmay Baidya, istock.com/heartstock, istock.com~Userba9fe9ab_931, istock .com/Avector Image sources:istock.com/Rakdee, istock.com/Alexander Ryabintsev, istock.com/bananajazz, istock.com/Hiranmay Baidya, istock.com/heartstock, istock.com~Userba9fe9ab_931, istock.com/Avector

Available at **resources.corwin.com/Long-Term SuccessforExperiencedMLs**

Developing learning strategies helps all learners take ownership of their learning and "when students take control over their learning, they see themselves as more effective and thereby gain in confidence with future learning activities" (Chamot & O'Malley, 2001, p. 18). When students begin applying learning strategies on their own, they may initially see them as an activity, such as asking clarifying questions while reading. However, as they practice these strategies regularly, they will internalize them. Then, they can choose or intentionally apply the learning strategy that best supports their learning in different contexts. When students intentionally use strategies to support their learning, they are practicing a form of metacognition, or thinking about their thinking. As students develop **metacognition**, they become much more effective at learning because they are able to

Metacognition: Awareness and understanding of your own thinking process

recognize when they need support and intentionally choose an appropriate tool to help themselves. (Echevarría et al., 2017; Hattie, 2021).

> "when students take control over their learning, they see themselves as more effective and thereby gain in confidence with future learning activities" (Chamot & O'Malley, 2001, p. 18).

However, many experienced multilinguals have not yet fully developed the learning strategies to effectively engage with school tasks independently, that is, strategies for tasks such as studying for an exam, reading a text, or completing multistep problems. When teachers advise students to study for an exam and give explicit instructions on *how* to study, students learn effective study strategies in addition to the content. Students are more likely to independently comprehend a text when teachers provide a purpose for reading and suggest ways to make meaning from that text (Tovani, 2000). When math teachers ask students to work through a problem set and explicitly teach strategies for how to solve that type of problem, they create the conditions for students to understand the process as well as complete the problem set. As the popular learning strategies program AVID (2016) states, "note-taking, studying, and organizing assignments are all skills that must be taught and practiced, but are not explicitly taught in schools." We believe all teachers can and should explicitly teach learning strategies. These strategies give experienced multilinguals confidence that they have the tools they need to tackle grade-level content.

> If experienced multilinguals know how to use effective learning strategies, they will find long-term success in any class they find themselves in.

When they learn how and when to ask questions, cooperate with others, visualize information, and take notes, then they are truly prepared for long-term success both in and out of school.

Mr. Nguyen teaches learning strategies throughout his seventh-grade math class with the hopes that students will transfer these skills to other math units and to other content areas. When he asks students to read the task aloud and ask each other questions about it before starting on the task, he lets them know that cooperation is a learning strategy that can help them understand complex problems. When he asks them to draw the lines and angles for their city map, he also explains that using imagery can help them visualize angle relationships. When Mr. Nguyen names each of these strategies during his lessons, students are able to apply them across the curriculum to become more autonomous learners.

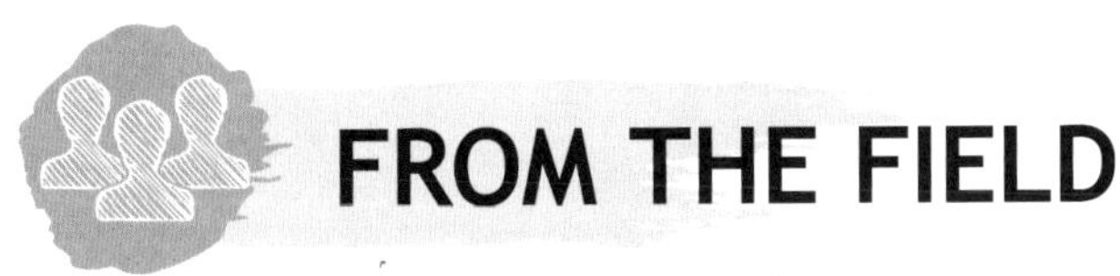

FROM THE FIELD

Learning Strategies in Action

Julio, a ninth-grade experienced multilingual, claimed his English language arts was his worst class. He knew that comprehending large chunks of text was his biggest challenge in the class and he seemed to understand the importance of different learning strategies as he reflected on his struggles with the class content and assignments.

When he asked the teacher to help him understand the texts, she recommended that he read more slowly. He tried that strategy, but it didn't work for him. He was undeterred. Being a natural problem-solver, Julio experimented with several different strategies on his own. He tried using an online bilingual dictionary and looked for cognates to understand the words in the stories, but he still struggled to understand the full page of text. Julio tried rereading, but that was not effective. Finally, he called a friend to talk about what they had read. Talking to someone in the class helped him the most.

Notice all the learning strategies Julio tried. Some were more successful than others in helping him comprehend texts in his most difficult class. The strategies that seemed to help him the most were monitoring his comprehension, using the dictionary and cognates, and cooperating with a friend. As Julio develops more effective learning and reading strategies, he may no longer consider English language arts class his "worst" class.

TRY IT OUT

Learning Strategies

1. Choose one of the learning strategies described in Figure 2.3 that you think would help your students learn content and academic English more independently.
2. Write where in a lesson you could model and name that strategy.

(Continued)

(Continued)

3. Plan an activity that would allow students to practice the learning strategy with your guidance.
4. Ask students how successful the strategy was for them.
5. Plan to teach additional strategies in future lessons.

REFLECTION

- Which learning strategies are you using to comprehend this text?

- taking notes
- look videos for more information
- use bilingual dictionary

- Which learning strategies do you teach your students to use in your classes?

- read more slowly, make conecciones
- cooperate
- scaffolds
- ABC exercises

- Review the list of learning strategies in Figure 2.3. Which ones could you explicitly model and teach in an upcoming lesson?

visualize
use resources

INSTRUCTIONAL FRAMEWORK FOR EXPERIENCED MULTILINGUALS

In this chapter, we have provided a rationale for teaching academic language to experienced multilinguals in content area classrooms. We have proposed that content teachers are the best teachers of the disciplinary language of their content. We whole-heartedly believe that

> experienced multilinguals can become successful, autonomous learners in every content area when teachers explicitly teach academic language, content, and learning strategies.

In order to guide teachers in unpacking and teaching the academic language for assessments and daily lessons, we have created a four-part framework. This framework, as shown in Figure 2.4, serves as the outline for the rest of the book. The visuals that accompany each part of the framework refer to an analogy of an orchard, which may help educators remember and process the concepts.

Part 1 of the framework is the summative assessment. In Chapter 3, we explain the need to begin planning a unit by first designing equitable summative assessments, and we guide teachers through the process. This assessment-first approach to planning comes from Wiggins and McTighe (2005) in their seminal book *Understanding by Design*. The authors encourage educators to start with the end in mind and finalize what students have to know and do by the end of the unit before planning the daily objectives and learning experiences. Knowing the assessment at the end of the unit helps us define what we have to teach, what skills we have to develop, and in what order to teach these things. We offer ways to support the content, academic language, and learning strategies needed to succeed on summative assessments. The visual of the orchard for this first part of the framework encourages educators to see the big picture of the unit from the beginning. We encourage teachers to think about the harvest or the final product of the unit as it guides our daily instruction.

By keeping the end-of-unit assessment in mind, teachers can more effectively plan lessons by first designing integrated objectives. Part 2 of the framework, discussed in Chapter 4, guides teachers through creating these integrated objectives that focus on both the

academic language and the content students need to be successful during each of the lessons leading up to the summative assessment. The visual of the individual tree in the orchard represents these daily objectives. Each tree contributes to the orchard's bountiful harvest just like each objective supports students in achieving the highest level of learning by the end of the unit.

Once the academic language demands are unpacked, teachers can plan scaffolds strategically so that content is accessible. In Part 3 of the framework, described in Chapter 5, we focus on five essential scaffolds that create comprehensible input, which is represented by the visual of the sun and rain. Like water and sun, comprehensible input in each lesson creates the conditions for experienced multilinguals to grow in their content and academic language skills.

Finally, in Part 4 of the framework, we share strategies that scaffold students' output. After lots of comprehensible input, students will also be ready to produce in speech and writing about their new content understandings. Chapter 6 describes strategies for speaking and scaffolds for writing across disciplines. The visual of the apple represents this output or production. After establishing the optimal conditions for growth with plenty of nurturing inputs, the trees finally can produce fruit.

The goal of the instructional framework is equitable instruction. That equity comes from unpacking and explicitly teaching the discipline-specific language hidden in the content curriculum. The framework guides content teachers in identifying and teaching the academic language so that students can successfully engage with assessment expectations and lesson objectives. We believe that experienced multilinguals will thrive when they have "equitable access to rigorous and authentic disciplinary instruction that effectively develops and deepens their understandings, learning, and language development" (Heineke & McTighe, 2018, p. 31).

> When educators reveal the hidden academic language of their content curriculum, they create conditions for experienced multilinguals' long-term success.

2.4 **Instructional Framework for Experienced Multilinguals**

Engineer the summative assessment

Write the integrated objective

Establish comprehensible input

Structure academic output

CLOSING REMARKS

By the end of this book, secondary content teachers will know how to design equitable assessments, write objectives that integrate content and academic language expectations, make lessons comprehensible, and structure speaking and writing. School administrators will also have a road map for implementing the framework schoolwide. With this framework, secondary teachers can use their content as the context for academic language development. When experienced multilinguals meet success in their content classes, they will also more likely see themselves as independent, capable learners who have increasingly diverse choices for their future. We hope that our framework provides a practical and streamlined approach for all content teachers to design the most equitable, clear, and scaffolded lessons for experienced multilinguals.

CHAPTER SUMMARY

- Experienced multilinguals deserve high grade-level expectations coupled with high support to successfully engage in content classes.
- Appropriate intentional scaffolding enables experienced multilinguals to succeed in grade-level content courses.
- Academic language includes vocabulary, complex sentence structures, transition phrases, and organizational patterns.
- Academic language is best taught *within* the context of the content classroom from a discipline-specific teacher.
- Experienced multilinguals develop metacognitive skills from explicit instruction that teaches them to independently apply learning strategies in new contexts.
- The instructional framework for experienced multilinguals includes engineering equitable summative assessments, writing integrated objectives focused on teaching content and academic language, establishing comprehensible input, and structuring academic output.

ENGINEERING SUMMATIVE ASSESSMENTS

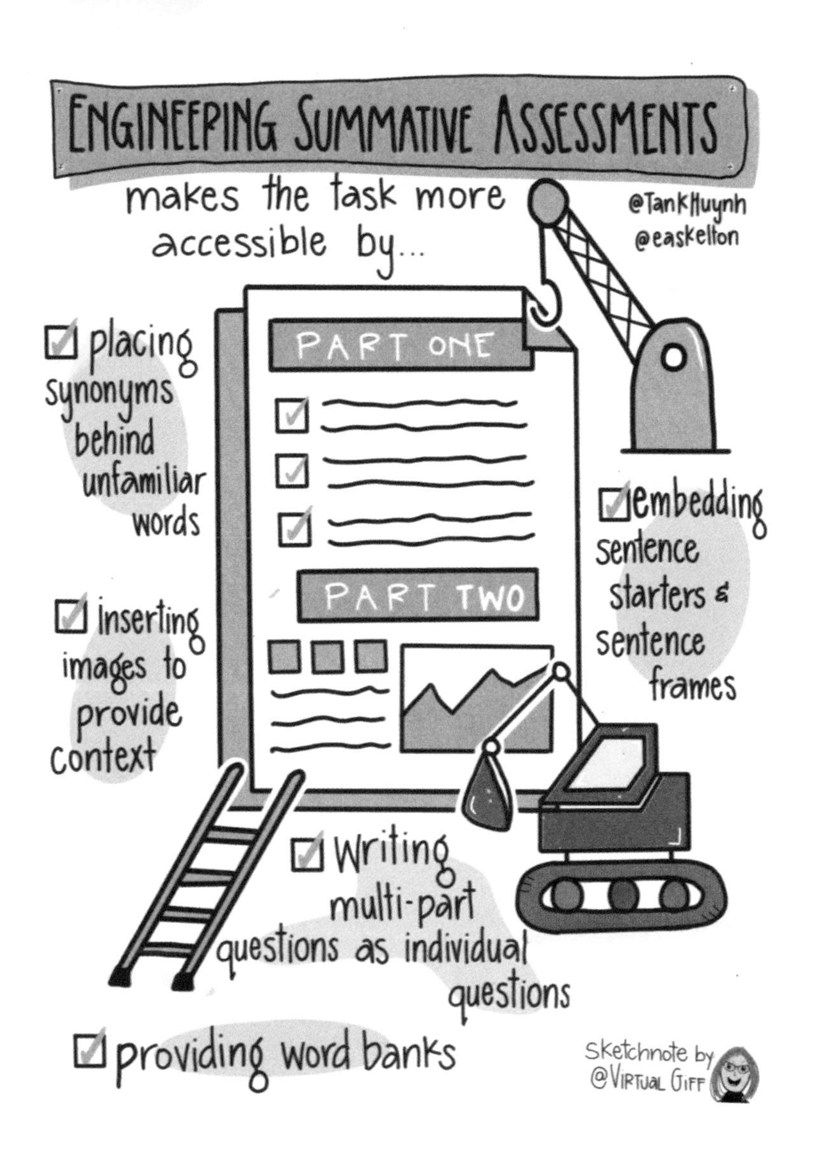

In two weeks, Mrs. Maple's next science unit will begin. One crisp October day, she decides to devote her planning time to designing the next unit on ecosystems. After the first unit of the year, she has a better sense of her students. Mrs. Maple knows she has some students who receive dedicated English language support classes, but she is surprised by some of her more English-fluent students like Min Woo, who still need support even though they have been attending the school for years. During Unit 1, she noticed that he was able to understand the instructions and complete the tasks, but the work revealed that he understood the concept at a surface level and produced few specific details taken from articles they had read in class. As Mrs. Maple thinks about students like Min Woo, she is not sure where to start. These experienced multilinguals need help understanding abstract concepts, using academic language accurately, and writing coherently to explain their thinking. As she stares at a laptop still closed, she takes a deep breath and thinks, *Where do I even begin?*

SUMMATIVE ASSESSMENTS

To best support experienced multilinguals for long-term success in the unit, we encourage teachers to first step back to see the whole picture of the unit. We use the analogy of the orchard when planning. With this analogy, we want teachers to also feel a sense of direction by starting with the assessment instead of being lost among the trees.

Planning the assessment first as recommended by Wiggins and McTighe (2005) creates the conditions so that all the lessons support the desired outcomes for understanding and using academic language. Intentionally planning the assessment first anchors all of our subsequent lessons and learning experiences. In the same way that orchards have a shape and defined boundaries, our assessment will shape and set the direction for our individual lessons.

Teachers usually design one of two main types of summative assessments: exams or performance-based assessments. We share our practical strategies to design exams and assessments so that they are more accessible and equitable to experienced multilinguals.

ENGINEERING EXAMS

Exams are generally completed in one class period, not over several days and weeks. They require students to memorize content concepts and practice skills prior to the exam date, which starts and ends at a certain time. Usually, these exams take place at the end of a unit or semester. There is no feedback from teachers during the exam. Experienced multilinguals should experience success on exams by design, not by accident.

"Paper-pencil" exams are commonly used to assess content knowledge. Whether students complete summative exams on paper or on the computer, typical elements of these exams include such things as matching, fill-in-the-blank, short and long answer response, word problems, interpreting graphs, multiple choice, labeling diagrams, and creating graphs. When these exam elements lack necessary scaffolding,

> un-scaffolded content exams can become reading tests instead of content exams.

Fortunately, content teachers can intentionally construct and scaffold their exams with a few simple techniques (Huynh, 2019). Employing techniques to scaffold summative tests is called exam engineering. Just like an engineer designs buildings with specific features to make it stable, content teachers can engineer exams with features that make the question more comprehensible and structure students' responses so that they are more accurate and better reflect their skill development. These techniques are summarized in Figure 3.1.

3.1 Exam Engineering Strategies

Exam Engineering Strategy	Places to Use This Technique
Synonyms	Written instructions, multiple choice, matching, creating graphs
Sentence Starters	Short and long responses, fill-in-the-blank, interpreting graphs
Chunking	Word problems, written scenarios
Images	Written instructions, multiple choice, matching
Word Banks	Matching, short and long responses, fill-in-the blank, labeling diagrams

Available at resources.corwin.com/Long-TermSuccessforExperiencedMLs

Exam engineering: Employing techniques to scaffold summative tests

When we share these strategies to make assessments more equitable, some teachers express concern that they give experienced multilinguals an "unfair advantage" or that the supports somehow help them "cheat." In response, we share that even highly experienced and skilled mountain climbers use scaffolds such as ropes and harnesses. Their tools do not shrink the height of the mountain. They just make climbing the mountain possible.

We also reference universal design for learning (UDL) to make instruction more equitable for all students by providing multiple pathways to the content (Novak, 2014). Designing accessible assessments means providing multiple scaffolds so students can engage successfully and meaningfully with content without English becoming a barrier. We encourage teachers to see scaffolded assessments as a product of designing for success, not a "gotcha" gauntlet. An equitable scaffolded assessment is designed with both academic language and content in mind.

The following section provides specific exam engineering techniques that scaffold typical elements of paper-pencil exams.

SYNONYMS

Vocabulary matching sections can sometimes feel like a reading comprehension test (Figure 3.2). One exam engineering technique is to

3.2 An Excerpt From the Original Version of the Vocabulary Matching Exam

1. Match the words with their definitions. Write your answers in the box below.

	WORD		DEFINITION
A.	Food chain		1. An organism which produces its own food usually through the use of light energy in the process of photosynthesis.
B.	Food web		2. An organism that feeds on dead organisms and causes them to decay.
C.	Producer		3. An organism that feeds only on producers (plants or algae).
D.	Consumer		4. A simple diagram to show the flow of energy from one organism to another in an ecosystem.
E.	Herbivore		5. An organism that feeds on both producers and animals.

provide synonyms behind non-content-related words as shown in Figure 3.3. Notice how *feeds* appears several times in the exam, but a synonym was provided only for the first appearance of *feeds*. After the first time it appears, students are responsible for the rest because scaffolds are temporary, not permanent.

3.3 An Excerpt of an Example of Synonyms Embedded in an Exam

Band 1-2 Questions (21 points)

1. Match the words with their definitions. Write your answers in the box below.

	WORD	Answer
A.	Food chain	
B.	Foodweb	4
C.	Producer	1
D.	Consumer	5
E.	Herbivore	3

	DEFINITION
1.	An organism that produces (makes) its own food by using light energy.
2.	An organism that feeds (eats) on dead organisms.
3.	An organism that feeds only on producers.
4.	A diagram (image) to show the flow of energy from one organism to another in an ecosytem.
5.	An organism that feeds on both producers and animals.

In another example, we want to assess students' understanding and application of discipline-specific words. When we ask students to describe a trophic cascade, we cannot water down the exams by providing a synonym for this term as it will be explicitly taught to all students during the lessons that lead up to the exam. Instead, we can write the instruction as such:

Identify (name) the secondary consumer that initiates (starts) a trophic cascade.

The two content words (*secondary consumer, trophic cascade*) receive no scaffolding but the words *identify* and *initiates* are followed by more accessible words to prevent this question from becoming a reading test.

IMAGES

Often the format of the question actually increases its complexity (Figure 3.4). Sometimes this increased complexity is due to a large amount of details students have to understand in the question. Other times, it is the way the question is written that causes comprehension issues. Teachers can meet this increased complexity by inserting images when appropriate (Figure 3.5).

> Images do not water down the exam's expectations. They simply make the question and choices comprehensible.

Teachers can insert an image to provide context for a word problem or provide images in a vocabulary matching section.

3.4 Examples of Highly Complex Concepts Written in a Highly Complex Format

1. Use the following food chain to answer questions (a) and (b).

lettuce → greenflies → ladybird insects → insect-eating birds → hawks

(a) Which organism is a **secondary consumer**? ____________

(b) If the hawks were removed from the food chain, what is most likely to happen to the number of other organisms in the food chain? Circle the best answer (a, b, c, or d).

	Greenflies	Ladybirds	Insect-eating birds
a.	decrease	increase	decrease
b.	decrease	increase	increase
c.	increase	decrease	decrease
d.	increase	decrease	increase

3.5 Example of a Science Exam With Images Strategically Embedded

1. Use the following food chain to answer questions A and B.

A. Which organism is a secondary consumer? ____________

lettuce → greenflies → ladybugs → sparrows → hawks

B. There is a forest ecosystem. In this ecosystem, there are greenflies, ladybugs, sparrows, and hawks. If the hawks were removed (taken away) from the food chain, what is most likely to happen to the number of other organisms in the food chain? Circle the best answer (a, b, c, or d).

greenflies	ladybug	sparrow
a. ↓decrease	↑increase	↓decrease
b. ↓decrease	↑increase	↑increase
c. ↑increase	↓decrease	↓decrease
d. ↑increase	↓decrease	↑increase

Images: istock.com/Mariia Meteleva, istock.com/asantosg, istock.com/Elena Brovko, istock.com/sceka, istock.com/Alfadanz

Furthermore, an image can appear with instructions for a higher-level question that requires students to apply content-specific information. For example, when presenting a word problem about a trophic cascade, teachers can provide an image of the specific cascade to add context to the word problem (see Figure 3.6).

3.6 Example of an Image Accompanying a Word Problem to Provide Context

This is a balanced marine food chain. Killer whales feed on seals, which in turn feed on otters. Otters help maintain the sea urchin population down. Sea urchin feed on sea kelp. Too many sea urchins would mean a disappearance of the sea kelp forest, which is vital to providing a habitat for a coastal ecosystem. Humans began hunting seals in large numbers for their fur, greatly reducing their populations.

Describe what happens as a result of this trophic cascade.

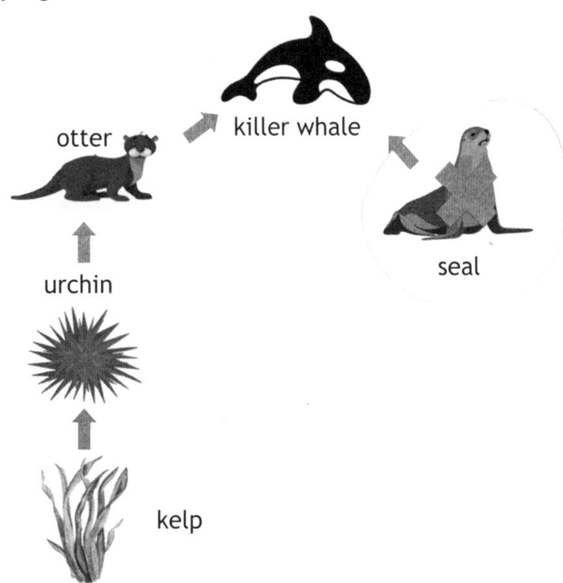

Images: istock.com/Logorilla, istock.com/pleshko74, istock.com/olgaserova, istock.com/Color_Brush, istock.com/Aghidel

Additionally, as text-only multiple-choice questions and word problems are void of context, this makes comprehending the question significantly more difficult. Therefore, we encourage teachers to incorporate images into word problems or lengthy texts. In Figure 3.7, an image of the food web accompanying the multiple-choice question ramps up the comprehensibility of the question. The image does not make the thinking less challenging. It only makes questions more comprehensible.

3.7 Example of a Scaffolded Multiple-Choice Question Containing a Labeled Diagram

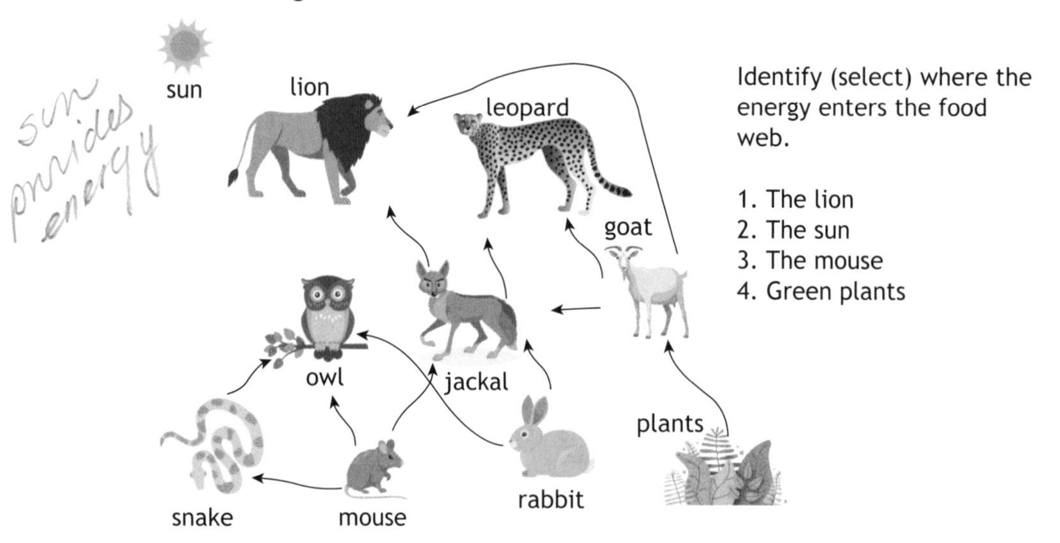

Images: iStock.com/StudioBarcelon, istock.com/BRO Vector, istock.com/andegro4ka, istock.com/Katernia Sisperova, istock.com/pleshkjo74, istock.com/Thomas Lydell, istock.com/adekvat, istock.cm/PCH-Vector, istock.com/Denis08131, istock.com/filo

SENTENCE STARTERS

At times, students can understand exam questions but not know how to answer them because there are few accompanying scaffolds (Figure 3.8). A third exam engineering strategy supports students as they answer short-response questions. We suggest providing sentence starters to scaffold student responses. Sentence starters spur students to think in certain ways about content, but they must still come up with the content in their responses. Figure 3.9 gives an example of how to provide a sentence starter for a short-response question.

3.8 Examples of Exam Questions Without Scaffolds

1. The arrows in a food web represent energy transfer. In what form does energy enter a food chain?

   ____

2. State clearly how energy is passed along a food chain.

   ____

3.9 Annotated Examples of Sentence Starters Embedded in Content-Based Exams

1. The arrows in a food web represent (show) energy transfer.
   In what form does energy enter this food web?

Add synonyms behind academic words.

The energy enters the food web through the . . . solor energy

2. State (say) clearly how energy is passed along a food chain.

Add sentence starters or sentence frames to help students communicate their ideas without giving away the answer.

The energy is passed through the food chain by . . .

CHUNKING

Chunking exam questions for multipart questions and long responses is a supportive exam engineering technique for experienced multilinguals. Tricky multipart questions ask students to provide at least two unique responses. Often, experienced multilingual students will provide only a partial answer to multipart questions. Instead, we suggest separating multipart questions into two or more single questions.

Multilingual students will then focus on one question at a time, increasing their likelihood of providing a complete answer. The question shown in Figure 3.10 asks students to *identify* and *explain*, for example.

3.10 Annotated Example of Breaking a Multipart Question Into a Series of Single-Part Questions

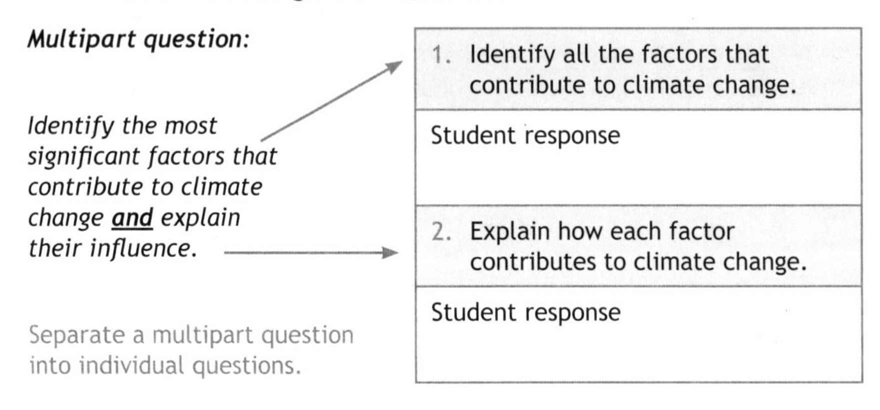

Teachers can also chunk long-response questions for students. Long-response questions present one of the most challenging exam questions for experienced multilinguals because of the amount of content that they require students to write. Often, students only answer part of the long-response question, resulting in missed opportunities to show the greatest level of understanding. We can prevent this from happening by chunking the response with guiding prompts or a list of reminders for students as shown in Figure 3.11. Students can use the reminders to provide the appropriate type of details and the sequence in which they appear.

3.11 Example of Chunking a Long-Response Question

Explain why trophic cascades can be devastating for the ecosystem. Remember to do the following:

- Use one of these case studies we've looked at.
  - Wolves in Yellowstone
  - Otters on the Pacific Coast
  - Geckos in Borneo
- Describe the food web in this case study.
- Describe how this food web was changed.
- Describe the consequences as a result of this change in the food web.

Type your response below.

WORD BANKS

Word banks are like treasure chests that contain the golden words students need to use to demonstrate understanding of content. A word bank increases students' likelihood of providing the most accurate response. Without the word bank, students are left wondering which words to use. Word banks can be added to matching, short and long responses, and fill-in-the-blank questions. The common objection to word banks is that they oversimplify the assessment. Some teachers think that if students have learned the content, they should be able to recall content-specific words and also spell them correctly. Without word banks, providing a response becomes a recall challenge and a spelling test rolled into one. Imagine the difficulty experienced multilinguals face when having to pick the correct vocabulary words from all the thousands of words read and spoken in the unit. A word bank does not ensure that students can apply words appropriately. It simply narrows down the menu of key words to those being assessed.

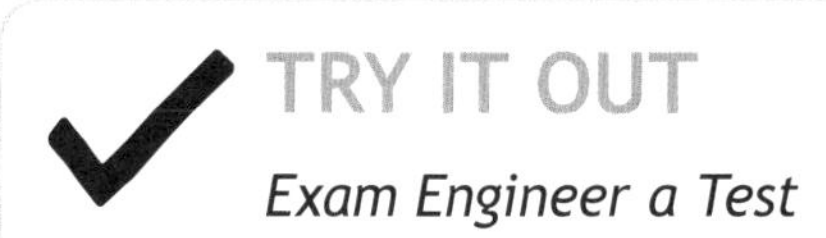

TRY IT OUT

Exam Engineer a Test

1. Choose a multipart test you have already created, or create a new one.
2. Use at least one or two engineering techniques from this section to scaffold different parts of the exam.
3. After the exam, notice if your experienced multilinguals perform differently on the engineered parts of the exam.

REFLECTION

- How would these exam engineering techniques be an example of educational equity?

with these Techniques teachers are able to adapt their teaching style to match a student's learning capabilities

(Continued)

(Continued)

- Which of these exam engineering techniques can you incorporate in your next exam?

____

____

____

____

- How would students feel if they started receiving exams with these techniques?

they will be more confident in themselves, less nervous because they will understand the question(s)

____

ENGINEERING PERFORMANCE-BASED ASSESSMENTS

PBAs.

As demanding as exams are, performance-based assessments (PBAs) present a completely different set of expectations. A PBA is an end-of-unit assessment that requires students to apply specific content skills and concepts to produce a product that can take a significant period of time to complete. Teachers who use PBAs want students to apply content-specific skills and academic language that experts in respective fields use to solve actual problems (Heineke & McTighe, 2018). For example, students might write a business plan for business class, a factsheet for global affairs class to summarize a problem, a science report for biology class, or a series of placards for a museum display. They may also be asked to orally present a design project to community members or participate in a debate as a form of PBA. Figure 3.12 shows a sample list of the common types of PBAs. As students are working on different parts of the PBA, they receive specific feedback to improve their work and develop their skills.

Performance-based assessment: Long-term project that requires the application of content concepts and skills

3.12 Types of Performance-Based Assessments

Oral	Written	Visual
Podcast	Reports	Poster
Panel discussion	Op-ed	Diagram
Debate	Reviews	Website
Speech	Executive summaries	Digital application
Plays	Factsheet	Scaled model
Demonstration	Short story	Infographic
Interview	Chapter book	Display
Proposal	Children's book	Pamphlet
Song	Newspaper article	Advertisement
Storytelling	Letter	Animated video
	Blog	Music video
	Song lyrics	Presentation slides
	Prologues	
	Epilogues	

Adapted from Heineke & McTighe (2018).

Available at **resources.corwin.com/Long-TermSuccessforExperiencedMLs**

Since there are numerous parts to a PBA and each of these parts work together to form a whole, PBAs are quite complex and academically rigorous (Figure 3.13). However, they also give students the opportunity to demonstrate their content understanding in more authentic ways than a conventional exam. Experienced multilinguals need teachers to scaffold the PBA because these academic tasks are highly complex, and students must possess and develop advanced academic skills to be successful (Cummins & Early, 2015).

When designing performance-based assessments, we suggest using an assessment template. A template is a document that is a hybrid

---

Assessment template: A document for scaffolding performance-based assessments that is a hybrid between written instructions and a graphic organizer

3.13 Original Instructions Provided for a Performance-Based Assessment Without Exam Engineering

Unit 1 Summative Task: Ecosystem

You have been learning about ecosystems, how they function, and consequences of significant stressors placed on them. We studied several cases of ecosystems in this unit. Now it's your turn to conduct research about different ecosystems other than rivers and coral reefs. Make sure to provide some details about your ecosystem, how humans are impacting them, and possible solutions to restore the health of your ecosystem.

Due: September 15

Word count: Between 800 and 1000

between written instructions and a graphic organizer. The template has instructions for each part of the assessment sequenced in a desired order. Along with the instructions, the template also includes student response boxes. Teachers can structure student response boxes by adding

- prompts,
- sentence frames, and
- guiding questions.

The template does not lower the cognitive or academic load of the assignment. Templates make succeeding on these assessments possible. An intentionally designed template will support students throughout the unit (see Figure 3.14). Since a PBA will take many days or even weeks to complete, the template can guide experienced multilinguals each step of the way. Once teachers create a PBA template, they might be inclined to share them with all students as even the most fluent students need academic language support.

In this section, we describe several scaffolds shown in Figure 3.15 that teachers can embed into the template to ensure experienced multilinguals have an equitable opportunity for success on performance-based assessments. These scaffolds for a template can be used for any type of PBA including an oral presentation or a performance.

3.14 Example of a Completed PBA Template With Annotations

Instructional boxes sequenced in a particular order by their topics

Your Ecosystem

- Where is your ecosystem found (countries, regions, hemispheres)?
- Describe the main food chain in your ecosystem: producers, primary consumers, secondary consumers, tertiary consumers (apex predator).
- Why is your ecosystem important (what does it produce, what does it protect)?

Student response box

[type here]

Guiding questions and prompts embedded in the instructional boxes to stimulate thinking

Human Impact

- What did humans do to this ecosystem?
- Describe how the food chain in your ecosystem changed because of this human activity.
  - What organism was reduced? How did this affect the ecosystem?
  - What organism was increased? How did this affect the ecosystem?

[type here]

Solution

- What is one possible solution to restore the balance in this ecosystem's food chain?
- What will happen to the food chain if the solution is successful?
- Why will the return to balance be beneficial to:
  - the ecosystem
  - humans

Guiding questions and prompts embedded in the student response boxes to stimulate thinking

One possible solution to restore the balance in the food chain in [your ecosystem] is . . . This solution works by . . . if the solution is successful, we will see more . . . and less . . . As a result, the ecosystem will . . . Furthermore, the restoration of the food chain will benefits humans by . . .

3.15 Exam Engineering Techniques for a Performance-Based Assessment Template

Engineering Technique	Purpose
Sequencing	To guide students to present specific information in a particular order
Instruction Boxes	To prompt students to communicate in specific ways (e.g., inform, narrate, explain, argue) and to provide particular details
Sentence Starters or Sentence Frames	To stimulate more content-specific student responses

Available at **resources.corwin.com/Long-TermSuccessforExperiencedMLs**

SEQUENCING

One central question when planning is *What steps do students have to follow to successfully complete the PBA?* Teachers can guide students on each step by engineering the sequence of the topics and questions on the assessment template. Each instruction box focuses on one topic, flagged by a particular heading. Each part of the PBA should have its own instructions. These instructions are strategically sequenced so that students complete the product in the most appropriate phases. We suggest seeing the PBA as interlocking puzzle pieces. The individual pieces only connect with other specific pieces. In the same way, experienced multilingual students need each part of the assessment presented in an intentional sequence for equitable learning.

For example, Mrs. Maple assessed students with two products: documentation of research and the report. For the research, she created a template that identified topics to research and the sequence of these topics (Figure 3.16). When students submitted their research documentation, the completed template served as the final product to demonstrate their researching skills.

Once the research was gathered, it was then time for the report. The sequencing technique was also applied to the template for the report, shown in Figure 3.14. Each part of the report template clearly identifies the content students have to present and the sequence the

3.16 Example of One Part of a Product Template to Assess Students' Researching Skills

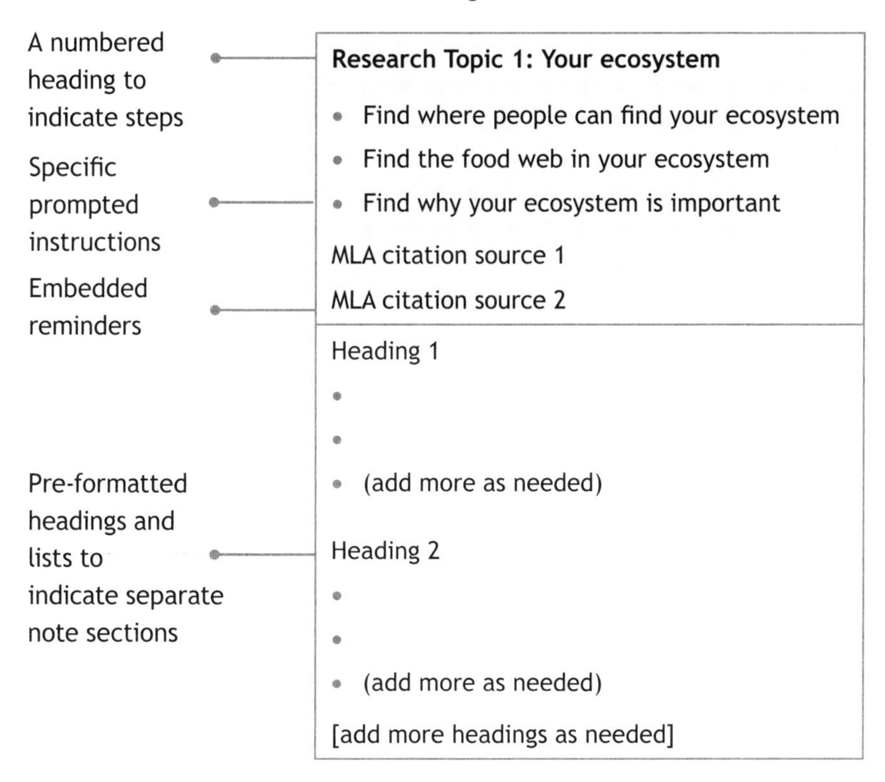

content needs to appear (Figure 3.16). Few, if any, of Mrs. Maple's students would know the order of a scientific report without having it provided. Even if they have experience with a science report, each report is different depending on the teacher and the unit. With the sequencing technique, students know the content to communicate and when to communicate it in the report. Additionally, the template implicitly teaches students that when writing a report, scientists can start with a broad idea, go into more specific details, and then end with a possible solution. Having this sequenced list of specific writing topics is far more comforting to students than simply explaining the instructions and then having students tackle a barren blank document.

> When reports are not scaffolded, they become writing assessments rather than content assessments.

TRY IT OUT

Sequencing

1. Design a template that walks students through creating the product for the PBA one step at a time.
2. Segment the different parts of the PBA in a desired order.
3. Label each section with a heading or title.

INSTRUCTION BOXES

Sequencing a template is just the first part of equitable PBA assessments. The next step is to weave in instruction boxes for each part of the assessment.

Each instruction box has its own set of instructions, and they're sequenced intentionally in a particular order. The instruction boxes contain headings to flag students to each segment of the report, presentation, product, or performance. However, having clearly marked components in a template is not enough. Many experienced multilinguals need further support to produce the ideas. Within the instruction boxes, teachers can prompt students' thinking by

- incorporating guiding questions,
- inserting writing prompts,
- linking to resources,
- adding visuals, and/or
- numbering steps.

These guiding questions and writing prompts can be sequenced in a desired order to scaffold the flow of ideas. In this way, we are teaching students how experts in their field string ideas together and bridge from one idea to another. For example, Mrs. Maple created the instruction box in Figure 3.17 to support students as they summarize their particular ecosystem. Some experienced multilingual students can fully understand their ecosystem from the research they gathered.

Instruction boxes: Specific instructions, prompts, and guiding questions students need to follow to engage successfully in the assessment

3.17 Example of an Instruction Box With Annotations

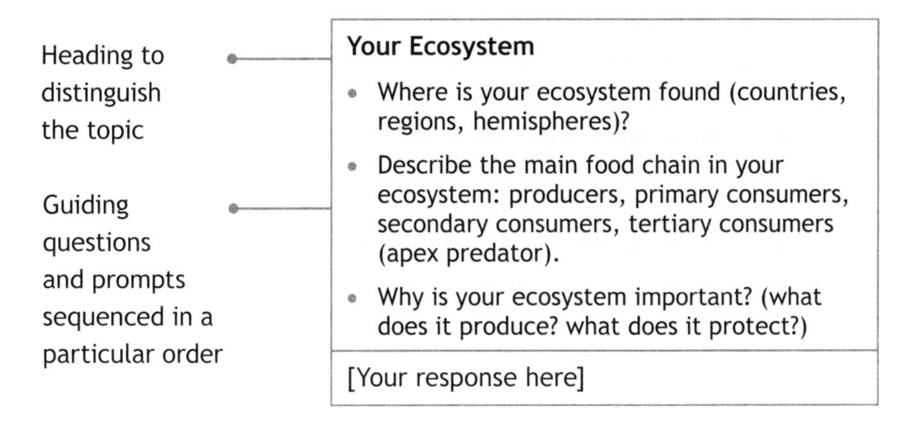

However, some might still struggle to structure their ideas effectively in writing to show deep understanding. With Mrs. Maple's thoughtful writing prompts, students now have a marked path to demonstrate their understanding of their ecosystem. With these prompts, Mrs. Maple can more accurately assess students' content knowledge. Embedding prompts in the instruction boxes exemplifies the spirit of equitable instruction. For a lesson from Mrs. Maple's unit on ecosystems, see Appendix B.

One frequent objection that content teachers have to this suggestion of providing the sequence of writing topics with embedded prompts is that there's no space for creativity. However, texts in many disciplines have a prescribed format for sharing ideas (e.g., lab reports, business contracts, peer-reviewed articles, summaries, news briefs, grant applications, business plans, factsheets, annual reports, stock prospectuses, etc.). For students to communicate like professionals in these disciplines, they must work within the confines of the content area. It's similar to jazz. The most innovative jazz performers must first learn the basics of music theory, musical scales, and the mechanics of playing the instrument before they can work creatively outside these confines. Students must first learn to work *within* the prescribed format before they innovate on the fringes. They are developing the foundational skills required for creativity.

Teachers can also create a simple PBA template without boxes, as shown in Figure 3.18, if they want students to work on a template that more resembles a finished product. With this version of the PBA template, students can draft their final report, presentation, or argument as a complete document. This instruction box-free approach can still intentionally sequence the content with prompts and guiding questions and provide linguistic scaffolds such as sentence starters and paragraph frames. Students do not have to then transfer their work from boxes to another document. They simply have to delete the prompts once they have written their paragraphs, and teachers can read a completed project report without the boxes or prompts.

3.18 Report Template Without Instructional or Student Response Boxes

Your Ecosystem

- Where is your ecosystem found (countries, regions, hemispheres)?
- Describe the main food chain in your ecosystem: producers, primary consumers, secondary consumers, tertiary consumers (apex predator).
- Why is your ecosystem important (what does it produce, what does it protect)?

[Your response here]

Human Impact

- What did humans do to this ecosystem?
- Describe how the food chain in your ecosystem changed because of this human activity
  - What organism was reduced? How did this affect the ecosystem?
  - What organism was increased? How did this affect the ecosystem?

[Your response here]

Solution

- What is one possible solution to restore the balance in this ecosystem's food chain?
- What will happen to the food chain if the solution is successful?
- Why will the return to balance be beneficial to each of the following?
  - The ecosystem
  - Humans

Use this paragraph frame: One possible solution to restore the balance in the food chain in [your ecosystem] is . . . This solution works by . . . If the solution is successful, we will see more . . . and less . . . As a result, the ecosystem will . . . Furthermore, the restoration of the food chain will benefit humans by . . .

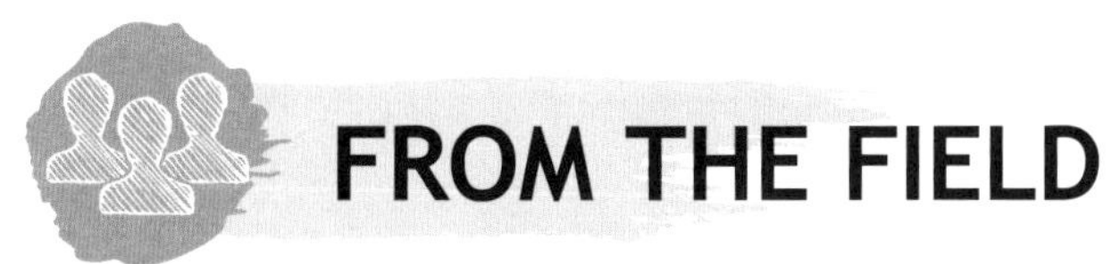

FROM THE FIELD

Instruction Boxes

Tan shares one way he explicitly supports student responses with instruction boxes.

I use the acronym SPEND when writing prompts and guiding questions in the instruction boxes. It helps students "spend" time thinking about the content of their writing. I do not use all of the components of SPEND at the same time, but I use them when they align with the content of the instruction boxes.

- S - Provide relevant **statistics** about this topic.
- P - Mention important **places** about this topic.
- E - Retell an important **event** about this topic.
- N - **Name** significant people or organizations.
- D - Cite an important **date** about this topic.

I also sequence the elements in the SPEND acronym. Depending on the topic, I have students start with a name, a place, and a date. With these elements in place, I have students narrate an event.

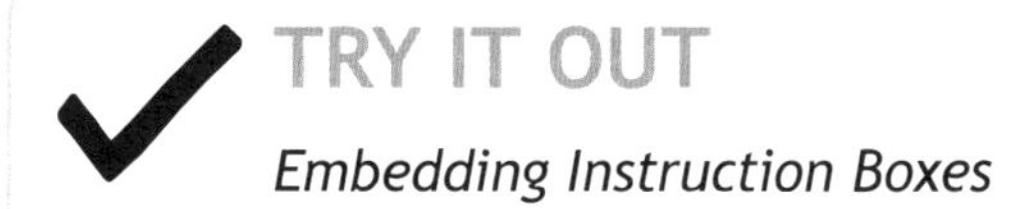

TRY IT OUT

Embedding Instruction Boxes

For each of the segments in your PBA template, write directions in the instruction boxes. Include guiding questions, prompts, useful links, visuals, and instructions.

ENGINEERING THE STUDENT RESPONSE BOXES

After creating the teacher instruction boxes, we work on the student response box in the assessment template.

Student response box: A box containing linguistic scaffolds such as sentence starters, sentence frames, and paragraph frames to structure student output

For many experienced multilingual students, having sequenced instruction boxes with embedded prompts is enough support. However, at times, some may need even more support, especially when communicating complex ideas.

In these situations, teachers can be proactive and provide optional sentence starters or frames in a few or all of the student response boxes. This judgment depends on the student and the content they have to communicate. A sentence starter provides the initial first few words of a sentence and strategically leaves the content for students to finish. For example, Mrs. Maple provides this sentence starter in the introduction section of the template: *[Insert ecosystems] are typically found in ...* This sentence starter spurs students' thinking but does not provide the answer. It intentionally trails off so students can generate their own ideas. Additionally, a sentence frame is like taking two sentence starters and putting them together to express more complex ideas. Mrs. Maple offers this sentence frame to scaffold the writing: *[Insert ecosystem] are important as they provide . . . and prevent . . .* In this way, two ideas are conjoined using a sentence frame. The key to sentence frames is to not have more than two blanks. Otherwise, it will become too difficult for students who end up guessing answers instead of composing authentic texts. Additionally, these linguistic scaffolds ensure that students can communicate like experts in the field. Sentence frames and starters also help content teachers become teachers of academic language. With strategic guidance, students can showcase all of their competence.

Sentence starters and frames are optional supports so students have the freedom and creativity to express their ideas their own way (see Figure 3.19). However, for some, that freedom is petrifying as the limitless options may actually limit progress, especially for students with perfectionist tendencies. In contrast, when teachers notice that students are using their freedom to produce ideas that meander aimlessly, they can help students lasso these ideas back by using the sentence starters and frames.

Teachers can apply this process of designing a template for writing assignments to presentations as well. For any presentation, students have to communicate specific content, in a particular sequence, and with specialized language. Of course, students will not be reading their presentation from the template. It simply scaffolds the process of organizing and structuring the content for the presentation.

3.19 Example of an Instruction Box With Prompts and a Paragraph Frame Embedded Into the Student Response Box

The instruction box has a label for referencing.

Prompts sequenced in order are embedded within the instruction box.

Paragraph frame to stimulate thinking and structure writing.

Part 2: Describe how humans have disrupted the ecosystem.

- **What were the human activities on this ecosystem?**
- **What was taken out, reduced in numbers, or lost in the ecosystem?**
  - **What was the result of this on the ecosystem?**
- **What was added or increased in numbers to the ecosystem?**
  - **What was the result of this on the ecosystem?**

Unfortunately, human activity has disrupted the [your ecosystem]. Some of the ways that humans have disrupted the balance of . . . are by . . . As a result of . . ., the [your ecosystem] lost . . . The loss of . . . caused . . . Now the ecosystem can no longer . . . Additionally, humans have . . . to increase. This increase means that . . . With too much . . ., the ecosystem cannot . . .

TRY IT OUT

Scaffold Student Responses With Starters and Frames

1. Identify student response boxes that are particularly complex and challenging.
2. Provide either sentence starters or sentence frames.
3. Sequence the sentence starters in a particular order.

REFLECTION

- How would creating PBA templates change the learning experience for your particular students?

___

___

___

___

- How would PBA templates support you in teaching content?

___

___

___

___

- How would PBA templates support you in teaching content-specific skills (e.g., evaluating sources for bias, designing an experiment, collecting data, etc.)?

___

___

___

___

- How would PBA templates support you in teaching content-specific language?

___

___

___

___

- How might you share the concept of templates with colleagues?

______

______

______

______

WORKSHOPPING PBAS

Once teachers have a clear, well-sequenced template with embedded linguistic scaffolds for the PBA, we cannot simply give students the template and walk away. This would be assigning and assessing only. For PBAs to be equitable, we need to directly teach students how to complete each part of the assessment. This is known as workshopping the assessment.

A workshopping lesson can mean modeling how to complete a section of the assessment template and also providing clear written instructions. Students then complete that part of the PBA as teachers circulate the room and conference with students.

For example, if the PBA requires students to conduct research, educators will need to teach and scaffold each part of the research process so students can use appropriate search terms, evaluate the usefulness and reliability of resources, organize notes effectively, and cite sources appropriately. All of these skills require explicit instruction and clear modeling. It would be inequitable for multilingual students to be sent off to engage with an assessment with only the oral and written instructions once the assessment is introduced. Workshopping a PBA makes it more equitable because students work on the project in manageable chunks. Each chunk might require different skills so devoting a day to each section develops proficiency in that skill. Through workshopping, students are guided on each chunk rather than languishing to figure out where to start or what to do.

Workshopping the assessment: Devoting a mini-lesson to teach one particular section of the assessment at a time

Mrs. Maple knows that students will have to gather sources for their food web report. She devotes one mini-lesson to showing students how to use appropriate search terms. Then, she briefly models typing in different search terms and scanning the results for the most appropriate sources based on their titles. After a quick discussion to synthesize this skill, students then apply the skill to their own searches. Mrs. Maple then circulates around the classroom to support students as they search.

The antithesis of workshopping assessment is providing all the instructions for the entire assessment in one lesson followed by class time for students to complete it independently. This assign-and-assess approach is not equitable as it lacks the intentional teaching of the assessment skills in accessible segments.

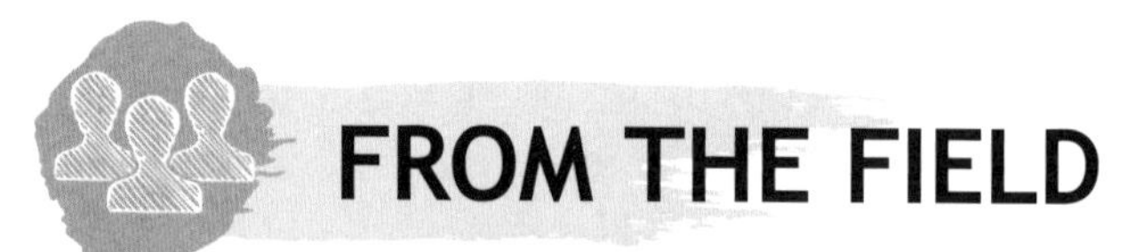

Workshopping a Lab Report

Tan shares his personal experience with a professor who workshopped a lab report in a college course.

I really enjoy science! When I was in college, I was so excited to take one of my two required science courses as part of the graduation requirements. That was until I learned that I had to complete a lab report. I was petrified as I did not have the slightest clue how to conduct a lab report or even what a lab report consisted of. In high school, I never once designed an experiment, collected data, analyzed the data, and communicated my findings in a lab report.

Fortunately for me, the professor who taught the course workshopped each part of the lab report instead of simply giving us the instructions, providing a due date, and setting us off to complete it. Each week, the professor guided students in completing one aspect of the lab report. We worked in a sequential order that provided the content required in the lab report. Gradually, my heightened anxiousness melted away with each passing class. By the end of the course, I submitted a finished lab report following my professor's expectations.

This sage professor lovingly nurtured my interest in science. Most importantly, she modeled how a skillful instructor guides students through an assessment step by step. I consider taking that science class as one of the most significant experiences that has shaped my instruction to this day.

When teachers create the product's template, it becomes a compass that guides their individual lessons.

Teachers will not waste time doing activities only for their "fun value" when teaching with the parts of the assessment template in mind. Instead, teachers can view all of their lessons critically for their relevance to the summative assessment. We offer this central guiding question when critiquing the relevance of a lesson: *How will this lesson help students during the summative assessment?* For example, after creating the research and report template, Mrs. Maple guided students through the research for two weeks. After that, she guided her students through the report for three weeks. During this month period, students are working independently on the assessment alongside Mrs. Maple's supportive attention. Creating these templates makes every lesson purposeful and anchored to the assessment.

TRY IT OUT

Workshopping a PBA

1. Look at your PBA template.
2. Identify parts of the template where a mini-lesson would help students be more successful.
3. Design a mini-lesson to teach these parts of the assessment.

REFLECTION

- How are workshopping assessments different or similar to the approach you're currently using?

____

____

____

____

(Continued)

(Continued)

- How might you have to restructure your lessons to workshop the PBA?

____

____

____

____

- What are the benefits of workshopping a future PBA?

____

____

____

____

- How might students feel if the PBA was taught through workshopping?

____

____

____

____

- How might workshopping a PBA support your ability to teach your curriculum?

____

____

____

____

GRADING A PBA

Since the PBA is how the content knowledge and skills are assessed, it's important to discuss grading students. Grading PBAs is a topic deserving of a book itself, but we will only address one point related to grading experienced multilinguals. We suggest grading only for content knowledge, discipline-specific vocabulary use, and skills explicitly taught in the workshops, not grammatical correctness. When grading for content, grade for

- thorough understanding of content-specific concepts,
- skillful application of content-specific skills, and
- appropriate and accurate use of content-specific language.

In terms of content-specific language beyond vocabulary, we can assess any of the dimensions of academic language that was taught in class, as explained in Chapter 2 in Figure 2.1. These include

- the use of content-specific details,
- organization of ideas,
- connection between ideas with appropriate transition phrases, and
- student responses that meet the lesson's objective (e.g., describe, explain, argue, narrate).

The content-specific language required by the PBA has largely been scaffolded at this point by the assessment template and by the workshopped lessons. Teachers can assess content-specific language because it has been taught and scaffolded through lessons and the template, but grading students for their grammatical correctness even though the content is accurate would be inequitable.

> When content teachers evaluate students only on grammar, they only see a narrow vision of students' full potential.

The examples in Figure 3.20 show the difference between grading for grammatical accuracy and for discipline-specific vocabulary use.

3.20 Examples of Grading for Content and Discipline-Specific Vocabulary Use

Student Response	Explanation of Grading for Academic Language
Student A *The plants are eaten by animals that only eat plants. Then these animals are eaten by other animals that eat the plant eaters. In the next level, bigger meat eaters eat the smaller meat eaters. Finally, the biggest meat eater eats the medium-sized meat eaters.*	The student response shows that this student understands energy transfer in a food web, but does not use specific terms such as *producers, primary consumers, secondary consumers,* and *apex predator*. Even though this response is grammatically correct, content-specific vocabulary is lacking.
Student B *Producers is plants. They get there energy from the sun. This energy move up a food web when consumers eats plants or other animals. Example: a rabbit is a primary consumer and it eat a plant, the energy from the plant transfer to the rabbits. This energy continues to the next level with the secondary consumers. These are usually huger predators that eat herbivores. At the top of the food web are the tertiary consumers. Usually this level have larger apex predators that have few or no other predators.*	Content wise, this student demonstrates a higher proficiency level than Student A at using content-specific words accurately. This student understands each layer of the food web, uses specific vocabulary words correctly at level, and can describe the relationship between each level more accurately than can Student A. Grammatically, this student needs support. However, the grammar approximations do not impede comprehension of the ideas.

online resources Available at **resources.corwin.com/Long-Term SuccessforExperiencedMLs**

CLOSING REMARKS

Beginning at the end is Mrs. Maple's first step when she plans the next unit. She is not lured by the temptation to plan the next fun lesson, nor is she distracted by the immediacy of the next lesson. Mrs. Maple knows that planning the assessment first is a titanic task. Yet, she knows it's one of the most time-multiplying activities. The time she invests now carefully planning the assessment will pay significant dividends when students engage in the assessment later.

She invests time creating the PBA template section by section proactively thinking about what experience multilinguals need to be successful. As she works, a sense of peace settles on her. The concerns she often feels when working with experienced multilinguals begins to evaporate. The assessment she designs presents the road map for the upcoming lessons. Now that she has an approach to engineering the assessment, instructing multilingual students feels more like gentle rolling hills than steep mountains.

Achievement occurs by design, not by accident. Summative assessments are challenging when the instructions are unclear or lack support. When this occurs, assessments cease being a curriculum issue and start becoming an equity problem. We can find a middle ground between assigning scaffold-less assessments and giving below-grade-level summative assessments to experienced multilinguals. Engineering equitable assessments is this middle ground. In this balanced place, we lay the sturdy foundation for the rest of learning to come.

CHAPTER SUMMARY

- Scaffolding summatives (e.g., exams and performance-based assessments) is equitable for experienced multilinguals.
- Design scaffolds into the assessment document within exam instructions.
- Exam engineering does not reduce the expectations but guides students to be successful in meeting grade-level expectations.
- Exam engineering techniques for tests include synonyms, sentence starters, chunking, images, and word banks.
- Exam engineering techniques for performance-based assessments include intentional sequencing, instruction boxes, sentence starters, and frames.

WRITING INTEGRATED OBJECTIVES

WRITING INTEGRATED OBJECTIVES

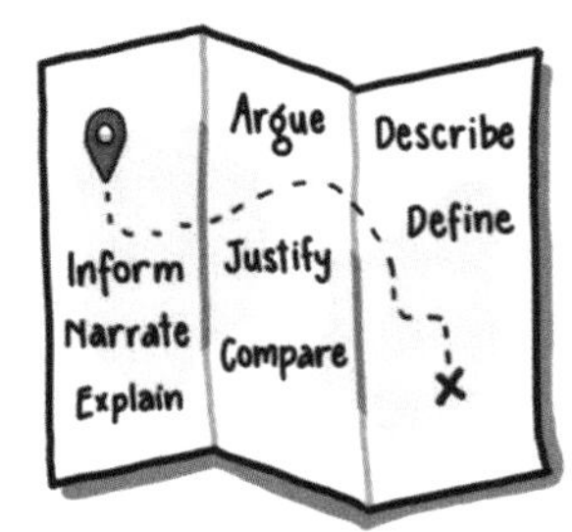

Write a prompt with a thinking verb for the exit ticket. Write a model response

Discipline-specific words and phrases
Sentence structures for thinking verbs

Analyze the language in the response

Thinking verb
+ content
+ academic language expectations

Create an integrated objective

@TanKHuynh @easKelton

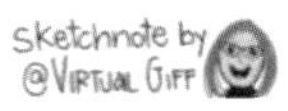

Graciela looks forward to her art class with Ms. Maita every morning. She not only loves learning elements of art and design, but she also loves interacting with her friends in the class. Graciela has developed a strong bond with Ms. Maita; she even told her friends that Ms. Maita "gets her." Graciela appreciates the choices she gets to make in art class, and she enjoys learning about other cultures through art. Today, she's excited about working on her line drawing of a *calavera*, a decorative skull made from sugar used in the celebration of Día de los Muertos, for the upcoming school art auction.

Ms. Maita explicitly plans for content and academic language development in her art classes, which is one reason students like Graciela experience such success. Ms. Maita followed the same instructional framework we introduced in Chapter 2 to intentionally integrate academic language development throughout her art lesson, as shown in Figure 4.1.

4.1 Instructional Framework for Ms. Maita's Art Unit

Design the summative assessment

At the end of the line drewing unit, Ms. Maita plans to display her students' work and hold an art auction at the school. Each student will write a critique of their own still life drawing referring to the lines and the tone using the style of an art critique.

Write the integrated objective

Explain why they chose to draw at least two lines in their artifact by stating the names of the lines and the phrase in order to show.

Establish comprehensible input

Ms. Maita decides to use a visual scaffold to make the concept of line usage more understandable for students. She models with her own drawing thinking aloud about her process. She also annotates the different type of lines used to create her picture.

Structure discipline-specific output

Ms. Maita asks students to tell a partner which lines they used and explain why they used them. To support the discipline-specific language in their explanations, she provides a word bank with the labeled lines and some sentence frames for how an artist might explain their process.

Ms. Maita's students could certainly learn to draw the five line types and complete the line drawing of a cultural artifact without speaking or writing much. However, just like professional artists outside of the school setting, they may be asked to describe their process or write an article about their work. In order to do that, Ms. Maita knows they will also need to use art-specific language.

Across the curriculum, secondary multilingual students need to learn not only the content but also the language related to that content. In Chapter 3, we focused on starting with the end in mind by centering our planning on the summative assessment (Covey, 2020; Wiggins & McTighe, 2005). We introduced a process teachers can use to consider the academic language students will need to successfully demonstrate their mastery of the content concepts on the summative assessment. Understanding the academic language demands inherent in this final assessment sets the foundation for the unit. Once the final assessment is planned, teachers can start planning the daily lessons guided by each day's objectives. These objectives focus on both the content-specific language skills and content knowledge that are necessary for success. Ms. Maita plans to display her students' line drawings at the end of the unit and hold an art auction at the school. To accompany their drawing, each student will write a critique of their own work referring to the lines and the tone using the style of an art critic.

Once the unit test or final performance assessment is clear, teachers can transition to planning for daily lessons that lead toward proficiency in the knowledge, skills, and academic language necessary for eventual success on that summative assessment. This chapter guides teachers through a step-by-step process that weaves academic language development into the objectives. We intentionally chose to model this process with an example from art class to demonstrate how academic language exists in every discipline, even in an inherently visual or hands-on class. Therefore, every content area educator needs to explicitly teach the language of their discipline. In the remaining chapters and in Appendix B, we share examples from several other content areas.

Authors Nguyen and Commins (2020) recommend, "Instead of planning instruction for 'the average learner' and then trying to accommodate instruction for students who are culturally and linguistically diverse through piecemeal resources, plan your instruction with them in mind from the beginning and intentionally incorporate their linguistic and cultural repertoire in your lessons" (p. 6). The approach in this chapter guides secondary content teachers through a three-step process that intentionally plans with experienced multilinguals in mind, not as an afterthought.

This three-step process for writing objectives uncovers the academic language that exists in texts, speaking tasks, and written assignments. As we described in Chapter 2, this academic language includes not only essential vocabulary students need to communicate about the topic but also the academic language they need for various purposes, audiences, and situations. Teachers can plan like an ELD specialist, even if they never had a course in linguistics or learned another language, with this practical process for writing integrated objectives (Figure 4.2).

4.2 Process for Writing Integrated Objectives

Step	Description
1	Write a prompt and model response for an exit ticket.
2	Analyze the academic language in the response.
3	Create an integrated objective.

INTEGRATED OBJECTIVES

Integrated objectives have a significant positive impact on multilingual learners' success in content classes. Both Marzano's et al. (2001) meta-analyses of studies on setting objectives and goals and Hattie's (2012) meta-analyses of studies related to teacher clarity revealed strong effect sizes for this influence on student achievement. These studies indicate that clear learning objectives can lead to increased student success because "when students understand what they are supposed to learn, the chances are much higher that they will actually learn it" (Knight, 2012, p. 32). The learning objectives give students a focus for the lesson. They also help teachers chunk complex content concepts into comprehensible, achievable learning goals.

The focus on academic language development is especially beneficial for multilingual learners. Teaching specific academic language objectives prepares "students for the type of academic language they need to understand the content and perform the activities of the lesson" (Echevarría et al., 2017, p. 32). An integrated language

---

Integrated objective: A statement that defines the desired outcomes for both the content and the content-specific language students need to use

Exit ticket: A short written or verbal formative assessment given at the end of the lesson

objective describes *how* students will develop reading, writing, listening, and speaking in the content classroom.

When an objective makes the academic language expectations clear, every lesson moves students one step closer to becoming content experts.

Integrating content and academic language objectives, rather than creating two *separate* objectives, is a practical way secondary teachers can focus on the requirements for success in their lessons. We offer a three-step process for crafting integrated objectives.

STEP 1: WRITE THE PROMPT AND MODEL RESPONSE

Step 1 in creating an integrated objective is to start with a prompt for an end-of-lesson exit ticket. This prompt could be a listening or reading comprehension check or require students to speak or write about their understanding of the lesson's objectives using academic language. It should challenge the students to demonstrate or apply their understanding of the content in some way.

We encourage teachers to start each prompt with a *verb* rather than a question word. Questions may be effective for assessing content knowledge, but they provide little guidance on the academic language students need to use in their response. For example, if Ms. Maita asks students, "*Which lines did you use?*" they may answer simply, "*straight, curved, and zigzag.*" However, if she changes the prompt to start with a verb, "*Describe each line you used,*" students would need to use complete sentences to give details about the lines they chose. While this second prompt is quite similar to the question, students are more likely to answer with complete sentences and extend their thinking into a full description because they have been prompted with a verb.

These verbs are important because they provide clarity on the purpose (or function) for using academic language, such as *describe, explain*, or *evaluate*, and

"if we are clear about the purposes that students will be expected to achieve, then we can better support them" (Derewianka & Jones, 2016, p. 9).

Experienced multilinguals benefit from explicit support in using language for different academic purposes. These purposes include comprehending grade-level texts, speaking about the content, writing discipline-specific texts, and listening to lectures, videos, and podcasts. Because the way we *describe* something is quite different from the way we *explain why* a phenomenon occurs, students need explicit support in comprehending or producing academic language for different purposes. The lesson's exit ticket prompt makes clear the essential purpose for using academic language by starting with a verb that students need to perform.

The verbs we use most often in our prompts can be categorized into four main groups:

- Inform
- Narrate
- Explain
- Argue

Each of these thinking verbs is a broad category for many different possible verbs that would prompt students to use academic language (WIDA, 2020). Across the content areas, students engage in using language for different academic purposes. For example, science teachers may ask students to describe a phenomenon, while math teachers may ask them to analyze a graph. Social studies teachers often ask students to defend a claim with reasoning, and language arts teachers ask students to recount key events in a narrative. Each of these types of thinking and language use, also known as language functions, are part of one of the four larger categories. The chart in Figure 4.3 shows the four main academic language uses and some of the common verbs associated with each category. This chart features some of the verbs that require students to use spoken or written language in their responses. In Appendix A, we provide a definition for each of these verbs and some possible sentence frames that could guide students to communicate the purpose of the verb. We acknowledge that the academic language students need to inform, narrate, explain, and argue often overlaps and that the listed verbs may belong in more than one category.

In order to figure out the academic English students need to address the verb in a prompt, we encourage teachers to write a response to their own prompt. Because this prompt usually happens at the end of a lesson, it should take students only about five minutes to write

4.3 Thinking Verbs (aka Language Functions or Command Terms)

Category	I Inform	N Narrate	E Explain	A Argue
Definition	Communicate factual information about a concept or a phenomenon or a topic	Share experiences through stories and histories, real or imagined	Give account for how or why things work	Support one's claim using evidence and reasoning
Additional verbs for exit tickets	Classify Compare Contrast Define Describe Estimate Identify Label List Outline Paraphrase Report Synthesize	Recall Recount Retell Sequence Summarize	Analyze Apply Conclude Connect Deduce Examine Exemplify Infer Interpret Investigate Predict Present Reflect	Agree Appraise Comment Defend Demonstrate Disagree Discuss Evaluate Form an opinion Justify Make a claim Persuade Prove Recommend Suggest

Adapted from WIDA (2020); International Baccalaureate (2019).

Available at **resources.corwin.com/Long-Term SuccessforExperiencedMLs**

or draw. That means it should take teachers just a couple of minutes to complete. Writing or drawing one model response is a quick way to determine what academic English students might need to express their own understanding at the end of a lesson. Teachers who use an inquiry-based approach to instruction may not be able to completely predict the direction the lesson will take. Therefore, there will be multiple ways to answer the prompt. However, writing one possible model response can still give teachers an indication of the vocabulary, sentence structures, and organization a student response might take. This model response can then guide instruction by helping teachers focus on what content and content-specific language are essential in the lesson.

Ms. Maita's prompt for her art students is to *explain why they chose each line to draw their artifact*, so she quickly writes a model response for her own drawing representing an artifact of her Senegalese heritage.

I drew a djembe, an African drum used in many traditional ceremonies. For this section of the drawing, I used horizontal lines at the base in order to show how stable this artifact is. Horizontal lines usually indicate calmness and stability. I used zigzag lines under the drumhead to indicate action and excitement. Although this djembe is stable, it also creates dynamic, exciting music.

Of course, her students will be talking and writing about completely different artifacts such as Graciela's *calavera*, but this model response provides an idea of the disciplinary language that most students will need in their responses. In the next step, we describe how to analyze the academic English in this model response. The examples in Figure 4.4 show some prompts from teachers in different content areas and at different points in their units.

4.4 Example Exit Ticket Prompts

Content Area	Sample Prompts for an Exit Ticket
Science	***Sort*** *the photos into categories of living, non-living, or dead.* ***Justify*** *whether the item in the photo is living, non-living, or dead.*
Social Studies	***List*** *the factors that created social inequality in nineteenth-century France.* ***Compare*** *the social inequality in nineteenth-century France to the reality of twenty-first-century Western society.*
Math	***Identify*** *the features of each of the transformed graphs.* ***Describe*** *how the graph has been transformed.*
Language Arts	***Identify*** *character traits of the main character.* ***Predict*** *what will happen to the main character in the next chapter.*
Art	***Identify*** *the lines in your drawing.* ***Explain*** *why you used each of the lines you did in your drawing.*

TRY IT OUT

Design a Prompt and Model Response

1. Write a prompt for an end-of-lesson exit ticket starting with a thinking verb.
2. Write or draw a model response to the prompt. Use the vocabulary and sentence structures you would expect a successful student in your grade-level content class to use.

Note: Generating a student response should take less than 5 minutes if you expect students to do it at the end of a class period.

STEP 2: ANALYZE THE ACADEMIC LANGUAGE IN THE MODEL RESPONSE

Secondary teachers are specialists in their content areas. They know the language of their content used by experts in the field better than other teachers do. We believe all teachers can notice the academic language students will need to succeed in their content classes without having to go to graduate school to be a linguist. In this step, we encourage content teachers to focus on two basic dimensions of the academic English in the model response: discipline-specific vocabulary and academic language based on the thinking verb.

Discipline-Specific Vocabulary

We suggest teachers first look for the discipline-specific vocabulary that students might need to successfully understand the content lessons and express that understanding. Developing this vocabulary is inextricably linked to students' academic success, especially in secondary classes. Every day, multilingual learners face a flood of specialized vocabulary in every class, so teachers need to carefully select which words will have the biggest impact on their comprehension of the concepts and their expression of that understanding (Beck et al., 2002; Calderón, 2007; Calderón & Minaya-Rowe, 2011; Farstrup & Samuels, 2009; Graves et al., 2013). Building comprehension of discipline-specific words like *totalitarianism* or *indigenous* in social studies, *amino acid* or *exoskeleton* in science, *place value* or *quadratic* in math, and *theme* or *literary device* in English language arts is equivalent to building comprehension of the concepts that make up those terms (Harmon et al., 2008). Chapter 5 will provide essential strategies for making terms like these comprehensible, but first teachers have to determine which words are most essential for their lessons.

If we analyze Ms. Maita's model response for art-specific vocabulary (underlined words), we would underline the terms for the different types of lines and the word *artifact*, since all students would need these words in their own responses.

> *I drew a djembe, an African drum used in many traditional ceremonies. For this section of the drawing, I used horizontal lines at the base in order to show how stable this artifact is. Horizontal lines usually indicate calmness and stability. I used zigzag lines under the drumhead to indicate action and excitement. Although this djembe is stable, it also creates dynamic, exciting music.*

Figure 4.5 provides examples of discipline-specific words for different prompts.

4.5 Discipline-Specific Words for Model Responses

Content Area	Prompts for an Exit Ticket	Discipline-Specific Words
Science	***Justify*** *whether the item in the photo is living, non-living, or dead.*	excretion nutrition respiration reproduction sensitivity
Social Studies	***Compare*** *the social inequality in nineteenth-century France to the reality of twenty-first-century Western society.*	clergy nobles exploitation monarchy inflation bankruptcy
Math	***Describe*** *how the graph has been transformed.*	translation reflection rotation scaling vertical horizontal

Content Area	Prompts for an Exit Ticket	Discipline-Specific Words
Language Arts	***Identify*** *character traits of the main character.*	character trait selfish compassionate courageous honest charismatic
Art	***Identify*** *the lines in your drawing.*	zigzag line horizontal line vertical line curved line diagonal line thick, thin

Academic Language for the Thinking Verb

In order to respond to a prompt in a content class, multilingual learners need more than just a list of discipline-specific words. They also need to understand what the thinking verb in the prompt is asking them to do and the words and phrases necessary to express this type of thinking. If the prompt asks students to *identify, label,* or *list,* students may need explicit instruction in how to respond with specific vocabulary only. However, if they are asked to *compare, justify, explain,* or *describe* they will need to write or speak in complete sentences that include phrases to form connections between their ideas and link the technical, discipline-specific words in context.

> Each thinking verb is a distinct cognitive move, and students need to know how to make each move.

For example, when students are asked to *compare* two texts, historical periods, or features, they will probably need to use language that indicates comparison like *more* or ____*er than* or *similar to.* When teachers analyze their model responses for the language of the thinking in the prompt, they will notice these types of phrases.

When Ms. Maita analyzed her model response to the prompt asking students to *explain why* they chose certain lines, she noticed expressions that showed purpose such as *in order to show* or *to indicate*. The chart in Figure 4.6 provides additional examples of the types of language often associated with the thinking verbs in example prompts.

Identifying the *essential* discipline-specific words and phrases to express thinking in a model response is a critical step in integrating academic language into content lessons. There are simply too many words in the English language or in any content area to teach all of them explicitly, so we focus on just the essential terms for responding to the prompt. Once we determine which words and phrases are expected, we have the ingredients necessary for the final step in writing an integrated objective.

4.6 Phrases and Sentence Structures in Model Responses

Content	Prompt	Language of the Thinking Verb
Science	***Justify*** *whether the item in the photo is living, non-living, or dead.*	It is ___ because ___ is composed of ___ therefore, it is ___
Social Studies	***Compare*** *the social inequality in nineteenth-century France to the reality of twenty-first-century Western society.*	both similar to just like in addition to on the other hand another characteristic of
Math	***Describe*** *how the graph has been transformed.*	translated by a factor of ___ across the ___ axis
Language Arts	***Predict*** *what will happen to the main character in the next chapter.*	in the future after that might could would if ___, then ___

TRY IT OUT

Analyze the Academic Language in the Model Response

Now that you have created the prompt and written the model response, you can analyze the academic language in that response using the following steps.

1. Highlight the discipline-specific terms students may need to successfully respond to the prompt.
2. Underline the words and phrases related to the language of the thinking verb (e.g., phrases, sentence structure, and transitions). Refer to Appendix A for some common phrases related to these verbs.
3. Consider alternative phrases used in your discipline to express a response to that prompt.

STEP 3: WRITE THE INTEGRATED OBJECTIVE

In Step 1, we wrote a prompt for the end-of-lesson exit ticket. This prompt addressed the essential content of the lesson. Then, in Step 2, we analyzed the academic language in the model response to find essential vocabulary and phrases students would need to successfully answer the prompt. Now we can add that academic language—either the discipline-specific vocabulary or the language for the thinking verbs—to our prompt. This creates an integrated objective. We encourage teachers to try this formula for creating integrated objectives.

Thinking Verb +	Content +	Academic Language Expectations (by . . .)

When writing this type of integrated objective, we encourage teachers to also consider whether the focus for the students is on developing listening, reading, speaking, or writing skills. Some possible integrated objectives from our examples in each content area are listed in Figure 4.7. In the far-right column of the table, we've also included the language domain(s) (listening, speaking, reading, and/or writing) that this objective focuses on.

This integrated objective gives teachers a focus for their instruction. They now have a goal for the knowledge and skills of the content lesson as well as the academic language they need to model, scaffold,

4.7 Example Content and Academic Language Objectives

Broad Category of Thinking Verb	Specific Thinking Verb	Content	Academic Language Expectations	Language Domain (Listening, Reading, Speaking, Writing)
Inform	Sort	photos into categories of living, non-living, or dead	by reading the descriptions of the life processes on the back of each photo.	Reading
Argue	Justify	whether the item in the photo is living, non-living, or dead	by citing the seven life processes (*movement*, *reproduction*, *sensitivity*, *nutrition*, *excretion*, *respiration*, and *growth*).	Speaking or writing
Inform	List	the factors that created social inequality in nineteenth-century France	by writing bullet points with specific examples from the text and video.	Reading and listening
Inform	Compare	the social inequality in nineteenth-century France to the reality of twenty-first-century Western society	by using comparative language to link inequalities in both centuries (e.g., *both*, *just like*, *a similarity between*).	Speaking or writing
Inform	Identify	the features of each of the transformed graphs	by labeling the graph with the terms such as *translation*, *reflection*, *rotation*, *scaling*, *horizontal*, and *vertical*.	Reading and writing
Explain	Describe	how the graph has been transformed	by using the precise term for the type of transformation and the phrase *by a factor of* or *by ___ units*.	Speaking or writing

Broad Category of Thinking Verb	Specific Thinking Verb	Content	Academic Language Expectations	Language Domain (Listening, Reading, Speaking, Writing)
Inform	Identify	character traits of the main character	by listing a character trait and writing a quotation that illustrates that trait.	Reading
Narrate	Predict	what will happen to the main character in the next chapter	by using conditional language such as *might* or *could* and a reference to previous chapters that support this belief.	Reading and writing
Explain	Explain	why you chose the lines you used	by stating the names of at least two lines and the phrase *in order to show.*	Speaking or writing

Available at **resources.corwin.com/Long-Term SuccessforExperiencedMLs**

and practice in class. Adding a focus on academic language to the prompt encourages students to use that language to more precisely and clearly express their thinking.

Writing an Integrated Objective

1. Create an integrated objective following the first two boxes in the structure below:

Thinking Verb	Content	Academic Language Expectations (by . . .)

(Continued)

(Continued)

2. In the Academic Language Expectations part of the integrated objective, add
   - the discipline-specific vocabulary or
   - the language of the thinking verb.

Note this integrated objective should require students to listen, read, speak, and/or write.

FROM THE FIELD

Co-Planning for Content and Academic Language

Beth had the opportunity to co-plan a lesson with Mr. Jones, the physics teacher at an international school. In the first lessons of the unit, students were tasked with designing and building their own tool for finding the focal length of a convex lens. They had light sources, objects, convex lenses, cardboard, paper, and tape available for the project. At the end of the first lesson, Mr. Jones prompted students to "*Describe what you learned about finding the focal length.*" When one student responded, "*It gets bigger when it gets closer,*" Mr. Jones knew he would need to focus more on technical vocabulary. Mr. Jones reviewed his model response for the prompt "*Describe what you learned about finding the focal length*" and highlighted all the discipline-specific vocabulary. Then he wrote an **integrated objective** for the next class, which was "*Describe what you learned about finding the focal length of a convex lens by using the precise vocabulary in the word bank.*"

Since the students didn't use this precise content-specific vocabulary at the end of the first class, Mr. Jones decided to label all the materials and write a word bank with these essential words on the board. In the next lesson, he circulated and prompted students to name the parts and purposes of the tool they were building. At the end of the lesson, he prompted the class to "*Describe what you learned about finding the focal length of a convex lens using the precise words in the word bank.*" Because Mr. Jones scaffolded the disciplinary language as well as content-based concepts throughout the class, students were able to use the precise vocabulary to express their understanding.

CLOSING REMARKS

Writing objectives using this process encourages teachers to put the puzzle pieces of content and content-specific language together.

When teachers are explicit about what academic language students need to be successful in a lesson, students develop both concept understanding and language proficiency in that discipline.

Teachers who use this process for creating an integrated objective find that it helps them focus each lesson on the most essential words and phrases their multilingual learners need for long-term success across the curriculum. Appendix B provides the completed lesson plan for this visual art lesson as well as lesson plans for the math, geometry, physics, social studies, language arts and business classes we discuss in the book. Each of these completed plans share a summative assessment (Chapter 3), one integrated objective (Chapter 4), scaffolds for input (Chapter 5), and ideas for structuring output (Chapter 6).

At the end of the art class, Ms. Maita prompts the students to explain why they used the lines they did in their drawings. Graciela turns to her partner to show her the line drawing of the *calavera* she brought to class. She and her partner, who also speaks Spanish, talk about their drawings for a few moments in Spanish. Then Graciela switches fluidly into English to address Ms. Maita's prompt. She uses the sentence frames on the board, which give her support for explaining *why* she used curved lines along the jaw bone but diagonal lines above the eyes. Then, Graciela writes down her explanation on an exit ticket, which she gives to Ms. Maita as she leaves. She feels confident about her drawing and explanation. Now she's excited and a bit nervous about displaying her work and writing a critique for the final art auction project.

After using this process to write the objective, teachers express enthusiasm about the difference it makes for their experienced multilinguals. Maggie Chen, a high school science teacher in Colorado, reflected, "I find myself being more intentional about language development over the course of a unit in regards to vocabulary words and how to use those words within science content. Color coding action words like *create, identify, explain* has really helped me support students with the structure of their responses." Margit McLaughlin, a humanities teacher at an international school in Sweden commented, "My humanities lessons became a lot more successful when I started implementing language development skills along with the content. . . . Now the students can write about what they know, or discuss it with their classmates. At this point, I can't imagine teaching content lessons without an academic language focus." Planning with an integrated objective in mind using the end-of-lesson prompt as a starting point helped these teachers more explicitly weave a focus on academic language into their lessons.

Experienced multilingual learners grow as learners when secondary teachers provide the support they need to express themselves as mathematicians, scientists, historians, authors, and artists. Once teachers identify the essential academic language for a lesson, they are ready to add the scaffolds and strategies we present in Chapters 5 and 6.

REFLECTION

- How could this process for creating integrated objectives benefit the multilingual learners in your context?

____

____

____

____

- How is this process similar to or different from the process you currently use to write objectives?

____

____

____

____

CHAPTER SUMMARY

- Experienced multilinguals need to learn not only the content but also the language related to that content.
- When teachers are explicit about what academic language students need to be successful in a lesson, students understand concepts and develop academic language proficiency.
- Clear integrated objectives lead to increased student success.
- Creating an integrated objective with a focus on academic language can be achieved in three steps:
    - Write an end-of-lesson prompt and model response.
    - Analyze the academic language in the response.
    - Write an integrated objective with a focus on the academic language expectations.

5

ESTABLISHING COMPREHENSIBLE INPUT

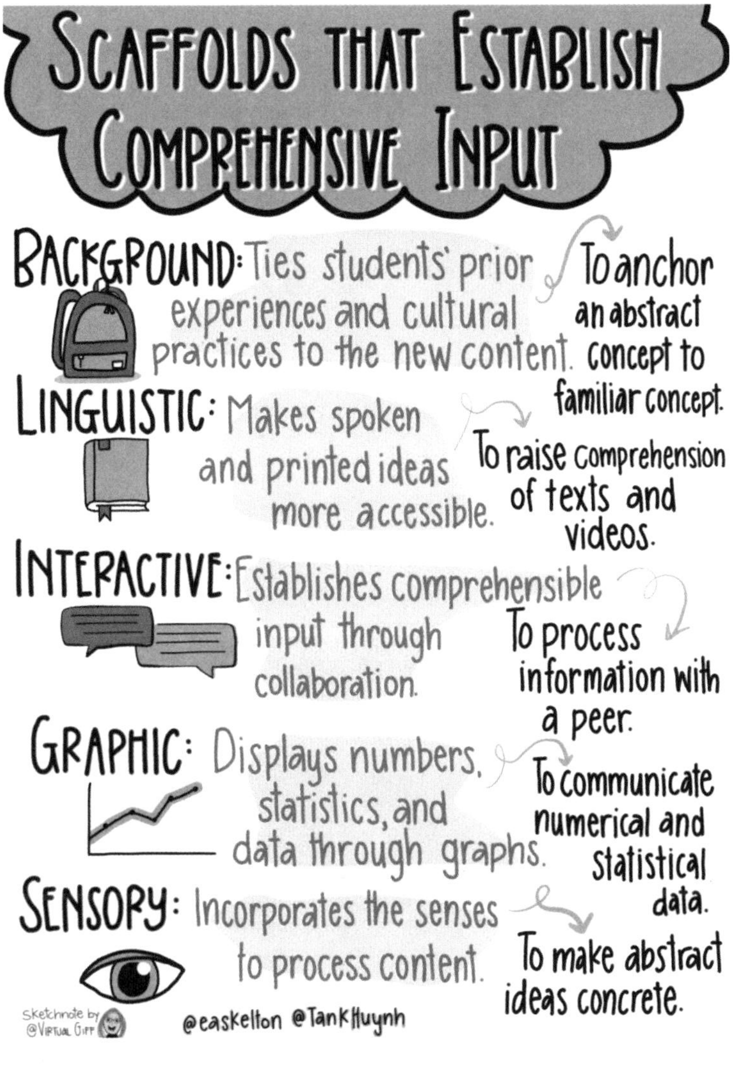

SCAFFOLDS THAT ESTABLISH COMPREHENSIVE INPUT

BACKGROUND: Ties students' prior experiences and cultural practices to the new content.
To anchor an abstract concept to familiar concept.

LINGUISTIC: Makes spoken and printed ideas more accessible.
To raise comprehension of texts and videos.

INTERACTIVE: Establishes comprehensible input through collaboration.
To process information with a peer.

GRAPHIC: Displays numbers, statistics, and data through graphs.
To communicate numerical and statistical data.

SENSORY: Incorporates the senses to process content.
To make abstract ideas concrete.

Sketchnote by @Virtual Giff

@easkelton @TankHuynh

Mx. Delgado, the seventh-grade design teacher, planned the bridge unit for their design class following the planning framework introduced in Chapter 2. Min Woo and his classmates will be learning about the physics behind bridges. They will create their own and compete to see which design can hold the most weight. Although Mx. Delgado already integrates discipline-specific vocabulary into every lesson, they are still concerned that some of their students need additional scaffolding to internalize the terms and be able to use them in the final report. Mx. Delgado realize they will need to focus on establishing comprehensible input to ensure that all students, especially the experienced multilinguals, grasp the essential terms. Mx. Delgado knows that for instruction to be kind, it must be clear, so they plan their unit using the instructional framework offered in this book (Figure 5.1).

5.1 Instructional Framework for a Science Unit

	Engineer the summative assessment	*At the end of the bridge unit, students will compete to see which bridge can hold the most weight. Then they will submit a report describing their design and reflecting on the engineering features they chose.*
	Write the integrated objective	*Describe the differences between tension and compression by using academic vocabulary.*
	Establish comprehensible input	*Students will to be manipulating different objects to feel the difference between tension and compression.*
	**Structure academic output**	*At each station, students will have the force exerted through the manipulatives and complete the sentence frames: This station demonstrates tension / compression because . . .*

In this chapter, we narrow in on the third phase of the planning framework and introduce five essential scaffolds for establishing comprehensible input, which is paramount for students' long-term success. This is the hard work of matching the integrated objective to the appropriate scaffolds that makes content meaningful to students.

WHAT IS COMPREHENSIBLE INPUT?

Imagine that you are joining two other long-time friends at a coffee shop to catch up. One of your friends is a stock analyst, and the other is a manager at a bank. As the three of you talk, the conversation meanders to the topic of retirement investing. They begin to talk about strategies for retirement investing. You are not familiar with investing, but you try to follow the conversation. You begin to get confused when terms such as *PE ratio, market cap, index funds, ETFs, large cap, midcap, small cap,* and *emerging markets* sprout up throughout the conversation. With each term, you feel more and more lost. You want to ask about each term, but the swarming words are just too many. You know that asking would obstruct the flow of the conversation. Feeling deflated, you let the conversation wander, give up trying to understand, lean back to sip on your pumpkin spice latte, nod throughout, and patiently wait for a topic about which all three of you share an understanding of the concepts.

In this scenario, you understood all of the words and even had a basic understanding of investing. However, when it became highly technical with industry-specific content, your comprehension plummeted because the terms were new to you. The conversation lacked the necessary context to make these words comprehensible. This is what many of our experienced multilinguals face in content classes. They can distinguish all of the words, but there is little comprehensible input as many discipline-specific terms lack meaning.

As explained in Chapter 2, comprehensible input is making ideas understandable. Krashen (1982) hypothesized that to acquire a language, we must understand what we hear and read. Speaking and writing will surface once words come to life with meaning. Once sounds and words have meaning, comprehension takes root.

Four decades of empirical research suggest that multilingual students can learn content as they are acquiring English if the instruction is comprehensible (Echevarría et al., 2017). Providing comprehensible input is essential for the long-term success of experienced multilinguals and a non-negotiable feature of equitable instruction. Experienced multilinguals cannot be successful if they do not understand the content. Often,

learning is less about students' intelligence and more about how we design instruction.

PLANNING SCAFFOLDS FOR COMPREHENSIBLE INPUT

With scaffolds, curriculum-specific concepts and new skills are within students' reach (Walqui & van Lier, 2010). A scaffold can make an abstract concept concrete and increase students' success with a new skill. Some teachers might think that scaffolds shrink the curriculum and "water down" the challenge. However, scaffolds simply make content more accessible by adding meaning to content-specific terms, complex sentence structures, and concepts. Figure 5.2 shows what a scaffold is and what it is not.

For Mx. Delgado's students to be successful during the bridge unit, they will have to learn two specific forces and five types of bridges. Therefore, Mx. Delgado intentionally weaves scaffolds in so that students learn the names of the forces and all five types of bridges. Less rigorous expectations would have students learn fewer types of bridges and forces.

Lowering expectations turns mountains into hills, whereas scaffolds equip students with the tools to climb the steepest mountains.

5.2 What Scaffolding Is and What It Is Not

Scaffolding is . . .	Scaffolding is not . . .
• temporary • preplanned and/or provided in the moment • used to maintain high expectations	• permanent • students learning less content • students doing easier work • students doing less work

Available at **resources.corwin.com/Long-TermSuccessforExperiencedMLs**

The most important feature of a scaffold is that it is temporary. Knowing when to *lose* a support is as important as knowing when to *use* one. When students can do the task independently, teachers can wean them off the support or students will forever latch onto the teacher's support instead of leaning into learning strategies. When a scaffold becomes an overused support, it robs opportunities for growth. As mentioned in Chapter 1, scaffolds such as writing bullet points actually prevent students from developing the academic skills necessary to succeed in content areas (Brooks, 2020).

The majority of scaffolds fall into five buckets: sensory, interactive, graphic (Gottlieb, 2013), linguistic (Zwiers, 2014), and background (Honigsfeld et al., 2022; Snyder & Staehr Fenner, 2021). Figure 5.3 shows each of these categories of scaffolds as distinct tools in a teacher's instructional toolbox. Scaffolds can be used by *teachers* to clarify instruction or by *students* to communicate ideas. It would be impossible to build a house with only a hammer, so it would be ineffective to use only one category of scaffolding when teaching different topics.

5.3 Descriptions of the Types of Scaffolds

Categories of Scaffolds		Application
	Background: ties students' prior experiences and cultural practices to the new content	• provides a familiar context to anchor an abstract concept • communicates personal connections and experiences
	Sensory: incorporates the senses to process content or to enhance communication of ideas	• makes abstract concepts more accessible through the senses • provides sensory experiences to communicate ideas
	Graphic: displays numbers, statistics, and data through graphs, charts, tables, scatter plots, timelines, etc.	• communicates numerical information visually charts, graphs, tables, timelines

(Continued)

(Continued)

Categories of Scaffolds		Application
	Interactive: facilitates processing of information through social interaction; structures engagement between participants	• increases comprehension through engagement with peers • provides opportunities to apply content-specific language and concepts
	Linguistic: increases comprehension of complex discipline-specific language and structures sentences for accuracy and clarity of content-specific concepts	• increases comprehension of content-specific texts • guides complex, discipline-specific output

Image sources: istock.com/PeterSnow, istock.com/matasabe, istock.com/Nadiinko, istock.com/Sergei Cherednichenko, istock.com/Momento Design

Available at **resources.corwin.com/Long-Term SuccessforExperiencedMLs**

> These scaffolds are not meant to be checkboxes in a lesson plan but rather intentional supports that maintain the highest expectations.

while creating the supportive conditions that make content accessible. As the academic challenges rise, so too can the number and types of scaffolds offered. A lesson does not have to be studded with all of these supports for students to be successful, nor do teachers have to offer them in any particular order. Teachers can mix and match these scaffolds to meet students' needs when they are struggling to comprehend instruction or complete a task independently. Additionally, secondary teachers can intentionally build in scaffolds to meet the academic language requirements (vocabulary, sentence structure, organization) of the integrated objective, which we will get to in this chapter and the following one. Most importantly, unlike a cooking recipe where every ingredient is essential and cannot be omitted, teachers do not have to design every lesson with a scaffold from *each* of the categories. That would be overwhelming and unrealistic. Instead, imagine the categories and the suggested strategies as colors in a paint tray. There's no need to use every color. Just like skilled artists who consciously choose particular colors to enhance a painting, skilled teachers choose scaffolds to enhance their lessons.

BACKGROUND SCAFFOLDS

ACTIVATE PRIOR KNOWLEDGE

Content can become relevant when students link their background knowledge to the new content. Students' knowledge of the world and their lived experiences form their schemata and serve as the stable foundation on which to build understanding of new concepts and skills (Chiesi et al., 1979). Experienced multilinguals already have a treasure chest of experiences in multiple cultures and languages, which teachers can connect to.

Activating prior knowledge is one of the first assets-based pathways to make content comprehensible. In activating students' prior knowledge, their experiences and cultures take center stage. Activating background knowledge is also culturally responsive instruction and assets-based teaching (Paris & Alim, 2017; Snyder & Staehr Fenner, 2021).

> Instead of planning for what gaps to fill, start with what students can do and already have.

When activating students' background knowledge, students' cultures are not something to be celebrated periodically in a given month but rather a keystone that supports every lesson throughout the year.

For experienced multilinguals in particular, connecting a new concept with something familiar is one way to lower the stress level associated with learning (Shevrin Venet, 2021). For example, when learning about nutrition in a physical education class, the teacher can incorporate meals from students' cultures as case studies of healthy dishes. Since these meals are part of students' lived experiences, learning abstract content becomes more familiar.

> When there's less school-produced stress, students can divert more mental resources to learning content and language (Hammond, 2015; Krashen, 1982).

Activating prior knowledge: Linking students' existing knowledge to new learning (Cummins, 2009; Marzano et al., 2001)

HOW TO ACTIVATE PRIOR KNOWLEDGE

When planning to activate students' background knowledge, teachers can think about experiences in a series of expanding circles from self to world. The expanding circles strategy in Figure 5.4 highlights a variety of opportunities for teachers to tap into students' schemata. The circles are self, country/community, and world.

- **Self**: Students can have specific personal experiences connected to the concept.
  - What belongings do students have that are connected to this concept?
  - When have students used this concept in their lives?
  - How does this concept affect students' lives even if they are unaware of it?
  - What hobbies do students have that connect to the concept?
- **Country/Community**: Countries and communities can provide examples of the concept.
  - How does this concept show up in their community?
  - How are people of that country or community experiencing a particular concept?
  - What part of a country's history can connect to this concept?
  - Which world or local leader can connect to this concept?
- **World**: World events can embody the concept.
  - Which cultures connect to this concept?
  - What historical event demonstrates this concept?
  - What recent world events demonstrate this concept?
  - What organization/business is deeply involved with this concept?

Expanding circles help activate prior knowledge and connect it to the content. Activating students' prior knowledge can occur at the beginning, middle, or end of the unit. It is often used at the introduction of the unit to contextualize an abstract concept. In the middle of the unit, activating prior knowledge provides opportunities for students to see examples of the concept in real life. Finally, at the end of the unit, teachers can activate students' prior knowledge to contextualize a summative project.

For Mx. Delgado, who works at a school in Bangkok, there are many opportunities to activate students' prior knowledge, particularly

5.4 Expanding Circles

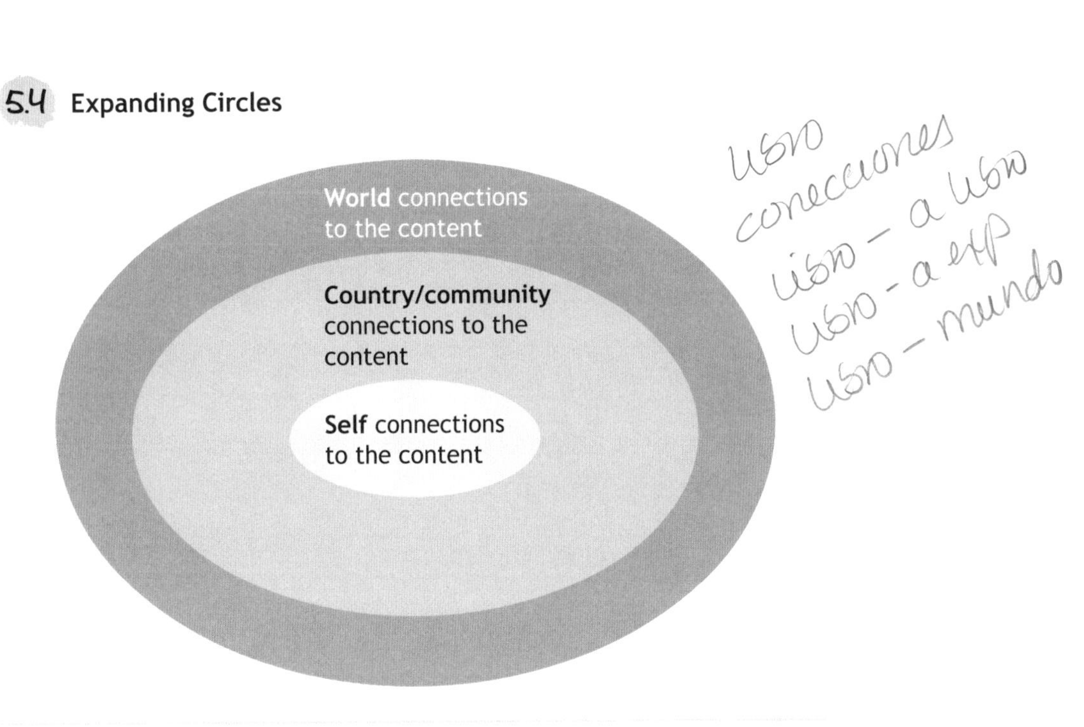

for students who come from Asian countries. Mx. Delgado used the expanding circles strategy to design the beginning, middle, and end of the unit.

- Beginning & Self
  - Students took pictures of bridges they came across throughout the week.
- Middle & Country
  - Mx. Delgado found famous bridges in Bangkok and Thailand to teach the different types of bridges used in Thailand.
- End & World
  - Mx. Delgado shared photos of famous bridges around the world as inspiration for students as they designed their bridges for the summative assessment.

BUILDING BACKGROUND KNOWLEDGE

While activating students' background knowledge is about what *students bring* to the content,

---

Building background knowledge: is what *teachers do* to make the content more familiar (Gay, 2018).

Sometimes students might not actually *have* a connection to the content. If this occurs, teachers will have to proactively *build* background knowledge through shared experiences to establish familiarity with key vocabulary words (Echevarría et al. 2017; Salva, 2017; Yzquierdo, 2017). Once the concept is initially introduced, it merges with students' background knowledge. Each subsequent learning experience, article, and text *builds up* students' knowledge base. In essence, when teachers establish comprehensible input, they develop students' background knowledge as a result.

TRY IT OUT

Background Scaffolds

Look at your current lesson or unit. Consider how you might do the following:

1. Integrate a world connection that links to the content.
2. Add a country/community connection that relates to the content.
3. Incorporate a reflection question where students think about how the content connects to their lives and cultures.
4. Create a shared experience through a video, experiment, hands-on activity, or skit that builds background knowledge.

SENSORY SCAFFOLDS

I hear and I forget, I see and I remember, I do and I understand.

—Confucius

Content teachers can also integrate sensory scaffolds to make content comprehensible (Gottlieb, 2013). One of the first things teachers think about when scaffolding for multilinguals is to use visuals, but vision is not the only sense we have. Other senses such as touch, hearing, and when appropriately safe, smell and taste can also make content more concrete for secondary multilinguals. When we present content mainly through text or presentations, it is heavily dependent

---

Sensory scaffolds: employ students' senses to learn content.

on written and oral academic language. Sensory scaffolds like pictures, lab experiments, and physical artifacts support multilinguals in grasping academic concepts through their senses, not just the text. When using sensory scaffolds, teachers can explicitly teach students to freely draw on their multiple senses to further their learning. Sensory scaffolds provide context and build the background students need to comprehend abstract academic content in every content area, as shown in Figure 5.5.

5.5 Sensory Scaffolds Across the Curriculum

Math	• Drawings • Protractors • Colored chips • Counting bars • Colored cubes • Graphing paper • Measuring tape • Circumference wheels • Models of geometry figures • Labeled visuals of types of angles
Science	• Scales • Weights • Test tubes • Demonstrations • Measuring tools • Natural materials • Labeled lab equipment • Videos of phenomenon • Models of organism or concept
Social Studies	• Simulations • Cultural artifacts • Food from the region • Videos about an event • Role plays of historical events • Music from a particular period in time • Artifacts or replicas from a historical period

(Continued)

(Continued)

Language Arts	• Sorting cards • Colored sentence strips • Videos of novels/stories • Pictures of vocabulary words • Acting out events in the story • Hanging pockets with vocabulary words • Creating a stage to demonstrate a scene
Arts, Physical Education, and Electives	• Fabric • Gears • Shop tools • Art supplies • Cooking utensils • Tablet computers • Sporting equipment • Musical instruments

Available at **resources.corwin.com/Long-Term SuccessforExperiencedMLs**

We encourage teachers to incorporate sensory scaffolds into their instruction to provide opportunities to interact with and manipulate objects. Manipulatives deepen students' understanding of how a concept works (Belenky & Nokes, 2009).

> Through multisensory learning, students are more likely to remember the content and understand abstract concepts (Marley & Carbonneau, 2014).

Manipulating objects provides rich opportunities for students to make observations, collect data, and discuss their insights. If a picture is worth a thousand words, then a manipulative can support a thousand words spoken during direct instruction.

Just like activating background knowledge, teachers can infuse sensory scaffolds at every phase of the unit so that multilinguals get to learn or interact with the concept to further cement their understanding at the beginning, middle, and end of the unit.

Mx. Delgado planned a lesson to teach the forces essential to bridges: *tension* and *compression*.

- **Beginning:**
    - Students experiment with wooden planks to understand fundamental bridge physics.
- **Middle:**
    - Students pull on cables to learn about tension.
- **End:**
    - Students create bridges that demonstrate application of bridge physics.

Mx. Delgado collected objects (e.g., bungee cords, rope, metal chains, and yoga bands) to demonstrate how tension is produced when objects are pulled from opposing directions. To illustrate how objects push down to produce compression, they used a gallon water bottle filled with water, a milk crate filled with books, a carry-on suitcase filled with clothes, and a bucket filled with sand. They placed these objects around the room so students could rotate between the objects and manipulate them by pulling and lifting to identify forces. Additionally, the students had to think about how these forces could be used to build a bridge. This learning experience utilized touch to make abstract concepts like tension and compression more concrete.

TRY IT OUT

Sensory Scaffolds

1. Create or collect manipulatives that students can move to establish greater comprehensible input.
2. Find a clear visual to communicate the concept and incorporate it into your presentation or a graphic organizer.
3. In addition to a text, provide students with a video that covers the same content.

GRAPHIC SCAFFOLDS

Graphic scaffolds make abstract numerical information easier to visualize. Inherent in most content classes are statistics, percentages, and dates. Authors deploy them to communicate changes, quantity, magnitude, and time periods. They pop up in printed texts, videos, and presentations. However, they are often quite confusing for experienced multilinguals because of their abstract, numerical nature. Many students need guidance to read and interpret them as they are essential to teaching content.

Graphic scaffolds also make content-specific details more comprehensible (Gottlieb, 2013). For example, when students read "methane is 25 times more potent than carbon dioxide as a climate-changing gas," they may not "see" this information or have an understanding of the magnitude of methane gas. Imagine all the parts students have to visualize and synthesize to understand these abstract concepts. Now, what if the science teacher shared that same fact as shown in Figure 5.6.

5.6 Visualizing a Statistic

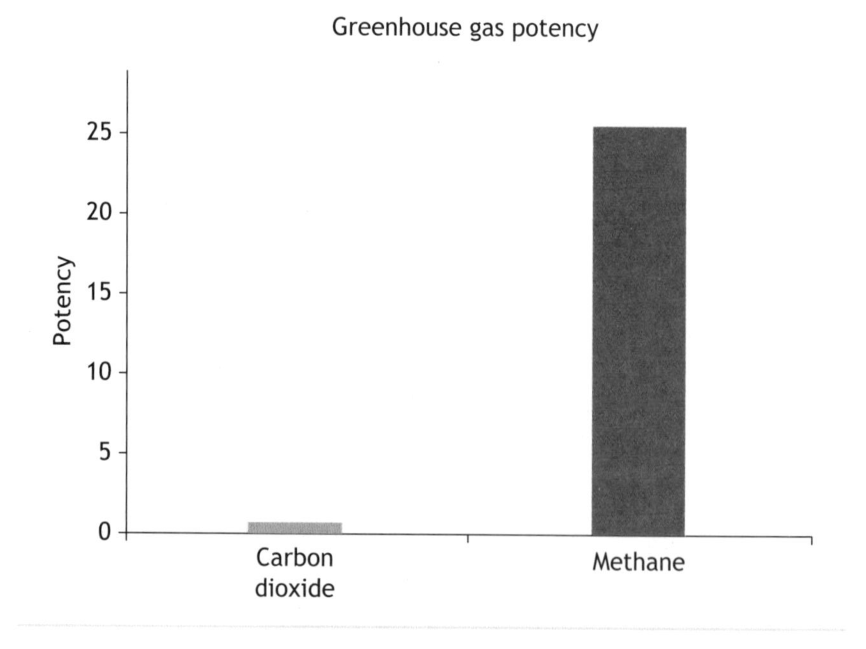

Graphic scaffolds: present information through charts, graphs, tables, and timelines that morph numbers and data points into visuals and images.

These supports communicate abstract concepts, show the magnitude of a phenomenon, or demonstrate the cause-effect relationship (Figure 5.7).

5.7 Types of Graphic Scaffolds

Charts		• A chart displays numerical data that can be represented in a diagram, table, or graph.
Graphs		• Graphs, a subset of charts, communicate numerical information by showing how numbers change and one number impacts another.
Tables		• Tables store and organize a data set in columns and rows.
Timelines		• Timelines visualize a sequence of events.

Image source: istock.com/Peacefull7, istock.com/limeart, istock.com/Yuriy Altukhov, istock.comm/Justicon

Graphs, charts, tables, and timelines are all forms of text. Therefore, it is important that teachers guide students in reading graphic scaffolds. The title of a graphic scaffold is often the most important place to start when reading graphs because it communicates the purpose of the graphic. Labels, captions, colors, and keys also provide essential information about the content of the graphic. They all need to be taught if students are to be able to read them.

Often data in informational texts do not come in the form of an accessible graphic. In this case, teachers can first convert statistics into visuals for students and hold a discussion to process the graph. After teachers demonstrate how to turn a data point into a visual, students can practice this skill within the context of the unit. Teaching students how to turn data into a visual fosters comprehension of numerical information in texts. When students develop the skill of transforming raw data into a visual graphic representation, they will be able to use this learning strategy in many content areas.

Mx. Delgado wanted students to compare the weight two types of bridges can support, so they created a bar graph using elephants stacked on each other to denote weight. They held a class conversation about this graph. This complex, abstract idea became more comprehensible through Mx. Delgado's thoughtful integration of a graphic scaffold (Figure 5.8).

5.8 Teaching Concepts Through a Graph

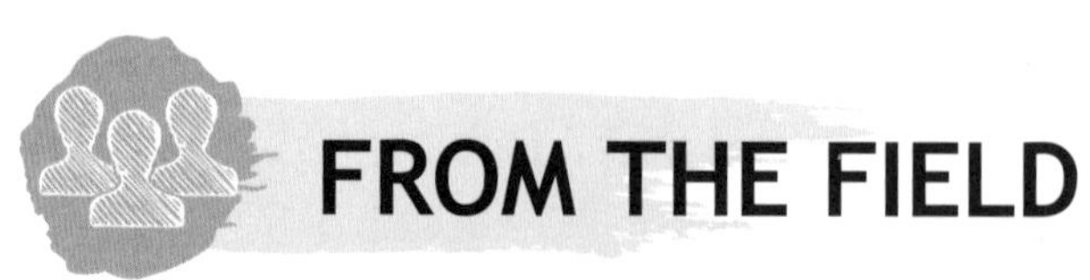

FROM THE FIELD

Graphic Scaffolds

Tan shares his experience with using a graphic scaffold to make a statistic from a video more comprehensible.

I joined Ananda in her eighth-grade science class. Ananda's teacher assigned a research project where students had to identify a contributor to climate change and propose something they can do to help the planet. From a list of options, Ananda chose to investigate how beef production exacerbates global warming.

As we watched a video explaining the topic, we came upon a statistic about how much water it takes to produce one pound of beef, pork, and poultry. I paused the video and asked her if she understood that statistic. She furrowed her forehead and shook her head. I explained that when we are given information in numbers, we can sometimes turn them into a graph to help see the numbers (see Figure 5.8). Then, I drew the axis of a bar graph.

I explained that the vertical axis represented the amount of water used in the production process, and the horizontal axis displayed the three categories of meat. We rewatched the video for the statistics, and I paused the video for each statistic. Ananda drew a bar to present the amount of water she heard. For experienced multilinguals like Ananda, turning number-laden information into a graph was one way to support her comprehension of the content-specific information and develop her ability to use this scaffold independently when watching other videos.

5.9 Turning Statistical Data Into a Visual Graph

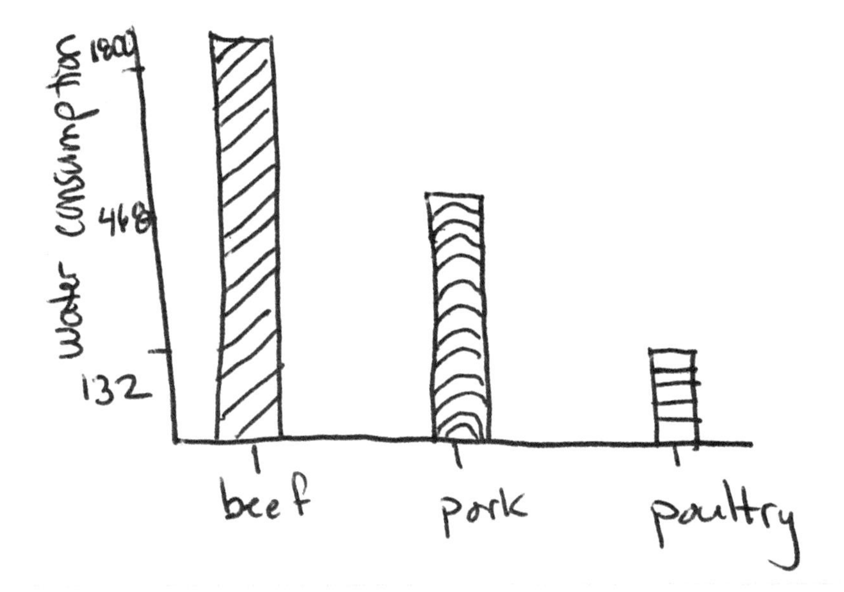

TRY IT OUT

Graphic Scaffolds

1. Take a graph and annotate it to show students what each part of the graph communicates. This develops graph-reading skills.
2. Take a statistic and turn it into a graph for students to understand the magnitude. Hold a discussion on how the graph made it easier to understand the statistic.
3. Have students turn a statistic into a type of graph. Have students explain why that particular graph is most appropriate for visualizing that exact statistic.

LINGUISTIC SCAFFOLDS

In this section, we will hone in on five linguistic scaffolds that make content texts, lectures, videos, and other forms of input more comprehensible. These five linguistic scaffolds make academic language used in school more accessible for experienced multilinguals.

Each element of academic language shown in Figure 5.10 can be made more comprehensible with a linguistic scaffold. For example, when Mx. Delgado planned the bridge lesson and analyzed the academic language in their plans, they noticed linguistic challenges for students in several areas. When they reviewed the articles about different types of bridges, they noticed a lack of context or pictures, complex sentence structures, and many specialized, abstract vocabulary words. Mx. Delgado knew they would have to provide several scaffolds for the academic language in the texts and videos in order to help experienced multilinguals like Min Woo overcome these linguistic hurdles.

5.10 Elements of Academic Language

Elements of Academic Language	Examples of Academic Language in Bridge Unit
Reduced context	Reading articles about the types of bridges, innovations, and the forces associated with bridges versus visiting actual bridges in the community
Academic sentence structures	A sentence about bridges: "In some cases, the deck area will be the load-bearing element, while in others it will be the towers." (Benson, 2019)
Specialized vocabulary	Arch, beam, cable-stayed, cantilever, suspension, truss, tied arch
Communicating abstract ideas	Tension, compression

Learning highly specialized content such as the physics of bridges becomes a hurdle rather than a joy when lessons are not scaffolded.

Linguistic scaffolds: make spoken and printed ideas more accessible.

The academic language used in content classes is a foreign language when the content is foreign.

Though Min Woo and his classmates have most likely seen, been on, and traveled over bridges, few if any are aware of the forces acting on and exerted by bridges. It is no wonder that experienced multilinguals like Min Woo benefit so much when lessons have linguistic scaffolds.

TRANSLANGUAGING

By definition, experienced multilinguals have many linguistic tools. Translanguaging is a pedagogical approach to instruction that invites and encourages students to use their entire linguistic repertoire to access content, communicate ideas, express their identities, and interact with others (García et al., 2016). There are multiple ways content teachers can incorporate students' heritage languages into learning content. Students who are highly literate in their heritage languages can read articles and watch videos in those languages. Students who can speak and understand various heritage languages but are not literate can talk together to process a lecture or a video played to the entire class. Figure 5.11 illustrates a continuum of how students can use their heritage languages in content classes.

5.11 Continuum of Students Using Their Heritage Languages

Can understand and speak the heritage language(s)	**Literate in the heritage language(s)**
Students speak in their heritage language(s) to process content	Students read, process, speak in the heritage language(s) to process content

Mx. Delgado knew that several of their students from Korea, such as Min Woo, were quite literate in Korean. When students conducted research on bridge types, Mx. Delgado encouraged them to read Korean articles if students found useful articles. Additionally, when students were co-constructing their bridges in groups, Mx. Delgado conferenced with a group of Hindi-fluent students and reminded them that it was perfectly appropriate for them to speak in Hindi as a tool to improve their comprehension and collaboration.

ANNOTATED VISUALS

Annotated visuals contain labels with words, phrases, and even whole sentences. These annotated visuals make the abstract content-specific vocabulary more comprehensible. Often academic language distills a long phrase into a single word to form a concept. For example, instead of saying *a force that is produced when something is stretched or pulled,* these 11 words are nestled within a single word: *tension.* Cramming a concept into one word makes it easier for people to communicate ideas accurately and efficiently. Unfortunately, it also reduces the context around the concept. Furthermore, abstract concepts like *tension* are invisible, making it even more slippery for multilinguals to grasp. Labeling these abstract terms on the visual teaches the content alongside discipline-specific vocabulary.

Mx. Delgado planned for annotated visuals in the bridge unit. They projected an image (Figure 5.12) of the school banner suspended by sturdy support cords and explained how the support cords exerted tension. Then they wrote the word *tension* followed by *force that pulls or stretches.*

5.12 Annotated Visual

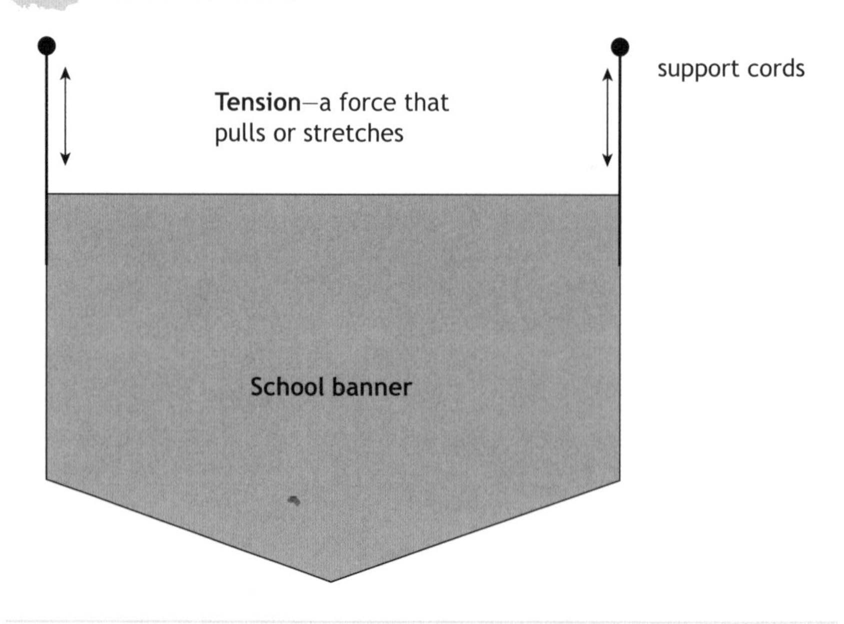

Stepping back to analyze this simple strategy, we can see how effective it is at making content comprehensible. The visual makes a concept more concrete while the annotation provides the technical language. Teachers from any discipline area can sprinkle in annotations to any visual they use to teach content.

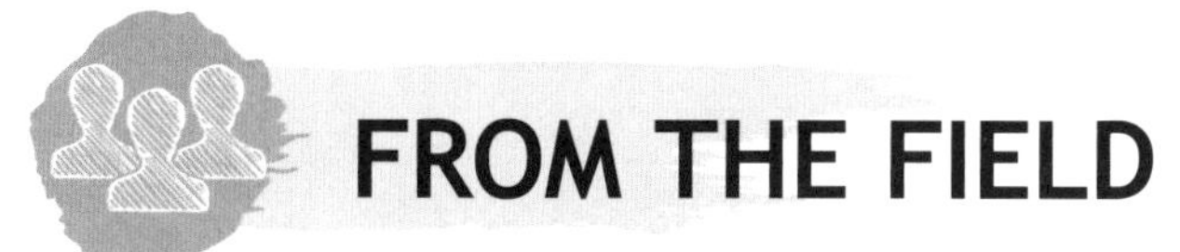

FROM THE FIELD

Annotated Visuals

Tan retells a time when he used an annotated visual to make students' responses more accurate.

We all have had those moments when we thought what we had planned was appropriately scaffolded, but when we showed up, students were lost in unexpected places during the lesson. I was teaching my students about the Industrial Revolution and how humans harnessed water to move machines such as a watermill. I played a video for students and even screenshotted the images to show the different parts of the watermill.

I saw their eyes glaze over and realized that the flood of new vocabulary words had confused them. There was input, but much of it was incomprehensible. For the next lesson, I created this slide with each part of the watermill displayed and clearly labeled (Figure 5.13). As I explained the watermill, students had the vocabulary words to go along with each part, making this lesson much more comprehensible. The annotated visuals turned an incomprehensible video lesson into a comprehensible one.

5.13 Slide With Labeled Visuals

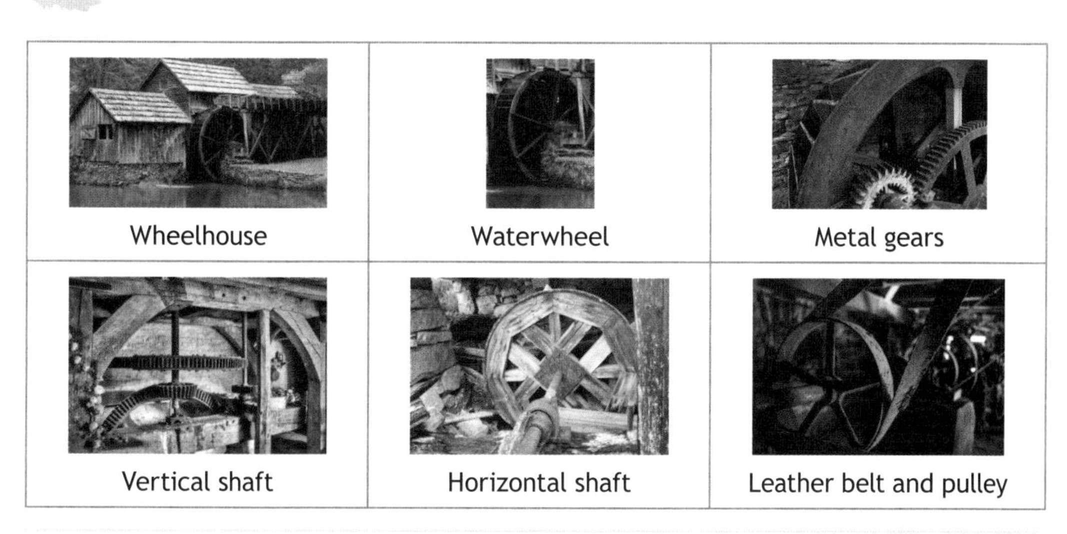

Image sources: pixabay.com/TranqjilGeo, istock.com'StockSoutions, istock.com/Gwenvidig, pixabay.com/Sorreisa, istock.com/ArtistGNDphotographyimage 22

CHUNKING CONTENT

Content teachers have a daunting amount of content to address, but for many experienced multilinguals, we have to downshift to go faster. When content is presented too quickly for multilinguals to process, very little is likely to be learned or retained. We may sacrifice comprehension at the price of coverage. This results in having to reallocate time, the most limited of resources teachers have, to reteach content.

Teachers can release the gas on the pedal by chunking information. Chunking instruction by segmenting information is one way to establish comprehensible input. Chunking content is like building a house one floor at a time. The subsequent floor is only built when the previous one is finished and stable. As students process one chunk at a time, they learn one concept or content-related concept or vocabulary word at a time.

We encourage teachers to build in frequent opportunities for students to pause to process one specific unit of knowledge before going to the next chunk of information. Options for engagement during an intentional pause to process include

- writing a brief note,
- drawing a simple sketch,
- summarizing information with a partner,
- typing a response on an online platform, and
- leaving a comment on a shared document.

For each chunk of the lesson, we recommend teachers plan a question or prompt for students to process the information using one of the options above. Teachers can braid questions or prompts into their presentation slides to help students summarize chunks of information throughout the class. Planning the prompts ahead of time tightens the lesson and guides students to focus on particular content. The questions can be open-ended or closed. For closed questions, we encourage teachers to ask a particular person in the pair to answer (e.g., the person closest to the right wall; Student A, Student B; Partner 1, Partner 2). This way everyone, and not just the more academically engaged partner, is afforded the opportunity to process. For open-ended questions, each student should have the opportunity to respond.

Teachers can use the following process to ensure that chunking occurs smoothly:

1. Teach one specific concept.
2. Stop before going on to the next concept.
3. Ask students to do one of the following:
   - Draw a simple sketch.
   - Summarize with a partner.
   - Write a brief note.
4. Repeat the first three steps for the next concept.

Asking students to draw a simple sketch during an intentional pause is also known as sketchnoting. Sketchnoting is a particularly beneficial strategy for making listening and reading input comprehensible for experienced multilinguals (McGregor, 2018). As teachers plan, they can flag moments to pause during the lesson to have students draw a concept and label their images with content-specific language. For example, when teaching about suspension bridges, Mx. Delgado paused at each part of the suspension bridge (Figure 5.14). Students then drew that part of the bridge and wrote a short text to describe that feature. In this way, students internalized each element of a suspension bridge in bitesize units.

5.14 Sketchnotes Taken During the Lesson to Process Each Part of a Suspension Bridge Through Chunking

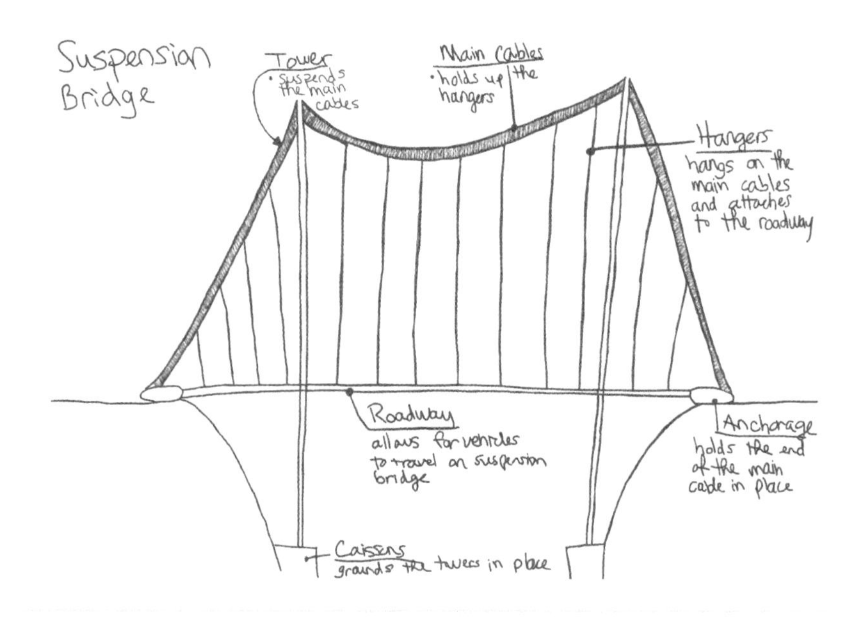

Inviting students to summarize a chunk of the lesson with a partner is another way to structure an intentional pause. When Mx. Delgado taught the evolution of bridges, they intentionally paused after teaching about each evolution. At each pause, Mx. Delgado posed a question tied to the evolution they just taught. They asked Student B to go first and Student A to listen to provide any missing detail or politely correct Student B. Imagine this lesson by Mx. Delgado without chunking. In this situation, Mx. Delgado could have bulldozed through the content, but students would not have internalized the content or the academic language.

Not only does sketchnoting work for direct instruction, it can also be used while reading a text or watching a video to learn content. Since information is built on previous information in text and video, it is imperative that students have opportunities to process one chunk before going onto the next one. While reading an article, students can draw simple sketches in the margins while they read or pause periodically to draw sketches on a separate document. Likewise, teachers can pause a video at strategic moments for students to sketch simple drawings to process the content. In addition, teachers can mention to students that chunking information while reading texts and watching videos is an effective learning strategy. This way, experienced multilinguals enjoy long-term success as they obtain a skill and learning strategy transferable to any class.

MODELING INSTRUCTION

We have focused the majority of this chapter on why content instruction needs to be comprehensible and shared strategies to reach that end. Making procedures and directions comprehensible is equally important. Modeling directions makes the classroom procedure clearer and builds rich context for content-specific words. As teachers hold up items such as specific chemical solutions, measuring equipment, or natural objects and use them in particular ways, they make the content-specific steps more concrete. Therefore, we encourage educators to invest time in intentionally, slowly, and clearly modeling each step of a classroom process or procedure. As we model, we

- narrate our actions,
- sequence the steps,
- point to specific objects, and
- demonstrate every step.

Before Mx. Delgado sent students out in pairs to identify tension and compression around the campus, they gave students a graphic organizer and modeled the procedure for the partner activity for the whole class with an example. In the room, Mx. Delgado placed a number around the room and asked students to help them find the number. Then Mx. Delgado theatrically sprinted to the science competition banner next to the posted #1 sign and drew a banner on the graphic organizer. They then modeled pausing to think about the force that is being exerted. They wrote down *tension* next to their sketchnote.

This simple modeling of the steps sets up all students, especially experienced multilinguals, for success. When experienced multilinguals are sometimes described as lacking motivation or misbehaving, a more accurate reality might be that they do not understand the instructions and might be too embarrassed to ask for clarification.

> If it is important for students to follow a procedure correctly, that procedure deserves to be modeled explicitly.

For routine and highly technical procedures, consider providing students with a three-minute screen recording. The video can walk students through each of the steps. The visual nature of the screen recording makes it comprehensible, and students have the added benefit of replaying and pausing at particular points.

TEXT ENGINEERING FOR READING COMPREHENSION

Reading texts is one path to learning content. Yet, texts present many challenges to experienced multilinguals for a multitude of reasons, including vocabulary, background knowledge, sentence structure, and topic. Experienced multilinguals have the ability to comprehend complex, grade-level text if that text includes some additional linguistic scaffolds. Similar to the exam engineering shared in Chapter 3, text engineering (Billings & Walqui, 2017) is one way to embed scaffolds for each element of the text including context, vocabulary, and sentence structure as shown in Figure 5.15. Similar to the way architects can design a bridge to be sturdy by adding cables and triangles, teachers can design supports *into* a text without simplifying it.

5.15 Ways to Engineer Text

- **Vocabulary:** Add a more accessible vocabulary word behind the academic word or add a short phrase.
- **Topic:** Use headings to section out each topic.

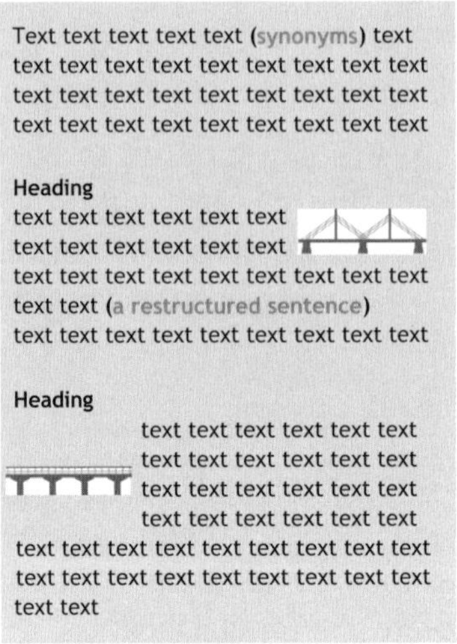

Text text text text text (synonyms) text text text text text text text text text text text text text text text text text text text text text text text text text text text text

Heading
text text text text text text text text text text text text text text text text text text text text text text text text (a restructured sentence) text text text text text text text text text

Heading
text text text text text text text text text text text text text text text text text text text text text text text text text text text text text text text text text text text text text text text text text text text text text text

- **Context:** Use labeled visuals to provide a visual context for the details.
- **Sentence structure:** Provide a restructured sentence behind the more complex one.

Image source: istock.com/alazur

When Mx. Delgado wanted students to read about the different types of bridges, they engineered the text in several ways, as shown in Figure 5.16. They chunked the information by adding a heading to group the paragraphs by bridge type. For each type of bridge, they added a labeled picture to help turn concepts into a visual representation. For a sentence with unfamiliar academic words like in the following sentence, Mx. Delgado added synonyms in parentheses to make the text more accessible: *The structure (design) of a stereotypical (common) suspension bridge looks very simple, but the design is extremely effective (works well)* (Benson, 2019). Although Mx. Delgado chunked the text, added labeled visuals, and included synonyms, they maintained the academic rigor of the grade-level text.

When texts are engineered to be more accessible, we stretch students' skills rather than snap their spirits.

5.16 An Excerpt From an Article That Has Been Engineered to Increase Comprehension

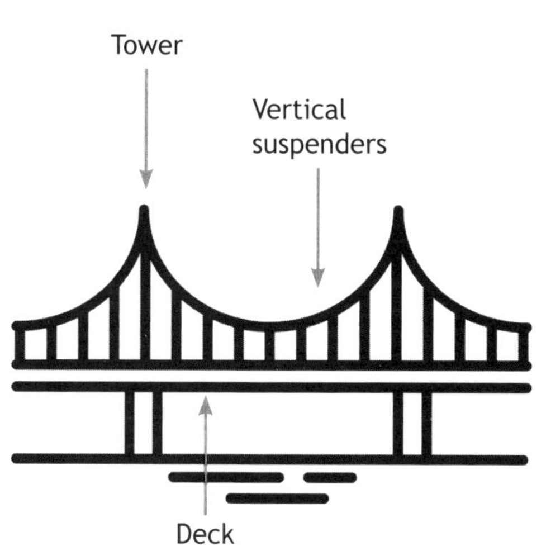

Suspension Bridge

The structure (design) of a stereotypical (common) suspension bridge looks very simple, but the design is extremely effective (works well). The deck of the suspension bridge is the load-bearing element of the structure (the deck holds the weight). This is held in place by vertical (top to bottom) suspenders that support the cables.

The suspension cables extend (reach) out beyond each side of the bridge and are anchored (placed) firmly into the ground. It will depend upon the size of the bridge, but a number of towers will be installed (built) to hold up the suspension cables. Any load applied to (placed on) the bridge is transformed into tension across the suspension cables, which are the integral (important) parts of the structure. As there is some "give" (flexibility) in the suspension cables, this can translate into slight (tiny) but measured (noticeable) bridge movement in difficult weather conditions.

Adapted from Benson (2019).

Image sources: istock.com/Rashad Aliyev

FROM THE FIELD

Annotating the Text

After learning about text engineering from Beth, one middle school English language arts teacher decided to teach her experienced multilinguals how to annotate their own texts to increase comprehension. She modeled how to

- write translations or synonyms for key words above the word in the text,
- write a note about the main idea of the paragraph in the margin,
- underline confusing sentences to discuss with a partner, and
- draw a labeled sketch of the context in the margin.

(Continued)

(Continued)

After modeling these techniques with the first two paragraphs of a text, she gave students time to practice with a partner on the next paragraphs. Students were completely engaged in the task. They shared their annotations with other teams of students and understood the text even better after the exchange. After several in-class practice sessions with partners, students were able to use the annotation strategies independently to better comprehend content texts in other classes as well. Through this scaffolded practice, the students gained a valuable learning strategy that increased their ability to independently communicate effectively using academic language.

SENTENCE LIFTING

While text engineering makes the text more accessible, experienced multilinguals still need to learn how to independently comprehend complex texts to develop long-term success. Often, in academic texts, the more complex and cryptic a sentence is, the more it is valued as being highly "scholarly." Independent readers can develop skills to make sense of such intricate sentences through explicit instruction such as sentence lifting.

To "lift a sentence," teachers first find one of the most challenging and complex sentences in the article. For example,

> *Born in the seventeenth century, Englishman Sir Isaac Newton, physicist and mathematician, father of calculus, changed the scientific world with his basic principles of physics, most significant of them all, the law of universal gravitation.*

Then, they analyze the sentence for the elements that make it difficult. The sentence about Sir Isaac Newton is quite challenging because of the many details condensed into dependent clauses. After reading the text, Mx. Delgado lifted this sentence for a quick mini-lesson to teach students reading comprehension skills. First, Mx. Delgado had students share why they think the sentence is so difficult or complex. Then, Mx. Delgado revealed an annotated version of the lifted sentence showing what exactly makes the sentence so challenging by highlighting all of the details the author provided about Newton in this condensed sentence (Figure 5.17). With the annotated sentence, Mx. Delgado discussed the main element that makes this sentence challenging and modeled the mental moves they used to make that aspect more comprehensible. There might be several elements that make it difficult, but we suggest just lasering in on one so that the lesson is not overwhelming to students.

5.17 Lifted Sentence for Modeling How to Read a Complex Sentence

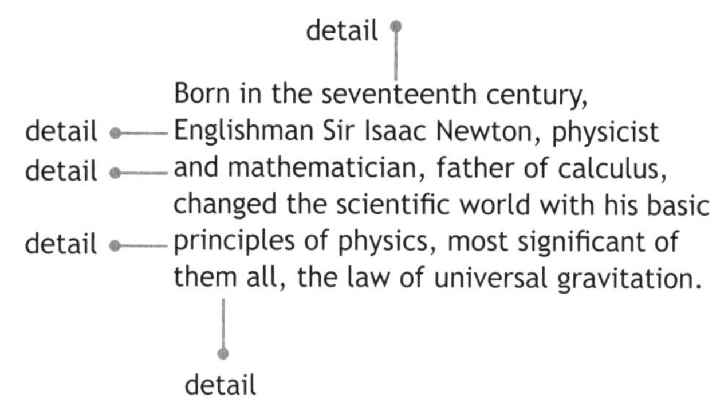

In the discussion, Mx. Delgado highlighted how the author packed many details into a single sentence. Then, he separated the details by a comma almost like a list. Mx. Delgado showed students how to read one detail at a time by stopping to pause every time there was a comma. To visualize this, Mx. Delgado wrote on the board all the details out in a series of sentences without commas (Figure 5.18). This makes the text about Newton more accessible, and by teaching them this skill, experienced multilinguals will be better prepared to read future challenging texts independently.

5.18 Making a Complex Sentence More Accessible by Writing Separate Simple Sentences

Sir Isaac Newton was an Englishman. He was born in the seventeenth century. He was a physicist and a mathematician. He invented calculus. Calculus led to the law of universal gravitation.

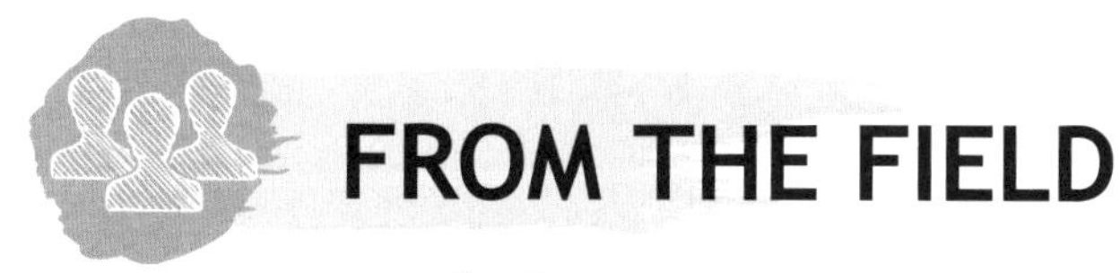

Guided Summary

Tan shares his experience of using a guided summary protocol to make a video more comprehensible.

When I taught social studies, I used videos and articles to teach students content. Sometimes, students would watch a video or read an article but still miss the key ideas. I could not allot more time to reread the article or rewatch the video as I had to adhere to my pacing guide. Therefore,

(Continued)

(Continued)

I created a protocol called "guided summary" to teach students content and the central ideas from a video or article.

Before students even read the article or watched the video, I created a series of comprehension prompts centered on the main concept of the course, not focused on minor details. I wrote prompts in the form of sentence starters that addressed the main concept (Figure 5.19). The sentence starters prompted students to think about the central concept, and they offered built-in linguistic scaffolds of sentence starters.

The sequence I use to conduct a guided summary is as follows:

1. Share the sentence starters.
2. Have students share their ideas with a partner.
3. Share the correct completed statement.
4. Repeat the process until all of the sentence starters are done.

At the end of the protocol, students have a summary of the text from the sentence starters. All students receive the clearest understanding of the central concept from the article and video when I reveal the completed prompts. This way, I am able to support students who struggle to understand the concept while reading or watching the video.

5.19 Series of Guided Summary Questions

Guided Summary

1. The Ancient Greeks valued . . . over . . .
2. The Ancient Greeks wanted men to be educated so they could . . .
3. The Ancient Greeks based their decisions on . . .
4. When creating art, the Ancient Greeks valued . . .
5. When designing buildings, the Ancient Greeks valued . . .

1. Annotate a visual to establish comprehensible input for a new concept.
2. Engineer a text by adding headings, photos with captions, and embedding more accessible synonyms or translations behind original words.

3. Teach students how to annotate a text with translations, drawings, and questions.
4. Model each step from written instructions.
5. Show students an annotated example of an expected response.

INTERACTIVE SCAFFOLDS

> Reading and writing float on a sea of talk.
>
> —James Britton

Interacting with others is another way to make complex concepts more accessible to experienced multilinguals. They benefit from frequent and consistent opportunities to explore, synthesize, and extend their understanding of the concepts with others (Baker et al., 2014). When students interact in these ways, they meaningfully process and internalize the content. As Mercer (1995) writes, "Information can be accumulated, but knowledge and understanding are only generated by working with information, selecting from it, organizing it, arguing for its relevance" (p. 67). As students participate in academic conversations, the content becomes meaningful as they work to make sense of it.

Translanguaging is an interactive scaffold that we encourage for establishing comprehensible input. Teachers can pair experienced multilinguals who speak the same heritage language to discuss academic content.

> When students have the opportunity to collaborate in their heritage language, their comprehension of content concepts increases significantly (Collier & Thomas, 2018; Cummins, 2021).

Experienced multilinguals can draw from their background to talk about the new content. If they are unfamiliar with the content, they can still process the content in their heritage language with a partner

---

Interactive scaffolds: Structures that establish comprehensible input through collaboration

to make sense of it. However, teachers have to be careful of using students' heritage language *only* as a tool to learn content in English. While it is important to develop students' academic English for success in schools, it is equally essential to foster students' entire linguistic repertoire (Carlo et al., 2004; Snyder & Staehr Fenner, 2021). Schools need to be places where students' connections to their heritage language is proactively maintained and nurtured (Garcia et al., 2016).

Students can learn another language without having to lose the ones they came with.

Because learning is a social experience (Vygotsky, 1978), we can design content-based instruction to be a collaborative journey. One form of collaboration is discussions, and there are several discussion moves that can enrich interactions in any language (Zwiers, 2014). Think of these moves like swings in tennis such as slices, backhand, forehand, topspin, etc. Teachers can design interactions that require these specific discussion moves (Figure 5.20).

5.20 Discussion Moves for Interactions

	Discussion Move	Sentence Starter
	Build on ideas	• I would like to add to . . . 's idea about . . .
	Link ideas	• . . . idea about ... connects to . . . because . . .
	Clarify information	• Who, what, where, when, why, how, how much
	Support ideas	• An example of . . . is . . .

Adapted from Zwiers (2014).

Image sources: istock.com/musmellow, istock.com/LysenkoAlexander, istock.com/Visual Generation, istock.com/Enis Aksoy

Available at **resources.corwin.com/Long-Term SuccessforExperiencedMLs**

Mx. Delgado planned for students to use these academic discussion moves to better comprehend tension and compression. They pasted numbers around the school campus to identify things that exerted tension or compression. Students worked in pairs and roamed around the campus to find the numbered items (e.g., columns, banners, curtains, railing, rope, swing, etc.). At each location, students drew a simple diagram of the item and then discussed if that item was exerting tension or compression. Once the groups were ready to return to the class, Mx. Delgado combined two pairs into a larger group of four to confirm their answers. Finally, in their groups of four, they answered guiding questions to help them see the connections between all the objects that exerted tension and compression.

In this activity, students had to clarify their understanding of tension and compression by coming to a consensus at each station. As students justified their ideas, they had to provide supporting evidence. During the closing activity, students discussed the connections between the items from each station, which they needed in order to write their own definitions of tension and compression. Through collaboration, they gained a greater understanding of the content because they were actively learning it rather than passively receiving information.

The Collaborative Processing Protocol

Mx. Delgado used a structured conversation protocol that asked students to work first in pairs and then in groups of four to explain their thinking. There are many different ways to structure student interactions in the classroom. With a little creativity and the discussion moves previously outlined in Figure 5.20, almost any learning experience can be interactive. Think of the typical learning experiences found in content classes: lectures, projects, experiments, presentations, reading articles, and writing text. Teachers can structure these reading, writing, and viewing experiences as shown in Figure 5.21 so that students have to interact with each other to learn content or produce something. When students interact with each other while reading a text or watching a video, they increase their understanding through structured discussions.

To make reading and watching a video an interactive experience, we recommend a partner activity that requires partners to regularly discuss chunks of text or video. The cycle of partner interactions for reading and viewing shown in Figure 5.21 provides experienced multilinguals the opportunity to engage with another student to make meaning. After participating in this collaborative reading activity in a high school social studies class, one multilingual student commented that he finally

5.21 Collaborative Processing Protocol

1. Read one paragraph at a time or pause at specific points during the video.

2. At the end of the paragraph or at specific sections in the video, stop to talk about the meaning.

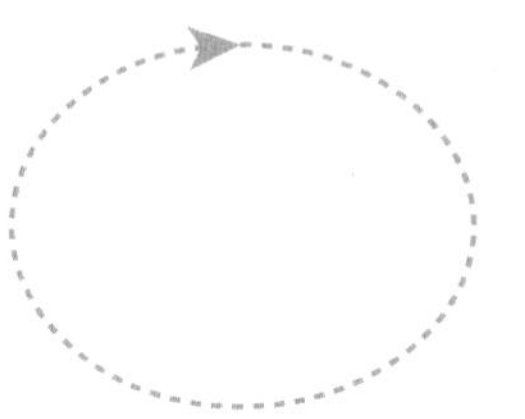

4. Continue on to the next paragraph or next section of the video and repeat the process.

3. Co-annotate the paragraph with a succinct sentence to capture the meaning of the paragraph, or take brief notes about this specific section of the video.

Image sources: istock.com/Vladislav Popov, istock.com/Momento Design, istock.com/appleuzr
Available at **resources.corwin.com/Long-Term SuccessforExperiencedMLs**

understood what he was reading. This reading process builds students' self-efficacy; they learn how to ask questions, clarify words, take notes, and comprehend texts and videos even when working independently.

FROM THE FIELD

Collaborative Processing Protocol

Johanna Carrazco-Gonzalez, a fourth-grade teacher of several multilingals, tried this collaborative reading strategy after one of Beth's workshops. Though her students would not technically be considered experienced multilinguals yet, they still benefitted from reading collaboratively with their peers. This is Johanna's reflection on the strategy:

After teaching a small group of students the partner reading strategy, I was able to observe a couple of things. When one partner was reading aloud, the other was following along and helping to read multisyllabic words. The reader seemed comfortable and appreciated the help. When it came to the second step of the strategy, one partner made a text-to-self connection, then both partners had an authentic conversation about the topic. Both students seemed to appreciate the time to talk and discuss before moving on to the next paragraph.

When teachers design a lesson to have **interactive scaffolds**, they have to consider the group size. There are many options for grouping students, as shown in Figure 5.22. The smaller groups provide for more interaction while more ideas are produced with larger groups. Smaller groups can have greater accountability as students can withdraw in larger groups.

5.22 Grouping Options and Example Activities

Number of Students	Example Activities
Pairs	• Two students work together to code an app. • Two students design and carry out an experiment in science. • Two students discuss the learning objectives for the day. • Two students pause after each paragraph to summarize the idea.
Triads	• Students work together using the design cycle to create a device that protects an egg when dropped from the third floor. • Students research a different aspect of a country and combine the ideas into a presentation. • Students analyze different characters in a novel and collaborate to show how each character impacted the others.
Small Group (Four Students)	• Students work together to write a script for characters in their five-minute play for drama. • Students compose a song for music. • Students design and install a new mural for the school. • Students develop and implement a program to meet a community need

Available at **resources.corwin.com/Long-TermSuccessforExperiencedMLs**

We also recommend that teachers create purposeful partnerships or small groups with multilingual students' heritage languages in mind. When interacting about a complex, grade-level text, pairing two experienced multilinguals with the same heritage language may be the most supportive partnership. On the other hand, when discussing a chunk of content-related video, a triad of students with different heritage languages and more English-proficient students may be the most effective grouping.

While interactive scaffolds are effective structures that establish comprehensible input (Motley, 2016), teachers still have to support the interaction. Just designing lessons with interactive scaffolds and having students talk to each other can sometimes induce stress. Some suggestions that can structure the conversation more can include the following:

- Word banks
- Talking points
- Sentence stems
- Guiding questions
- Written instructions
- Protocols for taking turns
- Roles such as time keeper, scribe, facilitator
- A defined task that requires collaborative conversations

> Talkers walk away from the conversation with much more than they could have thought up on their own. Like flowers that rely on bees to pollinate them, we need the ideas of others for our minds to thrive. (Zwiers & Crawford, 2011, *Kindle location 362*).

TRY IT OUT

Interactive Scaffolds

Create an activity where students collaborate to watch a video, read an article, or write a paragraph. Make sure to have students pause and summarize segments of the text or video with each other.

1. Insert a slide in the presentation that provides students with an opportunity to talk about the content. Ask students to first write or draw what they have understood so far and then take turns sharing their notes with their partner.
2. Write guiding questions that students need to answer with a partner at the end of the activity.

CLOSING REMARKS

At times, when referring to multilinguals, "kind" can be a euphemism for less rigorous, below grade level, and isolated experiences that soak up time but provide little educational value.

> The kindest thing we can do for multilinguals is to hold the highest expectations while providing equally high levels of scaffolds.

When we intentionally integrate scaffolds that make content comprehensible, we become the kind of teacher (pun intended) multilinguals need and deserve.

Min Woo and his partner, Rasheed, work together to put their miniature truss bridge to the test. The other teams' models were strong but collapsed at 7.5 kilos. At the start of the summative project, Min Woo and Rasheed debated over which type of bridge they should design. They returned to their notebooks to look at their labeled sketchnotes and scanned the annotated articles they read about the different types of bridges. They agreed on a truss bridge as they were confident that the triangles that formed the truss bridge would exert enough tension to counter the weights.

The students made way for Min Woo and Rasheed to nervously carry their bridge to the front of the room for Mx. Delgado to test it. Like with all the other miniature bridges, Mx. Delgado had Min Woo and Rasheed explain their design to the class. Both spoke eloquently and used bridge-specific terminology effectively to support their explanation. Min Woo traced some of the triangles and explained how they exerted tension to support the bridge.

Mx. Delgado smiled warmly and then placed the first three-kilo weight on the bridge. Min Woo and Rasheed held their breaths, but the bridge held strong. Mx. Delgado added another three-kilo weight and again, the bridge held. As the third three-kilo weight was placed on the bridge, students shouted out their predictions of doom for the bridge. Min Woo pulled down his hoodie to cover his eyes as Rasheed hid behind Min Woo. When Mx. Delgado lifted their fingers off the weight ever so gingerly, the class came to a hushed silence. Then the roar of applause and hooting from their classmates filled the room. Their bridge held the most weight thus far.

REFLECTIONS

- Explain how scaffolding instruction is a form of equitable instruction.

- Consider which types of scaffolds lend themselves most to your content area.

- Which types of scaffolds not currently used in your practice would benefit experienced multilinguals?

- How would the addition of this new scaffold support your experienced multilinguals?

CHAPTER SUMMARY

- Scaffolds support students in engaging with tasks that they would not otherwise be able to do independently.
- Scaffolds are meant to be temporary. Teachers should remove them when students can engage with the tasks independently.
- Scaffold categories include background, sensory, graphic, interactive, and linguistic.
- Teachers can scaffold for comprehensible input so that content, texts, and instructions are accessible.
- Teachers can scaffold every lesson, but they do not need to include all of the categories of scaffolding for each lesson.

6

STRUCTURING ACADEMIC OUTPUT

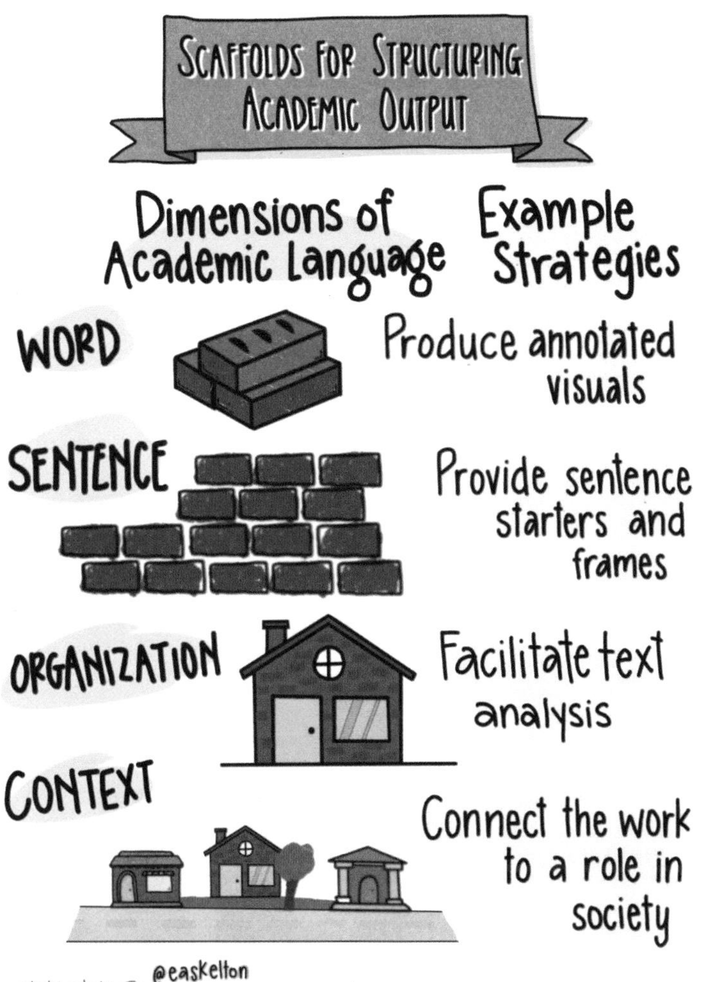

Min Woo really likes social studies, especially with Mr. Ichiro's approach to teaching. The annotated diagrams of social studies concepts and frequent opportunities to talk about them make Min Woo feel that he is a capable and competent person. Today, Mr. Ichiro wants students to write about how Greek philosophy influenced one aspect of ancient Greek society. Students will need to engage in this kind of thinking as they work as museum curators to create an exhibit about Greek philosophies' influence on ancient Greek society and many modern cultures. Min Woo and his classmates have already learned a lot about Greek philosophies through mini-lectures, visuals, video clips, and class discussions, so they have plenty of background knowledge. To scaffold the writing, Mr. Ichiro created Figure 6.1 as a prewriting activity. In pairs, students will talk about how Greek philosophies influenced Grecian society as represented by the icons on the slide. Min Woo turns to his partner to talk about each of the icons. They carefully listen to each other to add ideas, make connections, and clarify concepts. After this small group work, Mr. Ichiro has students share aloud as a whole group activity and take notes for each icon. He uses this opportunity to clarify their understanding. From this activity, Min Woo and his classmates are better prepared to write thoughtfully with content-specific details.

6.1 An Example of an Annotated Visual to Teach Ancient Greek Philosophy

Literate citizens

Democracy

Observation of natural laws

Physical health

Application of math and science to all aspects of life

Image sources: istock.com/da-vooda, istock.com/justinroque, istock.com/appleuzr, istock.com/cloudnumber9

Available at **resources.corwin.com/Long-Term SuccessforExperiencedMLs**

Like always, Mr. Ichiro has planned today's social studies lesson using the instructional framework for experienced multilinguals shown in Figure 6.2.

6.2 An Example of the Instructional Framewok Applied to a Social Studies Lesson

Engineer the summative assessment

Students will act as museum curators who are asked to design an exhibit to show how Greek philosophies have influenced ancient Greek society and also many modern societies.

Write the integrated objective

Explain how Greek philosophy influenced ancient Greek society by writing a paragraph that includes philosophy-based details.

Establish comprehensible input

The teacher reviews key Greek philosophies by providing images connected to the philosophy.

Structure academic output

The teacher will use the teaching and learning cycle approach to deconstruct and analyze a model text that describes the impact of a philosophy on society.

The integrated objective is *Explain how Greek philosophy influenced ancient Greek society by writing a paragraph that includes philosophy-based details.* Mr. Ichiro has identified academic language for this integrated objective as shown in Figure 6.3, including words and an authentic context for using highly academic language that will be new for many of his students. He has also planned structured opportunities for students to practice using academic language in class so experienced multilinguals like Min Woo will be successful writing about how a philosophy can influence society.

6.3 Academic Language in a Model Social Studies Response

Integrated Objective: *Explain how Greek philosophy influenced ancient Greek society by writing a paragraph that includes philosophy-based details.*	
Academic words and phrases	Greek philosophy, literate citizens, democracy, observation, natural world
Sentence structures	Past tense
Organizational patterns	Show connection between Greek philosophy and society by *first* describing the philosophy and *then* explaining how it influenced Greek society.
Context	Writing and thinking as a museum curator

Available at **resources.corwin.com/Long-Term SuccessforExperiencedMLs**

This social studies lesson and written assignment reveal the complexity of producing academic language and the cognitive demands it places on experienced multilinguals. As described in Chapter 2 with the architectural metaphor of academic language, every dimension of the final product or building has to work together to create a cohesive structure. The individual bricks (words), the walls (sentence structures), the support beams (organizational structure) and the surrounding landscape or neighborhood (context) work together to create that cohesive product (Zwiers, 2014). When students speak and write in content classes, they have to use discipline-specific vocabulary, sentence structures, organizational patterns, and contexts to produce essays, reports, and multimedia presentations. Today's lesson on writing a paragraph that explains the influence of a philosophy on society as a museum curator might write on an exhibit description is similar to the kind of writing students will produce on the summative report.

In Chapter 5, we presented five different categories of scaffolding that can establish comprehensible input for experienced multilinguals in content classes. Understanding the information and concepts is just the first step. Students also need to demonstrate mastery and understanding of the content through discussions, writing, presentations, and multimedia products. Just as experienced multilinguals need scaffolding for content to be comprehensible, they will also need careful scaffolding of academic language production in content classes to be successful (Snyder & Staehr Fenner, 2021).

Teachers can scaffold the production of academic language in all four dimensions as described in Chapter 2: word, sentence, organization, and context (Gottlieb & Ernst-Slavit, 2014):

- **Word dimension:** the content-specific vocabulary and phrases
- **Sentence dimension:** the way content-specific words are used together with other words to form a complete idea
- **Organizational dimension:** the way sentences and paragraphs are sequenced and organized to comprise an extended text
- **Context dimension:** the purpose for the written or spoken work, including the student's role in the project

The scaffolds presented in Chapter 3 to engineer the most equitable summative assessments can also be borrowed and applied to academic output in lessons. This chapter will also provide a few structures to teach academic language so that all educators can be teachers of that language. Again, teachers are not expected to use all of these strategies all the time in every lesson. We see these strategies as a deposit into teachers' existing bank of teaching techniques. Teachers are experts in knowing what approach to use, when, with whom, and for how long. Regardless of the strategies teachers use, it is essential that lessons be scaffolded for academic output. Otherwise, students will not be able to communicate with clarity and thoughtfulness. Experienced multilinguals often have clever and innovative ideas, but when they lack the words and structures to communicate effectively, their voices are lost or may be muted.

We understand that some teachers may be concerned that we are over-scaffolding with the strategies we present in this chapter. We believe that a diverse toolbox of strategies to use for different purposes will create the optimal and equitable conditions for student success. Returning to the principles of universal design for learning, teachers can use the scaffolds in this chapter as bridges where students can engage with the task. Whereas before the use of scaffolding, many experienced multilinguals were not able to cross the "gap," these scaffolds guide students as they travel through the unit without limitations.

WORD DIMENSION

Every discipline has its own bank of content-specific words. Research suggests that

> if multilingual students are to be successful in content classes, then content-specific words need to be taught explicitly (Cummins & Early, 2015; Fleenor & Beene, 2019).

The specificity of these words will help experienced multilinguals to communicate precisely and accurately about the content in their disciplines. For example, instead of referring to a concept in social studies vaguely as *that thingy*, students communicate with greater clarity when they say *stoicism* to discuss this Greek philosophy.

EMBED DISCIPLINE-SPECIFIC WORDS

One strategy used in engineering summative assessments—embedding the content-specific words within prompts and guiding questions—can be repurposed to structure students' use of discipline-specific output. When we do this, students use the words accurately in context. For example, Mr. Ichiro designed a graphic organizer with three panels to have students summarize the societal changes from Greek philosophies (Figure 6.4). The graphic organizer structures the written summary by asking a guiding question for each part of the summary using a specific, relevant content word.

6.4 An Example of Embedding Content-Specific Words Within the Instructions

Directions: Draw three pictures with captions that summarize what you learned about Greek philosophy and its role in changing society.		
Draw your picture here	Draw your picture here	Draw your picture here
What is a *philosophy*?	What were the core beliefs of Greek philosophy?	What was one way ancient Greek society changed?

Available at **resources.corwin.com/Long-Term SuccessforExperiencedMLs**

WORD BANKS

Just as word banks can support students on a summative assessment, they can remind students to use content-specific words during structured interactions in class or during daily writing prompts. Whether these word banks are written on the board or in students' notes, we recommend that the word lists be separated by nouns and verbs so that students can use them more accurately when speaking with partners or writing extended responses. When the verbs in this categorized word bank are presented in the appropriate tense, as shown in Figure 6.5, students will be able to produce complete sentences with discipline-specific vocabulary and appropriate verb tenses, too.

6.5 An Example of a Categorized Word Bank

Nouns	Verbs
• Greek philosophers • Stoicism • Ancient Greek philosophy	• valued • emphasized • included

TRY IT OUT

Categorized Word Banks

1. Review the nouns and verbs in a model response for a task.
2. Create a categorized word bank containing the discipline-specific nouns and essential verbs students are to use in the student response.

MORPHING VERBS

Teachers can also take this opportunity to explicitly model how to change academic verbs so they can use them in different sentence structures. The process of *morphing verbs* takes a specific verb and shows students how it can be changed into different forms to elevate students' writing and speech. To introduce the process of morphing verbs, teachers first write an academic verb such as *emphasize* on the board. Then they model how to change this present tense verb into a progressive verb, past tense verb, a noun, and how to include it in phrases as shown below.

- In *emphasizing* education, the ancient Greeks . . .
- Because the ancient Greek philosophers *emphasized* education, they . . .
- An *emphasis* was placed on education because . . .
- Ancient Greeks *placed an emphasis on* education because . . .
- Education was an *emphasis* during ancient Greece.

For example, after Mr. Ichiro modeled how to morph a verb, students worked in pairs to practice morphing the verb *influence* in the phrase *Greek philosophy influenced society.* Then Mr. Ichiro had students share the way they morphed the verb, and he wrote some examples they came up with on the board:

- Greek philosophy was influential in . . .
- Ancient Greek philosophies still influence Grecians today by . . .
- Greek philosophy greatly influenced the way . . .

Then students worked independently to complete their exit ticket to answer the prompt: *How did Greek philosophy influence society?*

Morphing verbs serves two purposes. The first is to show students that in English, verbs often change forms. Secondly, it shows students that when a verb changes, it often changes tense and can even change into a different part of speech (e.g., noun, adjective, adverb). Experienced multilinguals benefit from morphing verbs as it explicitly teaches grammar, which is sometimes a stumbling block for them.

SENTENCE DIMENSION

Knowing the discipline-specific words does not mean that students will know how to use them accurately in a sentence. Therefore, teachers need to scaffold academic language output in complete complex sentences. The following supports and activities provide opportunities for experienced multilinguals to extend their academic speech and writing at the sentence dimension.

CONCEPT MAPPING

One way students can practice using the new words and phrases in complete sentences in the context of the unit is to connect them to each other on a concept map. Concept mapping was originally developed to help students visually make connections between big ideas and details (Novak & Cañas, 2006). These visual maps can also provide experienced multilinguals with opportunities to use discipline-specific words and phrases in context. To create a concept map, students can work in teams to first write key words from the unit on a paper. Then, they write phrases to show the connection between the words, as shown in Figure 6.6. Teams of students can then orally share their connections with another team and ask questions about the different ways their partners connected two words. Finally, students can write sentences that show connections between the key words and concepts in a unit. This concept map not only builds comprehension of the big picture of the unit but also supports students when they speak and write about the academic concepts.

6.6 An Example of a Mind Map Showing the Connections Between Discipline-Specific Concepts

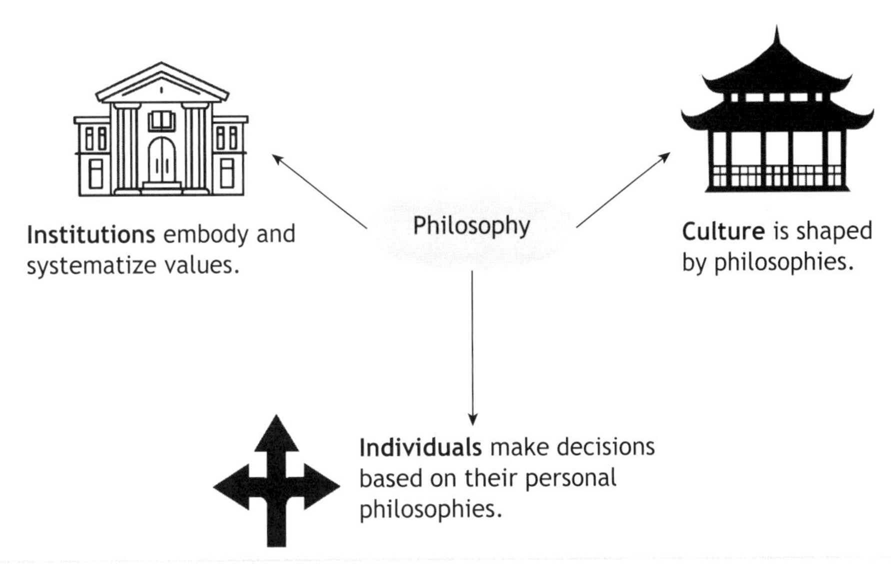

Image sources: istock.com/IconicBestiary, istcok.com/yangzai, istock.com/in8finity

Available at **resources.corwin.com/Long-Term SuccessforExperiencedMLs**

SENTENCE STARTERS AND FRAMES

Providing sentence starters and sentence frames is another effective practice introduced in Chapter 3. When used to structure academic speaking and writing in daily lessons, these supports, instead of providing students with the answers, prompt students to discuss the content with more complex structures and thinking. Additionally, these supports indirectly teach how content-specific language appears in context. Sentence starters and frames model mechanical aspects (e.g., punctuation, paragraphing, capitalization) and grammatical concepts (e.g., tenses, subject-verb agreement, articles, prepositions).

When content educators provide these supports,
they actually *are* teaching grammar.

As experienced multilinguals begin using sentence starters and frames, they too sound like confident and competent practitioners of a field.

One word of advice is to provide sentence starters and frames when needed and withdraw them when students already possess the skills to write in complete appropriate sentences (Echevarría, 2016). To avoid over-scaffolding or under-supporting students, provide sentence starters and frames but make them optional. This frees more proficient students to express themselves more creatively while still leaving the door open for students who need them. Another way teachers can determine if students need more support or challenge to use academic language is to carefully listen when they are speaking with their partners and monitor in-class written work. Many experienced multilinguals can effectively use social English. However, if they are not using the academic vocabulary or sentence structures, teachers can offer a sentence frame on the board, on a note card, or on a graphic organizer.

To support students, Mr. Ichiro provides sentence starters for the three-panel graphic organizer students will use to summarize their understanding (Figure 6.7). He pays careful attention to writing sentence starters that prompt students to think and leaving the rest of the sentence open for students to provide an answer. He makes sure that discipline-specific words are part of his sentence starters so as students read them, they internalize how those content-specific terms are used.

6.7 An Example of Content-Specific Sentence Starters and Frames

What is a philosophy?	What were the core beliefs of Greek philosophy?	What was one way ancient Greek society changed?
A philosophy is . . .	*In ancient Greece, the core philosophical beliefs were . . .*	*Ancient Greek society changed because of Greek philosophy by . . .*

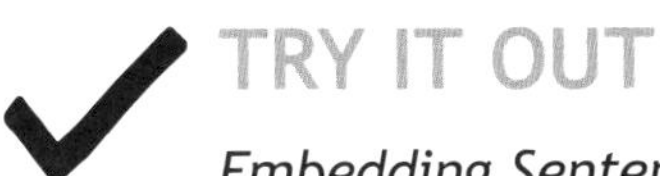

Embedding Sentence Starters and Frames

1. Write the instructions for a task.
2. Review the expected student response for a task.
3. Write the sentence starters for student responses. Include the key vocabulary words in the sentence starters when possible.

SENTENCE REDESIGN

Teachers can take a sentence starter or frame and elevate it from a scaffold to a writing lesson by using the *sentence redesign* approach. In this approach, teachers start by writing a complete sentence that uses the provided sentence starter or sentence frame. Then, they describe the role or function that sentence has such as a topic sentence, a sentence that provides an example, or a concluding sentence. For example, Mr. Ichiro wanted to teach students that a topic sentence can be redesigned or rewritten in many ways. He shared this sentence on the board: *Greek philosophy greatly influenced ancient Greek society*. Then he provided these sentence starters that could reconstruct the sentence:

- Without Greek philosophy, . . .
- Greek society was greatly shaped by . . .
- As the ancient Greeks started to adopt new philosophies . . .

The class worked together to generate the topic sentence using each of the new sentence starters. After the class had created new topic sentences, Mr. Ichiro gave them another topic sentence to practice with. Students worked in pairs to redesign the new topic sentence in three different ways. After the pairs worked together, he invited students to share their ideas to inspire others. Finally, he had students share all the ways that the sentences could be rewritten. The sentence redesign approach teaches students that

> language is like clay. It can be shaped into many different forms depending on the purpose.

ONE-SENTENCE SUMMARIES

Summarizing ideas can be difficult for students because knowing which ideas are essential to the summary is often difficult. Without scaffolding, students will often leave out important ideas or include insignificant details. Other times, students "summarize" by copying 99 percent of the text and changing just a word or two. Giving students acronyms for one-sentence summary frames that work with different text types is one way to scaffold the content of the one-sentence summary and the sentence structure. Acronyms are effective because they help students remember the structure of the summary.

The *someone wanted to but so* strategy (SWBS) strategy works well to scaffold one-sentence summaries of narratives (Beers, 2003; Macon et al., 1991). While this strategy works well with narratives, it can also be used for some nonfiction events as well (Figure 6.8). The acronym contains the main characters (someone), their desire (wanted to), the problem (but), and the solution (so) in a concise structure. The example in Figure 6.8 shows how students in Mr. Ichiro's class used SWBS to summarize what students learned about ancient Greek philosophy.

6.8 One-Sentence Summary

Someone: The ancient Greeks

Wanted to: have all of the male citizens participate in government

But: they needed to be educated

So: the men were expected to have private tutors

The *noun-verb-detail* (NVD) summarizing strategy provides a structure to summarize nonfiction text (Huynh, 2016). Students first identify the noun, which is taken from the text (e.g., philosophies, values, society, etc.). Then students describe what that noun is doing (e.g., influenced, emphasized, valued, etc.). Finally, students provide details to complete the idea (e.g., a literate citizenry, active participation in government, top physical health, application of science).

Noun: *Ancient Greeks*

Verb: *valued*

Detail: *active participation in the government*

These approaches to single-sentence summaries help students hone their summarization skills by focusing on the most essential details while communicating it in a comprehensible, well-structured format.

ORGANIZATION DIMENSION

Some teachers may have experienced this scenario: While reading a student's writing, you notice content-specific words and grammatically correct sentences, but the organization makes the text incomprehensible. Instead of the ideas flowing gently together, you are tossed around along the rapids of their ideas. This is our lived reality as well. Experienced multilinguals who produce text like this need support in organizing their ideas with academic organizational structures and clear transitions.

In the rest of the chapter, we offer scaffolds that structure longer written and spoken work. Additionally, we share approaches for teaching students to use different organizational structures for different purposes. The following menu of scaffolds and teaching approaches support experienced multilinguals as they produce academic oral presentations and written work in any content class. Secondary teachers can apply these ideas to support students as they engage in discussions and writing assignments. Each idea gives students ways to practice organizing and presenting their thoughts beyond single sentences.

GENRE-BASED WRITING AND PRESENTING

Genre-based writing and presenting refers to a deliberate process of teaching students content-specific language at the sentence and organization dimension. The teaching and learning cycle (TLC) is one approach to teaching different genres like narratives, informational reports, and arguments across the curriculum (Rothery, 1996). This approach scaffolds writing instruction or presentation formats through four specific steps:

1. Build content knowledge.
2. Analyze model writing or presentations.
3. Co-construct text.
4. Construct a text independently.

The first step of genre-based writing and presenting is to deepen students' understanding of the content and concepts. The scaffolds presented in Chapter 5 support this step by increasing the likelihood that students will comprehend the content material before they are asked to write or speak about it.

The more students understand the content, the more relevant details they can provide

in their writing and oral presentations and the more coherent their ideas become.

Once sufficient understanding has been established, the next step is to provide at least one model example of the text or presentation. Teachers can guide students in analyzing these examples for

- how the writing or presentation starts,
- use of content-specific words,
- phrases used to make connections,
- phrases that transition, and
- how the writing or presentation ends.

During the analysis, we encourage teachers to annotate the exemplar to make the writing or speaking expectations clearer. Because content teachers always feel the pressure of limited time, analyzing a written or spoken sample provides the basic scaffold for writing and speaking. Educators can also use this approach when honing in on a specific paragraph. However, some students would benefit from first seeing the finished product from a more global perspective. In this case, showing the entire example and giving an overview before going into paragraph analysis would be beneficial.

If teachers have more time, we encourage the third step, which is providing an opportunity for students to co-construct writing or speech that intentionally incorporates the expectations students found while analyzing the example text. To co-construct the text, the teacher asks students for the ideas and writes those ideas using the most accurate academic language. Co-writing with the teacher in this way makes the writing or speech expectations even more visible, increasing students' likelihood of incorporating these expectations into their work. Another option of co-constructing text is to have students work in pairs or triads to co-construct the text. The teacher can provide feedback as students work together. This form of co-construction is more engaging for students as the small group offers greater engagement and collaboration.

Regardless of the co-construction method used, having students co-construct a text right after the text analysis scaffolds the writing or oral presentation. Students now have greater clarity in the writing or speech they should produce when they write or speak independently.

When there is clarity of expectations, there is greater equity for multilingual students.

Writing and speaking successfully in content classes is not accidental, but rather by design.

Mr. Ichiro knew that his students would have to write a paragraph that describes the impact of Greek philosophy on ancient Greek society and current societies. To scaffold this kind of writing, Mr. Ichiro wrote a model paragraph on the impact of Greek philosophy on Greek society (Figure 6.9). He then led his students through an analysis of this paragraph, carefully annotating parts of the paragraph to highlight the writing decisions he made. Students then practiced by co-constructing a similar impact paragraph for the role Greek philosophy had on architecture. This lesson will prepare them to write their museum exhibit where they will be asked to explain the impact of Greek philosophy on the Italian Renaissance.

6.9 Mr. Ichiro's Exemplar Text Used to Analyze the Academic Language Needed in Students' Work

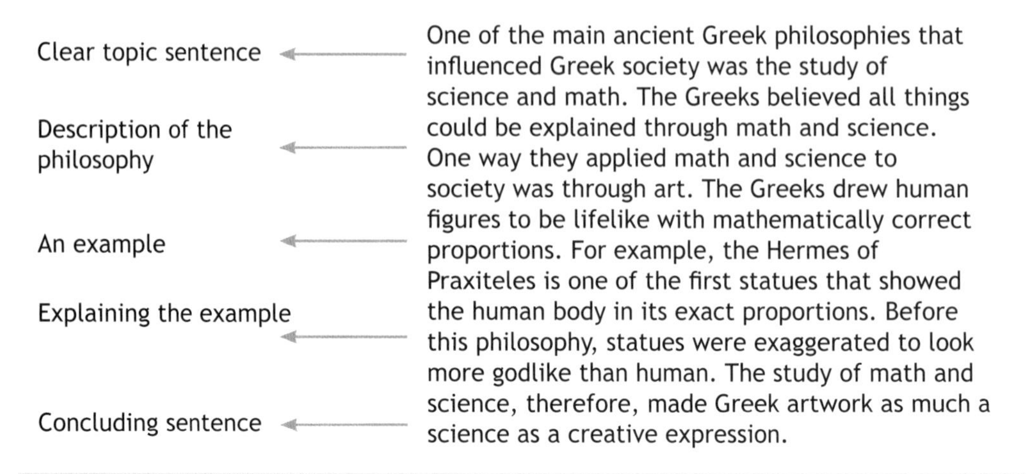

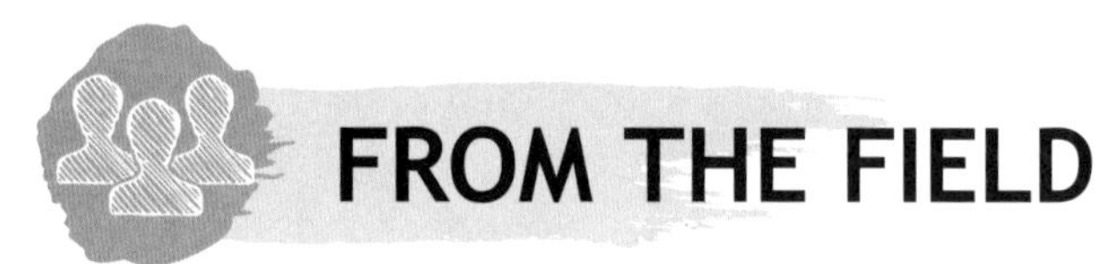

Structured Instructions

Tan shares his experience of not receiving structured instructions as a secondary student and how that impacted him as an adult.

I should not have graduated high school even though I had straight As. I was an unidentified long-term English learner. Teachers thought I didn't need help in middle and high school because I was diligent and highly fluent in social English. Everyone thought I was born in the United States by the time I was in middle school. However, I only realized how lacking my academic writing skills were in my senior year of college when I had to take the PRAXIS test to qualify for my teaching certificate. I had to produce a written text as a part of the examination. I thought my writing score would be one of the highest scoring parts of the examination. After all, I made it to the dean's list in college! I took the exam and waited nervously for the results. A few months later, I received my scores and my heart dropped. Luckily, my writing had earned just two points higher than the absolute minimum score allowed by the state. Without those two points, I would have failed.

How could this have happened? My teachers did the best they could. Unfortunately, I wasn't provided instruction on how to write during my secondary and college years. I just remember being assigned the writing task with no further guidance. In college, I often was required to "Read this book and write a response to it."

Maybe the lack of structure in the instructions for these assignments traumatized me. That is why my documents for my students are so highly organized, structured, descriptive, and detailed. I take this "guided" approach in hopes that my students learn how to write with clarity, organization, and flow.

One day, their lives will depend on these skills when applying for higher education, applying for a job, sitting for an entrance exam, or being considered for a promotion. I do not want to be the reason why they score only two points above the minimum requirement.

TRY IT OUT

Genre-Based Writing or Presenting

1. Think about the writing or speaking you want students to produce.
2. Identify one part of that writing or presentation that would benefit from scaffolding.
3. Find or write a model text for that one section, or find or make a video of a model presentation.
4. Guide students in analyzing that written or spoken work to discover the purpose of each sentence or section.
5. Annotate that example as you lead the guided analysis.
6. Invite students to co-construct a similar piece of writing or presentation (optional).
7. Encourage students to write or speak independently using the structures identified in the analysis.

EMBEDDING TRANSITIONS

The organization of a text hinges on the transitions between ideas. When we analyze academic writing and speaking, we notice the frequent and artful use of transitions that lead the audience from one idea to the next or spotlight a particular idea. Teachers can easily embed strategic transitions into sentence starters. With transitions, students can more effectively

- sequence ideas,
- connect ideas, and
- emphasize ideas.

Transitions can help students mirror the academic language used by experts in the field and more effectively communicate their content-specific ideas. We have found that with this single writing tool, students can elevate their writing to the next level.

To provide even more support to experienced multilinguals, these transitions can be sequenced into sentence starters intentionally (Figure 6.10). This way, students will have the transitions and the order the ideas are to appear, resulting in improved flow and clarity of ideas. We have found that proactively prompting for specific details is more effective in helping students generate ideas than writing "Add more details" when we review their work. The intentionally sequenced sentence starters already lead students to provide the necessary details.

6.10 An Example of Scaffolding the Discourse Dimension in an Assignment

Greek Philosophy's Influence on Society

- What is a philosophy?
- What were core beliefs of ancient Greek philosophies?
- How did society change based on one of the Greek philosophies?

A philosophy is . . . In ancient Greece, the core philosophical beliefs were . . . One example of how ancient Greek philosophies changed society was . . . Society changed because of this belief because . . .

SENTENCE BRIDGES

To help experienced multilinguals become more independent using effective transitions in their speech and writing, teachers can have them practice with an approach called *sentence bridges*. For example, Mr. Ichiro first takes two consecutive sentences in a paragraph and removes any transition between these sentences: *Greek philosophy emphasized education. Boys from wealthy families often had private tutors*. He projects these two sentences and models how to add a transition between them; for example, *Greek philosophy emphasized education.* ***As a result,*** *boys from wealthy families often had private tutors*. In this first part of the lesson, Mr. Ichiro highlights the importance of transitions to students.

In the second part, Mr. Ichiro takes an entire paragraph completely void of transitions. He then reads it aloud to students. He then asks students to explain what they noticed about a paragraph that does not have transitions. In the next phase, he gives students a list of transitions and instructs them to work in pairs to add transitions between sentences. When the class is ready, he has students share their completed paragraph with transitions. Then they compare and contrast how the meaning of the paragraph changes with different transition phrases. Finally, Mr. Ichiro has students discuss why writers use transitions.

Using the sentence bridges approach explicitly teaches students how writers enhance their communication through transitions. Through this lesson, students will see how

> transitions bridge the space between sentences so that readers have greater comprehension.

STRUCTURED PARAGRAPHS

If an entire summative performance-based assessment can be organized and scaffolded as shown in Chapter 3, then a single paragraph can too. Many paragraphs follow this sequence of ideas:

1. Topic sentence
2. Evidence/example (razonamiento, detalle)
3. Explanation of how the evidence supports the topic sentence

Together, this organization structure is called a TEE paragraph (topic sentence, evidence, explanation). Each sentence in a TEE paragraph has a role distinct from the other sentences, yet they all work together. A TEE paragraph scaffolds the sequence of ideas for students to communicate with a central topic, provide evidence, and use that evidence to support the message. Starting off the paragraph with a topic sentence keeps the paragraph focused. Identifying evidence makes the message come alive. Providing an explanation demonstrates understanding of the content. For example, Min Woo can use a TEE paragraph to respond to Mr. Ichiro's exit ticket prompt by

1. T: writing a topic sentence to introduce the societal impact of Greek philosophies,
2. E: providing an example of a specific societal impact due to a Greek philosophy, and
3. E: explaining how this part of society was influenced by a Greek philosophy.

Intentionally organizing a paragraph shows students that all sentences of a paragraph work together to communicate a central message.

Students begin to learn that writing is not just a collection of random sentences but an act of intentionality.

STICKY NOTE ORGANIZATION

Even when each paragraph in a report or section of a presentation is organized effectively, if the sequence of those paragraphs or sections is not thoughtfully arranged, communication loses its effect. Therefore, we encourage content teachers to provide students with a scaffold for organizing their longer written and spoken work. Sticky notes provide simple manipulatives students can use to arrange their ideas and topics into sections or categories. Once the notes are organized in a logical, effective order, students can use additional sticky notes to create headings and even greater clarity.

Mr. Ichiro models how to use sticky notes to organize the written response to the prompt about Greek philosophy. He writes one idea per sticky note. When he has them all laid out before him, he thinks aloud to show students his organizational logic. He first looks for a topic that would start his essay, picks up that sticky note, and places it at the top of the table. After that, he searches for a topic that would be the most appropriate following the first topic. Mr. Ichiro places that second topic right after the first sticky note, slowly forming a line. He continues until all of the topics are arranged in a particular order. Each of the sticky notes represents a paragraph in the final report. Teaching this transferable organizational skill will help multilinguals experience long-term success.

THINKING VERBS

One of the effective ways to scaffold academic discourse is to let the thinking verb of the prompt guide the organization of ideas, which we discussed in Chapter 4. Each thinking verb has a different flow of ideas (Figure 6.11). For example, when *compare* is the thinking verb, students can present the similarities first, then the differences. However, if the thinking verb is *narrate*, students usually need to present ideas chronologically. When teachers organize a response template according to the thinking verb in the prompt, students think more academically and connect ideas more eloquently. Over time, students will internalize these cognitive moves when they encounter them in other classes.

6.11 Organizational Pattern Based on Thinking Verbs

Thinking Verb	Example Organizational Pattern
Narrate	1. Establish the characters and setting. 2. Introduce the problem. 3. Develop the problem. 4. Attempt to solve the problem. 5. Describe the resolution or solution.
Explain	1. Identify the phenomenon (cycle, process, situation). 2. Describe the phenomenon. 3. Explain the causes of the phenomenon.
Inform	1. Identify the topic. 2. Introduce features, characteristics, or ideas about the topic. 3. Describe features, characteristics, or ideas with an example. 4. Summarize topic.
Argue	1. State claim/thesis/opinion. 2. Provide evidence. 3. Explain reasoning. 4. Describe a counterclaim. 5. Present a call for action.

Modified from Walqui & van Lier (2010).

Available at **resources.corwin.com/Long-Term SuccessforExperiencedMLs**

TRY IT OUT

Thinking Organization

1. Identify all the individual parts of a report or presentation.
2. Sequence the parts that best support the main thinking verb in the desired order using sentence starters, questions, or prompts.
3. Transfer this sequence onto a document.
4. Write instructions for students for each part of the document.
5. Give students the document to guide them as they write their own reports.

CONTEXT DIMENSION

In the way teachers can activate students' prior knowledge using the expanding circles strategy found in Chapter 5, teachers can also structure academic output through setting a context in one of the expanding circles for writing or speaking.

> By giving students a role that relates to real life in one of the expanding circles, the tasks transform from abstract to concrete.

For example, Mr. Ichiro used the community circle as the context. He has students work as museum curators, who serve the greater community. He contacted a nearby museum and asked the director to speak with the class about the project. The museum director has asked them to design a special exhibit to show how some modern societies trace their roots to ancient Greek philosophies. The goal of the exhibit is to demonstrate the ways Greek philosophies have influenced modern societies. As students write, they have to use content-specific words about Greek philosophies and examples from modern society to substantiate their ideas.

Establishing a context provides another way to structure the academic language because teachers have to help students write and produce academic language as particular experts in certain roles. For example, when Min Woo takes on the role of a museum curator, he will have to speak to an audience about the exhibit using content-specific vocabulary and complex sentences that are organized clearly and connected with transitional phrases. This means being mindful of vocabulary, sentence structure, and organization of the ideas.

CLOSING REMARKS

Min Woo leaves social studies class and goes to lunch feeling like he usually does when learning with Mr. Ichiro: welcomed, confident, and competent. Min Woo doesn't know it, but Mr. Ichiro planned for Min Woo and his classmates to feel this way. Mr. Ichiro's careful attention to structuring the four dimensions of language increased the chances that students would learn both content and academic language. As a result, students clearly understood the instructions and had scaffolds at their disposal to guide them to success. No wonder Min Woo and his classmates enjoy Mr. Ichiro's class because they experience small, daily successes by design. Because all of Min Woo's teachers (Mr. Nguyen, Mrs. Maple, Mx. Delgado, and Mr. Ichiro) intentionally and consistently scaffold their instruction and assessments for the language of their discipline, Min Woo has made significant gains in academic language development as well as content attainment this year. His teachers can see his increased engagement and confidence as he feels more supported and competent in his abilities.

Instruction that is intentionally designed with students' success in mind is the key to instruction that nurtures long-term success.

Since producing academic language is highly complex and invisible (Cummins & Early, 2015; Haynes & Zacarian, 2010), we encourage teachers to do everything within their power to coach to direct experienced multilinguals as they learn to produce that language. Figure 6.12 provides a summary of the strategies from this chapter that teachers can use to scaffold for students as they learn to speak and write using academic language.

As teachers shift from just *covering* to scaffolding the curriculum, long-term success becomes a fulfilled promise.

REFLECTION

- How do you scaffold students' production of discipline-specific vocabulary for your content area?

____

____

____

____

(Continued)

(Continued)

- How do you scaffold students' production of academic sentence structures for your content area?

____

____

____

____

- How do you scaffold students' production of academic organizational patterns for your content area?

____

____

____

____

- How do you scaffold students' production of academic contexts for your content area?

____

____

____

____

- How could students benefit from scaffolding language in these four dimensions?

____

____

____

____

- How might you start scaffolding one of these dimensions of language in your next lesson?

____

____

____

____

6.12 Strategies Categorized by Dimensions of Language

Dimensions	Output Strategies
Word	• Embedded discipline-specific words • Word banks • Morphing verbs
Sentence	• Concept mapping • Sentence starters and frames • Sentence redesign • One-sentence summaries
Organization	• Genre-based writing and presenting • Embedding transitions • Sentence bridges • TEE paragraphs • Sticky note organization • Thinking verbs
Context	• Expanding circles

Image sources: istock.com/da-vooda, istock.com/Antti Hekkinen, istock.com/Nadiinko, istock.com/yugoro

CHAPTER SUMMARY

- Structuring academic output scaffolds the language students need to use.
- Structuring academic output increases students' accuracy with words, facilitates thinking, sequences ideas in a logical order, and helps students address the audience appropriately.
- Scaffolding academic output can be focused ideally on the word, sentence, organization, or context dimension.

COLLABORATING FOR LONG-TERM SUCCESS

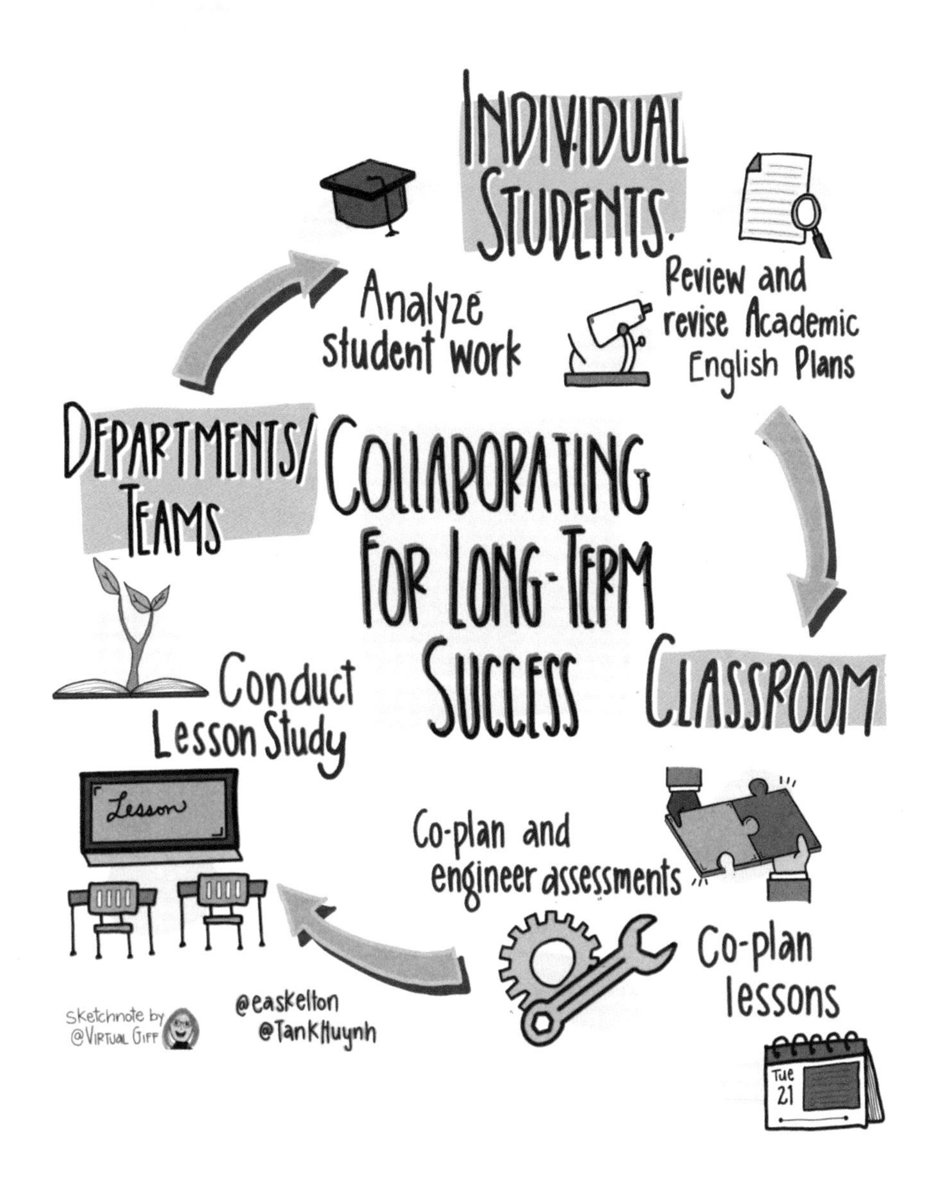

"If you want to go fast, go alone.
If you want to go far, go together."

—African proverb

Graciela leaves her art class chatting with her friends and heads to her business class. She greets Ms. Valladares as she walks in and notices a few other teachers in the room. She is used to these classroom observations as they happen often. At the beginning of the year, her principal explained that the teachers would be learning from each other all year and that they would be observing in different classes. Graciela wonders what the teachers might be learning today. Whatever they are learning, it is making a difference. She has noticed that all of her teachers now give her more time to talk with classmates about the topics and assignments, which helps her understand the content better. She also feels more confident writing and is beginning to succeed on tests this year, too.

This final chapter will share how schools such as Graciela's systematically established schoolwide systems of support for experienced multilinguals. In Graciela's high school, the principal worked with the entire faculty, especially department chairs, instructional coaches, and the English language development (ELD) specialist, to strategically implement the instructional framework schoolwide. They started small with a few collaborative sessions focused on individual students' assets and needs. Then, they created time in the schedule for the ELD teacher to co-plan with several content teachers focused on creating instruction and assessments that supported Graciela and other experienced multilinguals. Finally, teachers in each department began collaborating with the ELD specialist on a recurring basis. Their collaborative work included co-planning and lesson study. With each of these steps, teachers' beliefs about experienced multilinguals began to shift. Teachers noticed that students who would normally struggle were now successfully engaging with grade-level content. Content area teachers appreciated the collaboration with the ELD specialist and their department colleagues. They had renewed belief that they were collectively making a difference for experienced multilinguals. This belief that teachers working together can make a positive impact, also known as collective teacher efficacy, has been shown to have a tremendous positive influence on student achievement (Hattie, 2021).

Magic happens when every teacher in a school believes that through their collective effort, every student can be successful.

The collaborative structures presented in this chapter build that belief and transform every classroom into an academic language lab.

Implementing the instructional framework through collaborative efforts like those at Graciela's school will go far in creating the equitable long-term success all experienced multilinguals deserve. However, we would be remiss if we did not identify the other research-based schoolwide programs and policies beyond the instructional framework that can further create conditions for growth. The literature suggests that school leaders also consider

- creating programs that develop meaningful home-school connections (Cooper, 2020),
- offering an advisory or mentor program, and
- creating courses such as heritage language and English language development classes specifically designed for experienced multilinguals. (Ascenzi-Moreno et al., 2013; Buenrostro & Maxwell-Jolly, 2021; Calderón & Minaya-Rowe, 2011; Olsen, 2014)

While we encourage leadership teams to review these additional programming recommendations as feasible within their school context, this chapter introduces the collaborative implementation cycle as one approach to implementing the instructional framework described in the book.

COLLABORATIVE IMPLEMENTATION CYCLE

7.1 Collaborative Implementation Cycle

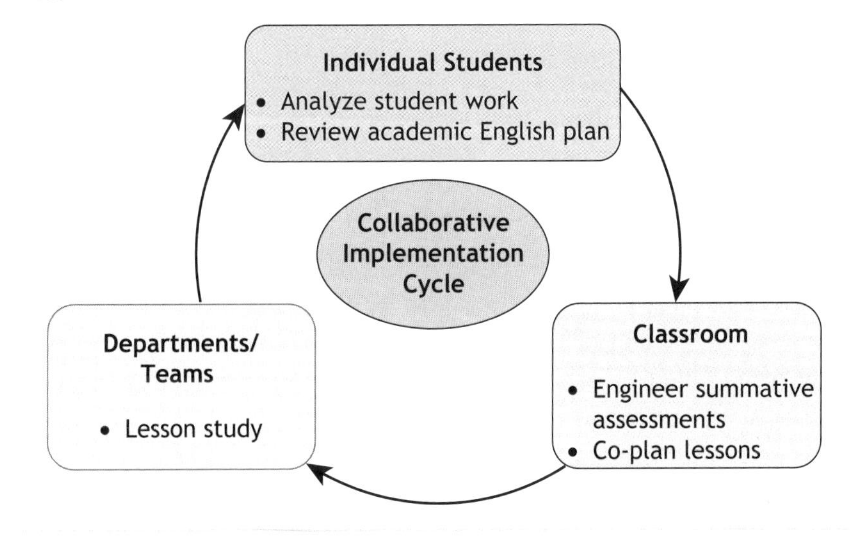

The collaborative implementation cycle shown in Figure 7.1 is used to methodically connect each element of the instructional framework to a schoolwide recommendation. The collaborative implementation cycle prioritizes teachers' actions as cultivating fertile ground for transformational learning for experienced multilinguals. Even small actions can lead to significant shifts in student learning. When teachers notice increased student achievement, their beliefs will also bloom (Fogarty & Pete, 2007). For example, when teachers engineer a summative assessment in collaboration with the ELD specialist and see improved exam results, their belief in experienced multilinguals' potential grows ever stronger. This belief in students creates equitable learning and closes the achievement gaps for experienced multilinguals.

We align the collaborative implementation cycle with each chapter in the book as outlined in Figure 7.2. First, we focus on individual students, just as we encouraged teachers in Chapter 1 to get to know the experienced multilinguals in their classes. In this phase of the implementation cycle, we introduce two ways teachers can become more aware of experienced multilinguals' academic strengths and needs: analyzing student work and implementing their academic English plans in collaboration with the school's ELD specialist. These two actions are manageable ways for the ELD specialist and the content area teachers to begin collaborating since they focus first on individual students rather than the whole class.

As content teachers collaborate with the ELD specialist, they nurture an awareness of the academic language expectations of their content. This awareness leads to opportunities to collaborate on classroom related items such as a summative assessment and lesson plans. Since the content and ELD teachers are in tune with the students' academic English needs, they can intentionally scaffold assessments and lessons as described in Chapters 3 through 6.

Then, teachers can share the fruits of their labor co-engineering and co-planning lesson experiences with departments and teams through a lesson study. Lesson study offers one form of job-embedded, teacher-driven professional learning that leads to systemic changes. During a lesson study, grade-level teams or departments observe how students engage with academic language and content based on the scaffolds designed during co-planning. Because teachers have the opportunity to observe students in another class during a lesson study, they see how experienced multilinguals are responding to intentionally designed instruction that is attuned to the lesson's academic language requirements. This understanding circles back to the first phase of the cycle, that is, looking at student work to determine next steps for instruction.

Later in the chapter, we provide a lesson study protocol that can structure professional learning for an entire department or grade-level team.

The collaborative implementation cycle is all about amplifying the effects of the instructional framework through teacher collaboration. When teachers collaborate, they

- apply their individual expertise,
- form new perspectives,
- share techniques, and
- agree on common practices.

This systematic approach to collaboration can be the most transformative form of professional learning because it provides opportunities for teachers to apply strategies most relevant to their context alongside colleagues in their department or team. Educators learning together is one of the hallmarks of effective professional learning (Darling-Hammond et al., 2009).

7.2 Connecting the Instructional Framework to the Collaborative Implementation Cycle

	Individual Teacher	Schoolwide Approach
Chapter 1: **An Affirming Shift**	Get to know students personally through surveys, journal entries, interviews, and informal chats.	• Analyze student work with colleagues to determine next steps for instruction. • Implement academic English plans for experienced multilinguals with colleagues.
Chapter 2: **Instructional Framework for Experienced Multilinguals**	Individual teachers integrate content and academic language in their classes.	Teams of teachers work together to integrate content and academic language across the curriculum.
Chapter 3: **Engineer the Summative Assessment**	Individually plan and engineer each summative assessment.	Co-plan and engineer summative assessments with an ELD specialist and/or a grade-level or content-specific team.
Chapters 4-6: **Plan Daily Lessons**	Individually plan daily lessons that establish comprehensible input and structure academic output.	• Co-plan scaffolded daily lessons for comprehensible input and structured output with an ELD specialist. • Conduct a lesson study to evaluate student engagement and academic language use in co-planned lessons.

MASTER SCHEDULE

Implementing this collaborative implementation cycle schoolwide relies on a master schedule that embeds regular opportunities for collaboration among colleagues.

The master schedule is the key that unlocks the potential for teachers to collaborate.

If the master schedule does not create space for different types of collaboration, students lose out on the schoolwide support that collaboration generates. In addition, teachers have to practice in isolation or find time on their own to engage in this critical work. However, expecting them to forgo lunch break or stay after contracted hours to collaborate leads to teacher burnout and is not sustainable. As John Hattie (2012) states, "Schools cannot help all students to learn if educators work in isolation. Schools must create the structures and cultures that foster effective educator collaboration" (p. 69). Designing a master schedule with collaborative structures in place is one way schools can foster effective collaboration.

According to Jen Hanson, an experienced district-level administrator of multilingual services, the school's master schedule is also one of the most important equity tools for serving experienced multilinguals (Huynh, 2023). In previous years, Ms. Valladares did not have a scheduled time for collaboration. She knew many students struggled in her class, but she was not sure how to best support them. This year, however, she has collaborative planning time with Mrs. Rivera, the ELD specialist. After planning assessments and daily lessons with the ELD specialist, Ms. Valladares has noticed that students like Graciela are experiencing more success in her class. Even students not identified as English learners are producing higher-quality work and are benefiting from their collaboration.

Collaboration creates the conditions for equitable learning in every corner of the school.

For the greatest success with implementing schoolwide approaches for experienced multilinguals, we recommend that the master schedule include time for each department or team to collaborate with the ELD specialist. There are many ways to schedule these collaborative opportunities during the school day. By adjusting the master schedule, schools can create time for departments to meet regularly (e.g., once a week or twice a month) for at least one class period (Honigsfeld & Dove, 2019). When the ELD teachers join the collaborative sessions, they have the opportunity to share their expertise in academic language development with content area specialists. We envision schools using the collaborative implementation cycle to structure different types of collaboration so that all students experience success. These structured collaborations involve a focus on

- **individual students,** by analyzing student work and implementing academic English plans;
- **classroom instruction,** by engineering assessments and designing lessons; and
- **departments,** through lesson study.

Depending on the master schedule, ELD specialists may have to occasionally miss teaching a class in order to find time to collaborate with content area colleagues. However, the time spent collaborating is a multiplier of time as the tools developed during collaborative planning can support students throughout the unit.

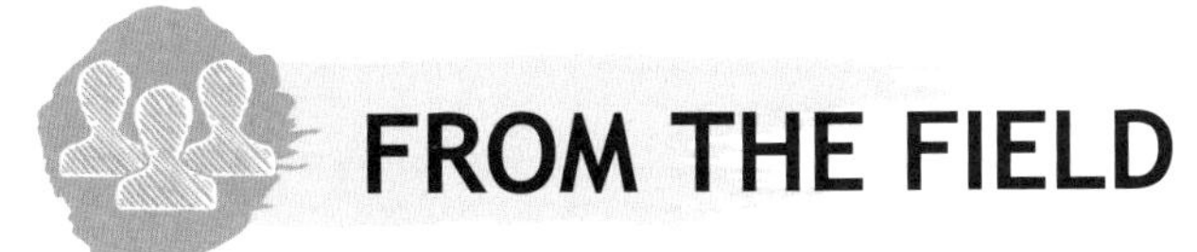

FROM THE FIELD

Scheduling Collaboration Time

Tan shares his experience in co-creating a schedule with time for collaboration.

When I first became an English language specialist, my administrator handed me a mostly blank teaching schedule. I saw where two English language development classes were scheduled, but there was nothing else blocked off. I went to my principal to ask when my schedule was going to be completed, but she said that I should create the rest of my schedule in collaboration with my co-teachers. She wanted me to co-create the co-planning and co-teaching schedule with the Grade 6, 7, and 8 science and social studies teachers. Since I was new to the school and the ELD position, I was surprised. But looking back, I realize that my principal was setting me, my students, and my colleagues up for success. Instead of using a program to design my schedule, she provided me with the freedom to collaborate with colleagues from the start. The almost

(Continued)

(Continued)

blank schedule gave my colleagues and me the flexibility to create a schedule to best support a cohort of students based on my colleagues' knowledge of the students and our examination of their previous year's work sample. My administrator had the wisdom to have teacher collaboration as part of the school's service to multilingual students and launched my collaboration with colleagues by having me co-create the schedule with them.

If school leaders are reading this chapter in the middle of the school year and do not have the ability to change the master schedule until the beginning of the next academic year, they can still implement parts of the collaborative implementation cycle. In each "Try It Out" feature, we suggest ways to get started with each type of collaboration, even if the master schedule has not yet been designed with embedded collaboration times.

TRY IT OUT

Master Schedule

In school leadership teams, do the following:

1. Identify teachers who would be willing to volunteer to collaborate all year.
   a. Co-create goals for the collaboration.
   b. Co-create a schedule for collaboration.
   c. Discuss how to balance the three focus areas for collaborative meetings: individual students, classroom, and departments.
2. Consider the following teams:
   a. Department teams
   b. Grade-level teams
   c. Co-teaching partnerships between content and ELD teachers
3. Review the current master schedule.
   a. Look for opportunities to provide each identified team scheduled time to meet on a regular basis.
   b. Share the suggested schedule with teachers for feedback and revision.

Whether looking at student work, co-planning a lesson, or participating in a lesson study, we encourage teachers to use some kind of protocol to structure this precious collaborative time. While informal interactions may foster collegial relationships, they alone do not lead to significant changes in instruction or student learning. Instead,

> following a protocol or formal structure will allow for all voices are heard and the focus remains on student learning and professional growth (Honigsfeld & Dove, 2019).

For each phase of the collaborative implementation cycle described in this chapter, we offer an example of a protocol or formal structure that supports a professional learning environment.

COLLABORATION FOCUSED ON INDIVIDUAL STUDENTS

In this phase of the collaborative implementation cycle, we focus on the assets and goals of individual students. Teachers can collaborate to understand students' academic strengths and needs by analyzing their work. Then, with a lens on what experienced multilinguals can do, teachers continue to support students with their goals on the academic English plan.

ANALYZE STUDENT WORK

As explained in Chapter 1, knowing the linguistic, cultural, and experiential assets students bring to the classroom enables teachers to provide equitable instruction that is more connected and relevant to students. In addition, knowing their academic strengths and areas for growth is essential for planning lessons that are at grade-level while still offering scaffolds.

One way to gain this important student-centered data is to analyze their work through both a content and a linguistic lens. When teachers meet in small groups to analyze student work, they can look at learning through their students' eyes. Analyzing student work can reveal understanding of an individual student's strengths, ideas for next steps in instruction, and wider insights into teaching and learning in general (Auslander & Yip, 2022).

Ms. Valladares and the ELD specialist meet once a month to look at student work from the previous unit before they begin planning the summative assessment for the next unit. This month, Ms. Valladares brings a sample of Graciela's work to review with the ELD teacher (Figure 7.3). First, Ms. Valladares explains the context for the written work they are about to analyze. For the summative assessment in the current persuasive writing unit, students were challenged to create a business plan for a food truck and write a persuasive and profitable business plan to attract investors. Ms. Valladares chunked the final assessment and as one part of the food truck business plan, she asked students to write a detailed description of their signature dish using descriptive adjectives that highlight the flavors of the dish. The writing should convince investors that the student's signature dish best represents their food truck theme. Ms. Valladares shared Graciela's work sample with the ELD specialist.

7.3 Student Work Sample

The taquitos of Mexico are crispy and flavorful. The taquitos are freshly made tortillas having the smell of the flour is used as the base. The chiles make the spicy flavors of the chicken filling. These chiles are then spreaded all over the tortilla base making the dish delicious. The raw chicken breast has salt, pepper, and chili powder is then well cooked and soon enough turned into tiny chicken bits with freshly grinded herbs, onion, and garlic. The taquitos use several techniques of kitchen mastery. The tortilla rolls with chicken inside are made in the burning, hot oil. The taquitos smell yummy when adding the rolls and oil to make them crunchy and tender. The taquitos are a wonderful way to introduce you to the flavors of Mexican cuisine.

Together, the ELD teacher and Ms. Valladares read through Graciela's writing about the signature dish looking for descriptive adjectives, her use of complex sentences, and transition phrases that connect one idea to another. The ELD teacher is able to guide Ms. Valladares to focus on Graciela's language development, not just content understanding. They notice that Graciela can use several cuisine-based individual adjectives that highlight Mexican food, but she needs support with describing using the five senses. The ELD teacher notes that Graciela writes most sentences with the same repeating sentence structure (*The + noun*), so she needs help writing with alternating sentence structures. Ms. Valladares also wonders how to support Graciela with the organization or sequencing of the descriptions that would make the writing more persuasive and convincing to a potential investor. Together they discuss ways of supporting not just Graciela but also other experienced multilinguals with structuring a piece of descriptive, persuasive writing like this for a business plan. They decide to find a few mentor texts for students to deconstruct and reconstruct.

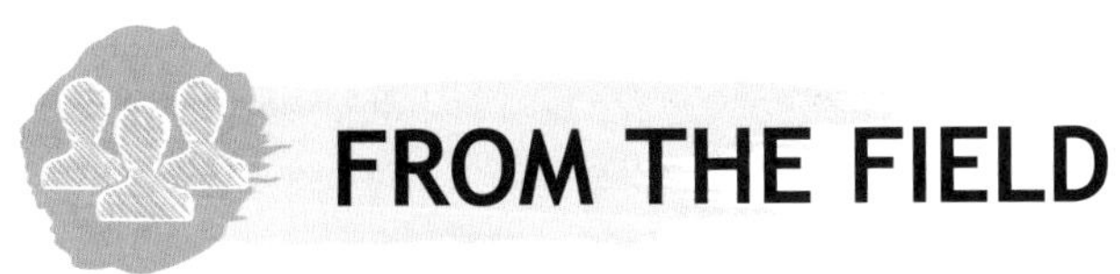

FROM THE FIELD

Analyzing Student Writing

Anastasia Mixcoatl-Martinez is an ELD specialist in California. She explains how analyzing student work with her grade-level colleagues supports and challenges experienced multilinguals across the curriculum.

As the only ELD teacher at my school, I am able to collaborate with my grade-level colleagues in history and English language arts. I support these two teachers with my input on what LTEL students can do in terms of their writing skills and what support they would need to continue improving their skills. I also share writing samples from my ELD classes to show what steps I have taken that led students to write successful paragraphs.

Aligning the writing expectations is beneficial because students notice consistency, meaning that all their teachers expect them to use higher-level words, check for run-on sentences, or write in complete sentences. Meeting with Grade 6 teachers and sharing students' writing samples is beneficial for all teachers. They see what students can do and what we need to do to help them improve.

Graciela's teachers look at student work at least once a month. They usually follow a protocol to guide what and how they analyze the work. Protocols help teams of teachers stay focused on the purpose of analyzing student work and provide a structure for the team meetings. While there are many protocols for looking at student work (National School Reform Faculty, 2022), we recommend following steps that focus the team on both content learning and academic language development in the student work. We have developed an assets-based protocol for analyzing student work that does just that (Figure 7.4). It provides explicit steps, designated roles, and time frames for analyzing the different dimensions of academic language in student work. As with all protocols, we invite teachers to modify the protocol to meet their context.

The purpose of this protocol is to use the information from student work to design next steps for instruction that will support the individual student and other students who have similar needs. One administrator commented on the impact of analyzing student work in teams, "It was really cool . . . for the team to sit there and dissect the writing. . . . Then for the team to walk away, having a strategic plan for each kid based upon their own individual samples is pretty powerful" (Thompson & Rodriguez-Mojica, 2022, p. 13). Although teachers may only be able to analyze a couple of students' work during one collaborative session, many students will benefit from the shifts in teaching practices that emerge from the rich discussions. All students, especially experienced multilinguals, benefit when teachers reflect on their practice. Tiny teaching tweaks and paradigm shifts can radically transform students' experience at school.

7.4 Protocol for Analyzing Student Work

Purpose:

To help grade-level teams analyze student work and design next steps for instruction.

Time: Approximately 20-25 minutes per student

Facilitator:

The facilitator's role is to maintain time frames and ensure that the participants follow the protocol.

<table>
<tr><th>Time</th><th>Description of Step</th><th>Notes</th></tr>
<tr><td>3-5 minutes</td><td>Individual Note Taking
Teachers record evidence in the student work of what students can do with academic words and phrases, sentence structures, and organization. This is done individually and silently.</td><td rowspan="2">Words/Phrases

Sentence Structures (grammar that shows the purpose for the writing)

Organization (transition phrases, cohesive devices, headings, etc.)</td></tr>
<tr><td>5-10 minutes</td><td>Individual Reports
Each educator reports what the student can do with academic words and phrases, sentence structures, and organization. Use evidence from the student work and the sentence starter "The student can . . ."</td></tr>
<tr><td>5-10 minutes</td><td>Next Steps for Instruction
Teachers individually write notes about next steps for instruction to support the student in this content area with academic words and phrases, sentence structures, and organization. Each teacher reports ideas individually.</td><td>Ideas for Next Steps</td></tr>
</table>

Time	Description of Step	Notes
3-5 minutes	**Reflection** Each teacher shares a brief reflection on what they learned from the work analysis and what they can apply to their own practice.	**Reflections on Work Analysis and Teaching Practice**
3-5 minutes	**Student Feedback** Teachers craft supportive feedback to conference with the particular student whose work sample was shared. The feedback should include at least one "glow" (something they did well) and *only one* "grow" (something to work on).	**Student Feedback**

Available at **resources.corwin.com/Long-Term SuccessforExperiencedMLs**

TRY IT OUT

Getting Started With Analyzing Student Work

If school leaders would like to get started with analyzing student work, we recommend following these steps:

1. Identify a grade-level team or department willing to volunteer to review student work with the ELD specialist.
2. Find time in the master schedule for the collaborative meeting to occur, or provide cover for teachers to participate.
3. Ask teachers to bring a work sample from one or two experienced multilinguals.
4. Facilitate the protocol for analyzing student work (Figure 7.4) for the team.
5. Share insights and reflections from this work with the rest of the staff.

IMPLEMENT ACADEMIC ENGLISH PLANS

Analyzing student work in collaborative teams gives educators insights into students' strengths and needs. This information can then be used in a collaborative session to revise and implement students' academic English plans.

These plans are also known as individualized language plans or English learner plans; we have chosen to call them **academic English plans (AEP)** to focus on the *academic English* experienced multilinguals need for long-term success. These goals and scaffolds can lead to success for experienced multilinguals as all teachers will be able to build on students' assets and support them with their goals.

Although the ELD teacher will most likely be responsible for creating the AEP, all content teachers are responsible for implementing it. Whenever possible, we encourage the ELD teacher to co-create the academic English goals and scaffolds with the students. This gives experienced multilinguals ownership in their own learning, motivates them, and lets them know that all teachers will be supporting them to achieve their personal language goals. Bringing student voice into the process of developing an AEP is one way to build caring relationships between adults and experienced multilinguals and truly value each student (Thompson & Rodriguez-Mojica, 2022). Finding time to co-create AEPs with experienced multilinguals is a challenge worth meeting. With administrative support, ELD teachers can meet one-on-one with students

- during their scheduled ELD class at the beginning of the school year,
- during co-taught classes in the first few weeks of the school year, or
- during a student's study hall or advisory period.

There are many different forms for academic English plans, and some schools now use software to generate the basics of each plan. Figure 7.5 shows a plan template that includes each recommended element: student background information, assets, recommended scaffolds, and language goals. Regardless of the format of the AEP, we encourage schools to make it a living document that guides instruction.

Academic English plan (AEP): describes students' linguistic strengths and recommends ways to support their development.

7.5 Academic English Plan Template

Student Background	**Student's preferred name** (with audio file of student pronouncing name, if possible): **Pronouns** the student wants the class to use when referring to them: **Current grade:** **Heritage language(s):** **Literacy level in the heritage language:** **Guardians:**			
English Proficiency Scores (from standardized language assessment)	**Listening proficiency score**	**Speaking proficiency score**	**Reading proficiency score**	**Writing proficiency score**
Assets What can this student do well?				
Scaffolds What are the recommended scaffolds?				
Language Goals Quarter ___				
Other Assets and Information				

Available at **resources.corwin.com/Long-Term SuccessforExperiencedMLs**

> Academic English plans should not become another box to check when serving multilingual students but rather a tool for amplifying each student's assets.

AEPs help to embed a can-do approach across the curriculum. We encourage teachers to reference the AEPs during co-planning sessions and grade-level meetings so they can embed appropriate scaffolds, build on students' strengths, and connect to their interests.

When collaborative teams analyze the work of an experienced multilingual, they can also reference students' AEP to see if they are making progress toward their language goals. In this way, the AEP can also be used to monitor progress toward language development.

The academic English plan is like a road map for teachers. It gives them a sense of direction as they work together toward the student's personalized language and educational goals (Staehr Fenner, 2014). It is critical that ELD teachers have time to meet with content area teachers at least twice a year to review and revise these language plans based on the analysis of actual student work in content classes. In a recent study about the effects of these meetings about the individualized plans, administrators noted that teachers across the school immediately implemented specific scaffolds from the AEP after each meeting (Thompson & Rodriguez-Mojica, 2022). When Ms. Valladares implemented the scaffolds on Graciela's AEP (Figure 7.6), she noticed that Graciela was able to use business-related vocabulary more accurately and communicate her ideas more coherently.

7.6 Graciela's Completed Academic English Plan

<table>
<tr><td>Student Background</td><td colspan="4">Preferred name: Graciela
Student pronouns: she/her/hers
Current Grade: 10
Home language(s): Spanish
Literacy level in the home language: basic skills in reading and writing
Guardians: parents</td></tr>
<tr><td>English Proficiency Scores</td><td>Listening
ACCESS*: 5.5</td><td>Speaking
ACCESS: 5.0</td><td>Reading
ACCESS: 3.8</td><td>Writing
ACCESS: 3.6</td></tr>
<tr><td>Assets
What can this student do well?</td><td>• Follow multistep directions.
• Comprehend classroom discussion and most information presented in videos.</td><td>• Recount main ideas and key details of information presented in class.
• Speak in complete sentences and link one idea to another in class discussions.</td><td>• Comprehend engineered grade-level content texts.
• Explain main ideas and key details of a chunk of text in small groups using Spanish and English.</td><td>• Write short answer responses about topic in complete sentences.
• Write extended papers using a graphic organizer and word bank.</td></tr>
</table>

Scaffolds What are the recommended scaffolds?	• Chunk videos and provide time for processing with a partner and sketchnoting. • Provide sensory scaffolds for new concepts.	• Structure academic discussions. • Provide sentence frames for academic discussion moves.	• Engineer content texts. • Build background knowledge before reading texts. • Provide graphic scaffolds for data.	• Engineer essay templates with additional linguistic supports. • Deconstruct mentor texts and label key features of the text.
Language Goals Quarter 1	Demonstrate comprehension of lectures and videos with sketchnotes.	Present a report individually on a content topic in front of the class.	Answer questions using evidence from grade-level texts.	Write extended informative papers using academic language.
Other Assets and Information	• Draws detailed designs and graphics. • Wants to study graphic design at the university. • Interacts professionally with customers at family store. • Speaks social Spanish fluently; reads and writes social Spanish texts.			

*ACCESS = English Language Proficiency Assessment from the WIDA Consortium used in over 40 states, territories, and federal agencies in the United States.

TRY IT OUT

Implementing Academic English Plans

If school leaders would like to get started with academic English plans, we recommend following these steps:

If the school already has an AEP for experienced multilinguals . . .	If the school does not yet have an AEP for experienced multilinguals . . .
1. Review the school's current AEP with the following questions: • To what extent do current plans include student assets, recommended scaffolds, and academic English goals?	1. Create a document that works for your school's context that includes assets, recommended scaffolds, and academic English goals. 2. As a leadership team, complete the AEP with several experienced multilinguals.

(Continued)

(Continued)

If the school already has an AEP for experienced multilinguals . . .	If the school does not yet have an AEP for experienced multilinguals . . .
• How do all teachers learn about the students' AEPs? • To what extent do teachers implement the plan? • To what extent are students involved in the creation of their AEP? 2. Ask for feedback on how teachers use the AEPs during planning and instruction.	3. Reflect on the process and make changes to the plan and process as necessary. 4. Provide time for the ELD specialist to begin meeting with experienced multilinguals to develop their AEPs.

REFLECTION

- How could analyzing student work support experienced multilinguals in your school?

____

____

____

____

- How could academic English plans support experienced multilinguals?

____

____

____

____

- How can AEPs become useful planning tools rather than check boxes?

____

____

____

____

- How does your school's AEP compare to the one presented in this section?

____

____

____

____

COLLABORATION FOCUSED ON THE CLASSROOM

From successfully planning for individual students' needs, the collaboration evolves to co-planning summative assessments and daily instruction for the entire class.

CO-PLAN AND ENGINEER SUMMATIVE ASSESSMENTS

Co-planning summative assessments is a high-leverage outcome for collaboration time. It has been shown that teacher collaboration focused on assessment yields strong and positive effects on student achievement (Killion, 2015).

When teachers learn about their students' needs and strengths in the first phase of the collaborative cycle, they can more effectively plan and engineer summative assessments for units. Co-planning these assessments with content area colleagues and an ELD specialist when possible is an effective way to take full advantage of precious collaboration time (Huynh, 2020). This form of co-planning draws on the content expertise of the subject teacher and the linguistic expertise of the language specialist. Since the summative assessment provides a focus for content and academic language learning for the entire unit,

> time spent co-engineering an equitable, authentic assessment will plant seeds of success for the entire unit.

In the same way that the instructional framework starts with planning the summative assessment, we encourage teachers to begin co-planning by co-engineering a summative assessment. We like to use the following vase metaphor (Covey, 2014) when sharing the importance of co-planning the assessment first. The vase represents the unit. The teacher's job is to fit a single large rock, a few stones, and a pile of sand into that vase. All of these materials can fit snugly within the vase without spilling out. In what order should the teacher put these items into the vase? The most efficient approach is to start with the big rock. It takes the largest space. The area that it does not cover can be filled in with the stones, and finally the granular sand fills up all the smallest spaces. If the teacher placed the sand in the vase first, there would be no space left for the rock or the stones. In the same way, if planning is focused on the granular daily lesson planning, there will be no space to plan for the biggest item in the unit: the summative assessment (Huynh, 2020).

If the summative assessment is a long-term project, the co-planning conversation can focus on

- identifying the content being assessed,
- identifying the product students have to produce to demonstrate mastery, and
- identifying the process students have to follow to complete the assessment.

Each member of the co-planning team can draw on their expertise to co-create the assessment. The content teachers can identify the content-specific words students have to use in the assessment. The language specialist can focus on ways to make those words comprehensible leading up to the summative assessment. The content teacher can identify the specific requirements of a performance-based assessment, and the language specialist can identify the academic language for each section of that assessment. Finally, the content teacher can describe the steps students have to follow to complete the performance-based assessment while the language specialist works to make these steps comprehensible and scaffolded for students.

For exam-based summative assessments, the conversation can focus on how to reformat the assessment so that reading and writing are scaffolded as described in Chapter 3.

> Students should be able to share their knowledge and use their skills in the content area without the academic language on the assessment becoming a barrier.

After collaborating with the ELD teacher to create the scaffolded project-based assessment document, Ms. Valladares gives each student a copy. Graciela is accustomed to these highly detailed, structured, and organized assessment templates. She and her classmates appreciate these so much because the assessment is not a mystery. Each section of the assessment is clearly labeled and accompanied by concise instructions and helpful prompts. Graciela especially appreciates the sentence starters and paragraph frames as she knows they'll help her sound like an actual food truck owner and think like one too. She knows that Ms. Valladares's carefully selected scaffolds light the path for a successful journey.

CO-PLAN LESSONS

Once teams have designed and engineered the summative assessment, they can then use the co-planning time to focus on lesson planning by using the template in Figure 7.7. We suggest co-planning teams start with the lesson's learning goal and the prompt for an exit ticket as described in Chapter 4. This helps the team focus on the essential content and academic language of that lesson. Next, each teacher on the team can write a model response and compare their responses with each other, noticing the academic language and content points everyone chose to include. After teams have determined the essential vocabulary and sentence structures in that model response, they can co-create an integrated lesson objective.

When the integrated objective is clear, teachers on the team can make suggestions for establishing comprehensible input with various scaffolds as described in Chapter 5. Then, they select approaches and activities for students to practice using academic words, sentences, and organizational patterns in the lesson as described in Chapter 6. The goal of a co-planned lesson is to collaboratively produce a product or activity that can be directly used in a future lesson. When such deliverables are produced, the session becomes more fruitful and productive. This spirit of collaborating on something that can be used immediately nurtures the co-teaching relationship (Huynh, 2021a). Everyone draws from their well of expertise to do what is best for experienced multilinguals.

Each time a scaffold or activity is successfully co-created and implemented, colleagues' belief in experienced multilinguals takes root.

Over time, this blossoms into the belief that all teachers have the responsibility and ability to meet the needs of experienced multilinguals.

7.7 Lesson Planning Template Based on the Instructional Framework

End-of-Unit Summative Assessment	
Integrated Objective	
What should students know or do by the end of the lesson?	
Exit Ticket Prompt	
Model Response	
Integrated Objective Thinking verb + content + academic language expectation (by . . .)	

Establish Comprehensible Input	
Scaffold(s) Background, Sensory, Graphic, Interactive, Linguistic	
Structure Academic Output	
Scaffold(s) Word, Sentence, Organization, and Context Dimension	

online resources Available at **resources.corwin.com/Long-Term SuccessforExperiencedMLs**

Ms. Valladares and Mrs. Rivera, the school's ELD specialist, used this lesson planning template to co-design the writing lesson about the food truck's signature dish. Mrs. Rivera started the co-planning session by asking what Ms. Valladares wanted students to know or be able to do by the end of the lesson. Ms. Valladares explained that she wanted students to describe their signature dish for the final business plan. Since the signature dish is the crown jewel of their menu, the dish's description would need to be particularly effective to set the food truck apart from competitors and thus entice investors. For the exit ticket, Ms. Valladares decided to ask students to describe their signature dish using sensory details. Then, they co-wrote a model response to this exit ticket. The pair noticed many adjectives and sensory details in their model response. Although every student would be writing about a different signature dish, they would still need to use this kind of descriptive language in their writing. Therefore, Ms. Valladares and Mrs. Rivera brainstormed scaffolds and learning experiences that would make the concept of sensory descriptions more comprehensible. They decided to use their model response to guide students through this style of writing. To structure the output, they created a graphic organizer with the five senses, so students could work collaboratively to brainstorm adjectives and phrases for each sense. Their completed lesson plan is shown in Figure 7.8.

7.8 A Completed Lesson Plan for Persuasive Writing in Business Class

<table>
<tr><th colspan="2"> End-of-Unit Summative Assessment</th></tr>
<tr><td colspan="2">Performance-Based Assessment

Create a business plan for a food truck, and write a persuasive and profitable business plan to attract investors.</td></tr>
<tr><th colspan="2"> Integrated Objective</th></tr>
<tr><td>What should students know or do by the end of the lesson?</td><td>Students will need to produce writing, including sensory details, about a signature dish.</td></tr>
<tr><td>Exit Ticket Prompt</td><td>Describe your signature dish with sensory details.</td></tr>
<tr><td>Model Response</td><td>Pad Thai is a sweet-savory dish that provides a treat for the taste buds. Lightly coated with a golden tamarind sauce, the straw-thin rice noodles form the base for the Kingdom of Thailand's national dish. The essential ingredients of chopped onion, egg, crispy bean sprouts, and warm roasted ground peanuts add texture to the salty, nutty taste. Customers customize the dish by adding their choice of shrimp, chicken, or tofu.</td></tr>
<tr><td>Integrated Objective</td><td>Thinking verb + content + academic language expectations (by . . .)

Describe your signature dish by using adjectives from the five senses to highlight the flavors of the dish.</td></tr>
<tr><th colspan="2"> Establish Comprehensible Input</th></tr>
<tr><td>Scaffold(s)

Background, Sensory, Graphic, Interactive, Linguistic</td><td>Linguistic: Provide an annotated mentor text of descriptions of signature dishes from restaurants' menus and websites.</td></tr>
<tr><th colspan="2"> Structure Academic Output</th></tr>
<tr><td>Scaffold(s)

Word, Sentence, Organization, Context Dimension</td><td>Word: Co-create a graphic organizer with sensory-based adjectives, verbs, and phrases.</td></tr>
</table>

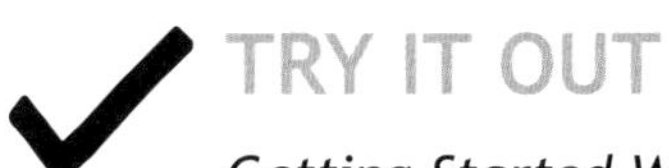

TRY IT OUT

Getting Started With Co-Planning

If school leaders would like to get started with co-planning, we recommend following these steps:

1. Invite one or more content teachers to pilot co-planning with the ELD specialist.
2. Co-create a special schedule to pilot co-planning with the partnership(s).
3. Support the collaboration with time, an allocated space, resources, and protocols for each meeting.
4. Facilitate a discussion in teams to reflect on their co-planning efforts.
5. Celebrate the results of co-planning such as engineered assessments or scaffolds for lessons with the rest of the staff and encourage other teachers to participate next time.

REFLECTION

- How could co-engineering summative assessments support the experienced multilinguals in your school?

____

____

____

____

- How could co-planning lessons support experienced multilinguals?

____

____

____

____

(Continued)

(Continued)

- How could co-planning contribute to ongoing, job-embedded professional learning?

____

____

____

____

- How could you overcome barriers to providing regular times for co-planning in the master schedule?

____

____

____

____

COLLABORATION FOCUSED ON DEPARTMENTS OR TEAMS

In this phase of the collaborative implementation cycle, we introduce the lesson study, which is a form of professional learning that involves an entire department or grade-level team. The trust earned when two teachers co-plan successfully together sets the stage for the rest of the grade or department to join in the collaborative work.

LESSON STUDY

The goal of a lesson study is to improve teacher practice. The lesson study, first pioneered in Japan, has become "one of the most potent known approaches to teacher professional learning" (Collet, 2019, p. ix). In brief, a lesson study is a process in which a team of teachers co-plan a lesson that one teacher volunteers to teach. During the lesson, others observe with a focus on student learning. After the lesson, teachers meet to reflect on the lesson and student learning. An overview of this process is shown in Figure 7.9.

Lesson study: A collaborative form of job-embedded professional learning in which teams of teachers plan, teach, and reflect on a lesson (Lewis, 2022)

7.9 Overview of Lesson Study

Step	Approximate Time	Description
Before the Lesson Co-plan	45 minutes or one planning period	Teams of teachers meet to plan a lesson for a lesson study. Part 1: Generate a question about teaching and learning (3-5 min.). Part 2: Co-plan (35 min.). Teachers contribute ideas and strategies to support the learning outcome and address the guiding question. Part 3: Data (3-5 min.). Teachers decide how they will gather student-centered data about the question.
During the Lesson Teach and Observe	45 minutes or one class period	• One teacher delivers the co-planned lesson. • Observers focus on gathering student-centered data.
After the Lesson Collaborative Reflection	45 minutes or one planning period	The lesson study team meets to • share student-centered data, • reflect on student learning, and • determine next steps for instruction.

Available at **resources.corwin.com/Long-Term SuccessforExperiencedMLs**

Before the Lesson: Co-Plan

The first step of a lesson study is the co-planning session. At the beginning of this session, teams decide on a question about student learning they would like to focus on. Here are some examples:

- Which strategies will make the social studies texts more comprehensible for experienced multilinguals?
- How can I encourage experienced multilinguals to share their thinking with their peers?
- How can I develop experienced multilinguals' writing skills on the science report?

With this guiding question in mind, teachers now contribute ideas and strategies to support the learning outcome. At the end of this co-planning session, one teacher volunteers to teach the co-planned lesson. Then, the team decides how they will collect student-centered data to determine if the strategies they planned addressed their guiding question.

There are many ways to gather student-centered data during an observation, including transcribing student responses during discussions, tallying the number of times students use content-specific words, or charting which students are responding. For example, if teachers want to know if the planned scaffolds are improving comprehension of grade-level texts, they can write down the discussion points students make during structured collaborative reading. If the focus is on improving students' academic writing, teachers could take snapshots of the students' writing process during independent writing time. To monitor if discussion moves are increasing students' use of academic language during group talk time, teachers can transcribe student responses during an academic discussion. Although only one teacher will deliver the initial lesson, the entire team shares the responsibility for the lesson.

During the Lesson: Teach and Observe

The next step in the lesson study is the observation. At this point, administrators may have to provide cover for a few classes, so the team members can observe the co-planned lesson. This additional administrative support is critical for the success of the lesson study. Having several additional sets of eyes and ears in the classroom focused on students' thinking and language use is key to the lesson study. Teaching and learning are complex, so the more the observers notice, the better (Collet, 2019). Observing teachers focus on gathering student-centered data. Depending on the guiding question, one observer may be focused on the big picture of the class environment and overall student engagement while another listens and records an academic discussion. Observers "are not there to critique the teacher, but to learn from watching the students navigate the complexities of teaching and learning" (Collet, 2019, p. 70). The focus of each phase of the lesson study is always on student learning.

After the Lesson: Collaborative Reflection

The final step of a lesson study is the reflection on the co-planned lesson with colleagues who observed the lesson. We recommend using a protocol to guide the reflection and keep it focused on student learning. An additional facilitator such as an instructional coach, school leader, or ELD specialist can help keep the team on track and center the reflection on collaborative learning. The protocol shared in Figure 7.10 provides a structure so that everyone on the team feels safe and has the opportunity to share their observations.

7.10 Protocol for Reflecting on Lesson Study

Time	Description of Step	Notes
5 minutes	**Instructor's Observations** The instructor restates the learning outcomes for the lesson and comments on any aspect of teaching the lesson such as the following: • Student engagement • Clarity of instruction • Any insights from the teacher's perspective	
10-15 minutes	**Share Observation Data** Each observing teacher • individually presents the data gathered and • explains what these data reveal about student learning.	
15 minutes	**Discussion of Data and Learning** After each team member has presented their data, they all discuss any of the following questions: • What are the implications for our teaching and learning from these data? • What new understandings or questions do we now have based on the data? • What did we learn from the lesson study cycle in general? Note: Build on each other's ideas and refer to the observational data or student work gathered during the discussion. Facilitator will make notes of key points raised.	
3-5 minutes	**Closing Comments** Facilitator • provides a synopsis of the discussion and • schedules the next lesson study.	**Next Steps for Instruction**

Available at **resources.corwin.com/Long-Term SuccessforExperiencedMLs**

The reflection protocol starts off with the teacher who implemented the co-planned lesson sharing their reflection on the lesson. They may also want to mention any changes made to the co-planned lesson, on-the-spot decisions they made, and anything unexpected that came up. Then, observers share actual student-centered data and discuss what those data reveal about student learning. For example, one observing teacher may share students' transcribed responses during discussions. The TEAM might notice if students used discipline-specific vocabulary, if they comprehended the main ideas, and if they used any of the scaffolds provided. Another observer may have transcribed all student questions during the class. In this case, the team would consider what those questions reveal about students' engagement, their comprehension, and their connection to background knowledge. Focusing the observations on individual students also loops back to collaboration at the individual student level.

During the reflection, the observing teachers may also discuss how they will revise the lesson or future lessons for their own students. If they are not going to teach the same lesson, they can commit to trying one of the strategies that worked in their next lesson. In this way, the lesson study can positively impact instruction well beyond one class. If there is a facilitator for the reflection session, they should provide a synopsis of the discussion, including next steps for instruction and information on the next lesson study. A lesson study is not just about improving that particular lesson; it is about improving the overall teaching and learning process (Collet, 2019). As Alice Collins, ELD Senior Consultant at the Colorado Department of Education, says, "Teaching is a growth profession" (A. Collins, personal communication, June 23, 2022). When teachers work collaboratively, they learn together and students benefit as a result.

LESSON STUDY IN MS. VALLADARES'S CLASSROOM

Ms. Valladares, Graciela's business teacher, had agreed to teach the lesson for the rest of the social studies team. She requested that the observers carefully watch the seven identified experienced multilinguals in the class throughout the lesson and transcribe their discussions in the small group activity. She was curious about their use of academic language during team interactions and wanted to know if the sensory words on the graphic organizer would make a difference for Graciela and others. During the co-planning session, the team of teachers decided to use the teaching and learning cycle shared in Chapter 6 to teach food-specific writing. To teach the sensory descriptions that students will need to write for their signature dish, the teachers co-created a model signature dish text for students to analyze.

When the lesson began, all of the observers sat near a different pair of students, including Graciela and her partner. The teachers transcribed what they heard the students saying and noted what the students wrote on their papers. At the end of the lesson, Ms. Valladares gathered the exit tickets to share with the team during the reflection on the lesson study.

During the reflection, the team followed the protocol described in Figure 7.10. After Ms. Valladares gave her impression of the lesson, the observers shared their transcribed sentences of the students' conversations. Ms. Valladares also shared the exit tickets for the seven experienced multilinguals, including Graciela. When the team reflected on the oral and written responses, they were pleased that the students used sensory adjectives and wrote their descriptions using the expected organization. However, they noticed that many students still used simple sentences like *Tacos are crispy* and *Falafel is crunchy* when describing their signature dishes, which made their oral and written language less persuasive. Ms. Valladares decided to keep these writing samples to analyze in more depth with the ELD teacher during next week's collaborative session, returning to the beginning of the collaborative implementation cycle with a focus on an individual student.

The team wondered how they could support students' use of more complex sentence structures. One of the teachers suggested that they could provide a couple of minutes for students to practice a sentence frame from the mentor text and ask them to use that structure in their written responses as well. They chose one sentence from the mentor text *Pad Thai is a sweet-savory dish that provides a treat for the taste buds* and gave students the frame: ______ is a ______ dish that ______. Since the rest of the team was planning to teach the same lesson the following day, they agreed to give students time to orally practice with that frame before writing.

The next day, the observing teachers made these changes to their lessons and support materials. When they reviewed their exit tickets, they were pleased that students had indeed written more complex sentences, including the one modeled. The lesson study gave them valuable insights and immediate ideas for improving their own practice.

TRY IT OUT

Getting Started With Lesson Study

If school leaders would like to get started with lesson study, we recommend following these steps:

1. Invite a department or grade-level team to participate in a lesson study.
2. Choose a facilitator for the co-planning and reflection sessions.
3. Create a schedule that includes cover for participating teachers during the
   - co-planning session,
   - classroom observation, and
   - reflection session.
4. Participate in each phase of the lesson study as a learner.
5. Celebrate the insights from the lesson study with the rest of the staff and encourage other teachers to participate in future sessions.

REFLECTION

- How could lesson study support the experienced multilinguals in your school?

____

____

____

____

- How could a lesson study contribute to ongoing, job-embedded professional learning?

____

____

____

____

CLOSING REMARKS

The collaborative implementation cycle and specific structures presented in this chapter can build the capacity of all educators to serve the needs of experienced multilinguals across the curriculum. Designing a master schedule that creates opportunities for collaboration is essential for bringing the instructional framework to educators across the school.

> Even if school leaders take just one step toward creating the conditions for long-term success, they can positively change the trajectory of experienced multilinguals.

Graciela and other experienced multilinguals in her high school are having a successful academic year. All of her content teachers now implement the instructional framework presented in this book, so instruction is consistent, comprehensible, connected to her background, and interactive. She has noticed that her teachers refer to her academic English goals and encourage her to speak more in class. Graciela still needs support when writing essays, but this year her teachers explicitly show her how to write each type of assignment and give her feedback along the way. Her grades have improved, and she is excited about taking an Advanced Placement Art History class next school year. The culture of the school makes Graciela feel welcomed, competent, and supported.

This culture of excellence does not happen by accident. Gradually, it is nurtured one teacher at a time, planting seeds of belief in what students can do. The famous American investor Warren Buffet once said, "Someone is sitting in the shade today because someone planted a tree a long time ago." The experienced multilinguals in schools today will one day be sitting in the shade, enjoying the fruits of their labor if we start today and come together to create the conditions for their long-term success.

CHAPTER SUMMARY

- Teacher collaboration is essential for long-term success of experienced multilinguals.
- The school's master schedule can open the door for successful, sustainable teacher collaboration.
- The instructional framework can be applied schoolwide through the collaborative implementation cycle.
- Teachers can collaborate focusing on individual students by analyzing their work samples and implementing their academic English plans.
- Co-planning summative assessments is a high-yield use of collaborative time.
- Co-planning lessons using a lesson planning template integrates content learning and academic English development.
- Teachers on a grade-level team or department team can collaborate on a lesson study for experienced multilinguals.

APPENDIX A

Thinking Verbs

Verb	Definition	Possible sentence starters/frames
Agree	Justify one's claim with reasoning and evidence.	• I agree that ___ because ___ • There are several advantages of ___ such as ___
Analyze	Break down into parts. Identify parts and relationships.	• ___ are essential for ___ • ___ supports the idea that ___ • ___ are connected to ___ • ___ consists of various ___, such as ___
Apply	Use knowledge and understanding in response to a given situation or real circumstances.	• ___ was used to ___ • I used ___ because ___ • ___ demonstrates how ___ • ___ shows the application of ___
Appraise	Evaluate, judge, or consider text or a piece of work.	• ___ uses more ___ • The part that functioned as hypothesized was ___ because ___ • ___ did not work well as a ___ • ___ was ineffective in ___ • The ___ was more effective than the ___, because ___
Classify	Arrange or order by class or category. Explain reasoning for grouping the items in this way.	• The things in this group all belong together because ___ • I grouped these items because ___

(Continued)

(Continued)

Verb	Definition	Possible sentence starters/frames
Comment	Give a judgment based on a given statement or result of a calculation.	• I disagree with ___ because ___ • I agree with ___ because ___ • ___ effectively ___ • ___ ineffectively ___ • ___ successfully ___ • ___ unsuccessfully ___
Compare	Highlight the similarities between two concepts or texts.	• There are several similarities between ___ and ___ such as ___, ___, and ___ • The common threads between ___ and ___ include ___, ___, and ___ • ___ has ___, while ___ has___
Conclude	State a judgment using reasoning.	• ___ suggests that ___ • ___ is the result of ___ • The results suggests ___
Connect	Show the relationship between two things.	• ___ relates to___ because ___ • ___ reminds me of ___ because ___
Contrast	Highlight the differences between two concepts or texts.	• These ___ differ in the following ways: • The main differences between ___ and ___ are ___ • Unlike ___, ___ has ___
Deduce	Reach a conclusion from the information given.	• ___ occurred because ___ • ___ is an effect of ___
Defend	Speak or write in favor of an idea, solution, or suggestion.	• ___ is more effective at ___ because ___ • It is best to use ___ because ___
Define	Give the precise meaning of a word, phrase, concept, or physical quantity.	• ___ is when ___ • ___ occurs when ___ • When ___, this is called ___ • ___ means ___

Verb	Definition	Possible sentence starters/frames
Demonstrate	Make clear with examples or practical application.	• ___ is one example of ___ • ___ demonstrates the principle of ___
Describe	Give a detailed account or picture of a situation, event, pattern, or process.	• ___ has ___, ___, and ___ • ___is ___, ___, and ___ • Some characteristics of __ are __ • The features of ___ are___
Disagree	Refute a statement; give the negative features; list the disadvantages.	• ___ does not show ___ because___ • ___ is not an example of ___ because ___
Discuss	Offer a considered and balanced review that includes a range of arguments, factors, or hypotheses. Opinions or conclusions should be presented clearly and supported by appropriate evidence.	• One perspective is from ___, who believes that ___ • Another perspective on ___ is ___ • An opposing perspective is ___ • One point of view is ___ • Some believe ___, while others suggest ___ • Considering these points, I conclude ___
Estimate	Approximately judge or calculate the amount, value, or extent of something	• ___ will be about ___ • ___ will most likely be ___ • It is probable that the sum of ___ will be ___
Evaluate	Make judgments by weighing the strengths and limitations.	• ___ has more advantages than ___ because ___ • A disadvantage of ___ is ___ because ___ • The limitations of ___ are ___ • Considering the evidence, ___ is the best/ most effective/ strongest ___

(Continued)

(Continued)

Verb	Definition	Possible sentence starters/frames
Examine	Consider an argument or concept in a way that uncovers the assumptions and interrelationships of the issue.	• ___ suggests that ___. However, ___ • ___ is believed to ___, but ___ • Close analysis shows that ___ • The data suggests that ___
Exemplify	Substantiate with an example.	• ___ is an example of ___ because ___ • For example, ___ • To illustrate, ___
Form an Opinion	State belief about a topic and the reasons for that belief.	• ___ is more ___ because ___ • ___ is less ___ because ___
Identify	Provide an answer from a number of possibilities. Recognize and state briefly a distinguishing factor or feature.	• ___ has ___, ___, and ___ • A feature of ___ is ___ • A characteristic of ___ is ___ • This is the ___, which ___
Infer	Deduce; reason from premises to a conclusion. Listen or read beyond what has been literally expressed.	• ___ suggests that ___ • The result of ___ is ___ • The cause of ___ is ___ • ___ is the consequence of ___
Interpret	Use knowledge and understanding to recognize trends and draw conclusions from given information.	• ___ increases from ___ to ___ • ___ decreases ___ to ___ • When ___ increases, ___ • When ___ decreases, ___
Investigate	Observe, study, or make a detailed and systematic examination, in order to establish facts and reach new conclusions.	• I observe that ___ • ___ has ___

Verb	Definition	Possible sentence starters/frames
Justify	Give valid reasons or evidence to support an answer or conclusion.	• ___ is important because ___ • ___ is more advantageous because ___ • ___ is less beneficial because ___ • Therefore, I believe ___
Label	Add title, labels, or brief explanation(s) to a diagram or graph.	• Use content-specific vocabulary • Use short content-specific phrases
List	Provide a series of ideas back to back without explanation.	• The causes of ___ are ___ and ___ • The consequences of ___ are ___ and ___ • The factors that ___ are ___ and ___
Make a Claim	State the main argument or position on a topic.	• ___ is caused by ___ • ___ is the result of ___ • ___ is better than ___ • ___ is worse than ___ • The main reason for ___ • The most significant ___ of ___
Outline	Give a brief account or summary.	• ___ wanted to ___, but ___ • In the beginning ___. In the middle, ___. At the end, ___
Paraphrase	Express meaning or text/video/quote using different words to provide clarity.	• In other words, this quote states ___. • ___ said ___ • The text states ___ • The author said ___
Persuade	Provide sound reasons for someone to do something.	• It is better to ___ because ___ • One reason to ___ is to ___ • The best way to ___ • It is advised that ___

(Continued)

(Continued)

Verb	Definition	Possible sentence starters/frames
Predict	Give an expected result of an upcoming action or event.	• When ___, this will ___ • When ___ increases, ___ • When ___ decreases, ___
Present/Report	Offer for display, observation, examination, or consideration.	• Features a report can include: labels, subtitles, heading, list of ideas, captions, timelines, graphs, statistics, anecdotes, dates, names, locations, significant events • This report focuses on ___ features / categories/ characteristics of ___. • This report presents/ provides/ attempts to ___.
Prove	Use a sequence of logical steps to obtain the required result in a formal way.	• ___ and ___ are ___ numbers. • Therefore, ___ is also ___. • If ___ , then ___ equals ___. • If ___ is true, then ___ is true.
Recall	Recognize or identify.	• ___ has ___ • ___ is ___
Recommend/ Suggest	Propose a solution, hypothesis, answer, or idea.	• A suggestion for ___ is to ___ • It is best to ___ because ___ • An advantage of ___ is ___ • I suggest ___ • I think we should ___
Recount/Retell	Present key details and essential concepts, events, plot of a story, or process in chronological order.	• ___ was ___ • ___ wanted to ___ • ___ tried to ___ • ___ needed ___
Reflect	Consider implications, perspectives, or effects of an experience.	• ___ could have improved if ___ • Next time, ___ • If the future, ___ • To improve on ___

Verb	Definition	Possible sentence starters/frames
Sequence	Arrange events or processes in a specific order.	• First, ___. Then, ___. After that, ___ • In the beginning, ___ • At the start, ___
State Causes	State in completed sentences any event or action that created or led to a reaction.	• ___ caused ___ because ___ • ___ impacted ___ by ___ • ___ altered ___ because ___ • ___ changed ___ by • ___ changed as a result of ___
State Effects	State in complete sentences the condition, occurrence, or result generated by one or more causes.	• Due to ___, it resulted in ___ • A consequence of ___ is ___ • Because of ___, it produced ___ • ___ changed as a result of ___ • ___ leads to ___
Summarize/ Synthesize	Produce a brief statement of the main points.	• The main idea of ___ is ___ • ___ occurs when ___ • ___ works by ___ • ___ is a period of time when ___ • This text/video argues that ___ • Basically, this text/video/concept is about ___

online resources Available at **resources.corwin.com/Long-Term SuccessforExperiencedMLs**

APPENDIX B

Sample Lesson Plans

These sample lesson plans are based on the scenarios with Graciela and Min Woo in each chapter. Each lesson plan is completed following the instructional framework for experienced multilinguals and the template presented in Chapter 7.

CHAPTER 1: ENGLISH LANGUAGE ARTS

End-of-Unit Summative Assessment

Performance-Based Assessment

Write any style of poem about an aspect of your life using at least three different types of figurative language.

Integrated Objective

What should students know or do by the end of the lesson?	Identify the types of figurative language used in a poem.
Exit Ticket Prompt	After reading the poem, identify one type of figurative language used.
Model Response	In the poem "Dreams" by Langston Hughes, the phrase "Life is a broken-winged bird" is a metaphor because it compares two unlike things: life and a bird.
Integrated Objective	Thinking verb + content + language use (by . . .) Identify one type of figurative language by using the structure *the ____ is a ____ because ____*.

Establish Comprehensible Input

Scaffold(s) Background, Sensory, Graphic, Interactive, Linguistic	**Interactive:** Students work in teams to identify and categorize the types of figurative language used in lines from several famous poems. They use a cooperative structure to take turns reading a line from a poem on a strip of paper and explaining which type of figurative language it is.

Structure Academic Output

Scaffold(s) Word, Sentence, Organization, and Context Dimension	**Word:** Provide visual word bank poster with names and concrete examples of each type of figurative language for each team.

Available at **resources.corwin.com/Long-Term SuccessforExperiencedMLs**

CHAPTER 2: GEOMETRY

<table>
<tr><td colspan="2">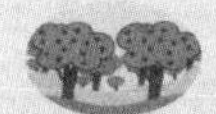 End-of-Unit Summative Assessment</td></tr>
<tr><td colspan="2">Performance-Based Assessment
Propose a street map to city planners for an expansion project using purposeful lines and angles.</td></tr>
<tr><td colspan="2"> Integrated Objective</td></tr>
<tr><td>What should students know or do by the end of the lesson?</td><td>Describe the position of lines (streets) and angles on their city map.</td></tr>
<tr><td>Exit Ticket Prompt</td><td>Justify the placement of two of the lines and angles on your street map.</td></tr>
<tr><td>Model Response</td><td>I drew two one-way streets that were parallel to each other, because they create a smoother traffic flow and more green space between the one-way streets. I created an obtuse angle in the northwest corner because it makes a large space for a public park at the edge of the city.</td></tr>
<tr><td>Integrated Objective</td><td>Thinking verb + content + language use (by . . .)
Justify the placement of the lines and angles on your street map by using the names of lines and angles and the structure I drew ___, because ___.</td></tr>
<tr><td colspan="2"> Establish Comprehensible Input</td></tr>
<tr><td>Scaffold(s)
Background, Sensory, Graphic, Interactive, Linguistic</td><td>Linguistic: Draw and label lines and angles on the board.
Background: Show basic street maps from students' home towns and local cities as models.</td></tr>
<tr><td colspan="2"> Structure Academic Output</td></tr>
<tr><td>Scaffold(s)
Word, Sentence, Organization, and Context Dimension</td><td>Sentence: Model how to justify the placement of lines and angles, and provide sentence frames.</td></tr>
</table>

Available at **resources.corwin.com/Long-Term SuccessforExperiencedMLs**

CHAPTER 3: SCIENCE

 **End-of-Unit Summative Assessment**	
Summative Exam: Students will complete a printed exam about energy transfer in ecosystems. The exam will consist of matching, multiple choice, fill in the blanks, and short response.	
 **Integrated Objective**	
What should students know or do by the end of the lesson?	Describe a trophic cascade.
Exit Ticket Prompt	Describe one of the trophic cascades that we learned today.
Model Response	One of the trophic cascades we learned today was about the wolves of Yellowstone. The wolves were one of the apex predators in the forest ecosystem. They preyed on primary consumers such as deer. When the wolves were hunted heavily, the deer's population increased significantly. They then overgrazed on producers such as seedlings. This caused more land erosion as there were fewer trees to hold the soil in place.
Integrated Objective	Thinking verb + content + language use (by . . .) Describe a trophic cascade by using words in a food chain.
 **Establish Comprehensible Input**	
Scaffold(s) Background, Sensory, Graphic, Interactive, Linguistic	**Sensory:** Cut out different organisms in different ecosystems and arrows for students to manipulate to show the energy transfer and the organisms in the food chain.
 **Structure Academic Output**	
Scaffold(s) Word, Sentence, Organization, and Context Dimension	**Linguistic:** Provide word bank that contains the content words *apex predator*, *secondary consumer*, *primary consumer*, *primary producers*.

Available at **resources.corwin.com/Long-Term SuccessforExperiencedMLs**

CHAPTER 4: VISUAL ARTS

<table>
<tr><th colspan="2"> End-of-Unit Summative Assessment</th></tr>
<tr><td colspan="2">Performance-Based Assessment
Create a line drawing of a cultural artifact for an art auction at school. Write a critique of your work referring to the lines and the tone; use the writing style of an art critic.</td></tr>
<tr><th colspan="2"> Integrated Objective</th></tr>
<tr><td>What should students know or do by the end of the lesson?</td><td>Use five line techniques in a still-life drawing of an artifact used in a cultural festival.</td></tr>
<tr><td>Exit Ticket Prompt</td><td>Explain why you chose to draw each line in your artifact.</td></tr>
<tr><td>Model Response</td><td>I drew a djembe, an African drum used in many traditional ceremonies. For this section of the drawing, I used horizontal lines in order to show how stable this artifact is. Horizontal lines usually indicate calmness and stability. I used zigzag lines above the horizontal lines to indicate action and excitement. Although this djembe is stable, it also creates dynamic, exciting music.</td></tr>
<tr><td>Integrated Objective</td><td>Thinking verb + content + language use (by . . .)
Explain why you chose to draw at least two lines in your artifact by stating the names of the lines and the phrase in order to show.</td></tr>
<tr><th colspan="2"> Establish Comprehensible Input</th></tr>
<tr><td>Scaffold(s)
Background, Sensory, Graphic, Interactive, Linguistic</td><td>Sensory and linguistic: Label an example drawing of djembe with names of lines, and annotate the purposes for those lines.
Interactive: Students tell their partner which lines they used and the purpose of those lines using the phrase in order to show before writing the exit ticket.</td></tr>
<tr><th colspan="2"> Structure Academic Output</th></tr>
<tr><td>Scaffold(s)
Word, Sentence, Organization, and Context Dimension</td><td>Sentence: Provide a sentence frame I used a ___ line in order to show ____.</td></tr>
</table>

Available at **resources.corwin.com/Long-Term SuccessforExperiencedMLs**

 **End-of-Unit Summative Assessment**	
Performance-Based Assessment Students will work in pairs to design a miniature cardboard bridge that applies the physics of tension and compression. Students will describe their design plan during a presentation and in a report.	
Integrated Objective	
What should students know or do by the end of the lesson?	Describe the tension and compression acting on a bridge design.
Exit Ticket Prompt	Describe where tension and compression are acting on your bridge design.
Model Response	We decided to design a truss bridge. The top beam of the truss bridge experiences compression because it is being pulled down by the rest of the bridge and the load. To balance this compression, the bottom beam experiences tension because it is being stretched by the top beam. The triangular supports in the middle provide additional compression while the vertical supports produce tension.
Integrated Objective	Thinking verb + content + language use (by . . .) Describe the tension and compression in your bridge design by describing how the different members (parts) experience one of these forces.
 **Establish Comprehensible Input**	
Scaffold(s) Background, Sensory, Graphic, Interactive, Linguistic	**Sensory:** Students will read the labeled diagram of different types of bridges in a Britannica article. **Interactive:** Students will co-read the Britannica article, stopping at each sentence to explain what that sentence means.
 **Structure Academic Output**	
Scaffold(s) Word, Sentence, Organization, and Context Dimension	**Organization:** Provide the following paragraph frame: *We decided to design a . . . bridge. The . . . of the . . . bridge experiences . . . because . . . To balance this . . ., the . . . experiences ... because . . .*

Available at **resources.corwin.com/Long-Term SuccessforExperiencedMLs**

CHAPTER 6: SOCIAL STUDIES

End-of-Unit Summative Assessment

Performance-Based Assessment

Students will create an exhibit for a traveling Greek museum. Students will pretend they are museum curators and have to work in teams to design an exhibit to explain how Greek philosophies influenced both ancient Greek society and many modern societies.

Integrated Objective

What should students know or do by the end of the lesson?	Describe how Greek philosophy influenced ancient Greek society.
Exit Ticket Prompt	Describe how a particular Greek philosophy influenced Greek society.
Model Response	One of the most important Greek philosophies was democracy. This philosophy influenced society by expecting the male children to attend school so they could read, write, and speak in public. For example, families would pay for their sons to have tutors who would teach them to read, write, and speak. The citizens needed to read proposed laws, write laws clearly, and argue for why these laws should exist or not exist.
Integrated Objective	Thinking verb + content + language use (by . . .) Describe how Greek philosophies influenced Greek society by providing an example.

Establish Comprehensible Input

Scaffold(s) Background, Sensory, Graphic, Interactive, Linguistic	**Sensory:** Provide a video about Greek philosophies. **Linguistic and interactive:** Pause after teaching each philosophy. Have students talk about the philosophy in pairs. Clarify understanding as a whole group. Repeat.

Structure Academic Output

Scaffold(s) Word, Sentence, Organization, and Context Dimension	**Word:** Provide a labeled visual for the main Grecian philosophies. **Organization:** One of the most important Greek philosophies was ... This philosophy influenced society by ... For example, . . .

Available at **resources.corwin.com/Long-Term SuccessforExperiencedMLs**

CHAPTER 7: BUSINESS

End-of-Unit Summative Assessment

Performance-Based Assessment:

Create a business plan for a food truck, and write a persuasive and profitable business plan to attract investors.

Integrated Objective

What should students know or do by the end of the lesson?	Write a paragraph that uses sensory details to describe a signature dish.
Exit Ticket Prompt	Describe your signature dish with sensory details.
Model Response	*Pad Thai is a sweet-savory dish that provides a treat for the taste buds. Lightly coated with a golden tamarind sauce, the straw-thin rice noodles form the base for the Kingdom of Thailand's national dish. The essential ingredients of chopped onion, egg, crispy bean sprouts, and warm roasted ground peanuts add texture to the salty, nutty taste. Customers customize the dish by adding their choice of shrimp, chicken, or tofu.*
Integrated Objective	Thinking verb + content + language use (by . . .) Describe your signature dish by using adjectives from the five senses to highlight the flavors of the dish.

Establish Comprehensible Input

Scaffold(s) Background, Sensory, Graphic, Interactive, Linguistic	**Linguistic:** Provide an annotated mentor text of descriptions of signature dishes from restaurant menus and websites.

Structure Academic Output

Scaffold(s) Word, Sentence, Organization, Context Dimension	**Word:** Provide a table with examples of highly effective sensory-based adjectives, verbs, and phrases.

Available at **resources.corwin.com/Long-Term SuccessforExperiencedMLs**

GLOSSARY

Term	Definition
Academic English plan	Plan that describes students' linguistic strengths and recommends ways to support their development
Academic language	Discipline-specific and transferable vocabulary, sentence structures, and discourse patterns needed to comprehend and communicate ideas in content areas
Activating prior knowledge	Linking students' existing knowledge to new learning
Assessment template	Document for scaffolding performance-based assessments that is a hybrid between written instructions and a graphic organizer
Building background knowledge	Actions teachers do to make new content more familiar
Comprehensible input	Making ideas understandable
Discipline-specific language	Words and phrases specific to each content area
DLL	Dual language learner
ELL	English language learner
English-medium schools	Schools where English is the primary language of instruction
Exam engineering	Employing techniques to scaffold summative tests
Exit ticket	A short written or verbal formative assessment given at the end of the lesson
FELL	Former English language learner
FEP	Fully English proficient
Graphic scaffolds	Present information through charts, graphs, tables, and timelines that morph numbers and data points into visuals and images
Instruction boxes	Specific instructions, prompts, and guiding questions students need to follow to engage successfully in the assessment

(Continued)

(Continued)

Term	Definition
Integrated objective	Statement that defines the desired outcomes for both the content and the academic language students need to use
Interactive scaffolds	Structures that establish comprehensible input through collaboration
Learning strategies	Any action a student does to boost their understanding of new content and use of discipline-specific language
LEP	Limited English proficient
Lesson study	A collaborative form of job-embedded professional learning in which teams of teachers plan, teach, and reflect on a lesson
Linguistic scaffolds	Make spoken and printed ideas more accessible
LTEL	Long-term English learner
Metacognition	Awareness and understanding of your own thinking process
ML	Multilingual learner
Multilinguals	Students who speak more than one language
NEP	Non-English proficient
Performance-based assessment	Long-term project that requires the application of content concepts and skills
PHLOTE	Primary home language other than English
Reclassified	When students classified as English learners (ELs) achieve a state-required level of English proficiency and receive the status "fully English proficient (FEP)"; also known as "redesignation" or "exit" in some states
Scaffold	Anything that temporarily supports students in engaging in tasks that they would not be able to do independently
Sensory scaffolds	Employ students' senses to learn content
SIFE	Students with interrupted formal education
SLIFE	Students with limited or interrupted formal education
Student response box	Box containing linguistic scaffolds such as sentence starters, sentence frames, and paragraph frames to structure student output
Unpack academic language	Analyze academic language used in the curriculum to make it explicit to students
Workshopping the assessment	Devoting a mini-lesson to teach one particular section of the assessment at a time

REFERENCES

Ascenzi-Moreno, L., Kleyn, T., Menken, K., Collins, B., Ebe, A., Hesson, S., & Pappas, L. (2013). *A CUNY-NYSIEB framework for the education of "long-term English learners": 6-12 grades*. CUNY-NYSIEB.

Auslander, L., & Yip, J. (2022). *School-wide systems for multilingual learner success*. Routledge.

AVID. (2016). *Closing the achievement gap in education*. https://www.avid.org/

Baker, S. K., Geva, E., Lesnick, J., McCallum, D., & Monroe Gersten, R. (2014). *Teaching academic content and literacy to English learners in elementary and middle school*. Institute of Education Sciences.

Batalova, J., Fix, M., & Murray, J. (2007). *The demography and literacy of adolescent English learners: A report to the Carnegie Corporation of New York*. Migration Policy Institute.

Beck, I. L., Mckeown, M. G., & Kucan, L. (2002). *Bringing words to life: Robust vocabulary instruction*. Guilford Press.

Beers, K. (2003). *When kids can't read: What teachers can do*. Heinemann.

Belenky, D. M., & Nokes, T. J. (2009). Examining the role of manipulatives and metacognition on engagement, learning, and transfer. *Journal of Problem Solving*, 2(2), 102-128.

Benson, M. (2019, September 4). Types of bridges. The 7 main types. *EngineeringClicks*. https://www.engineeringclicks.com/types-of-bridg es/#:~:text=The%20deck%20of%20the%20suspension

Billings, E., & Walqui, A. (2017). *De-mystifying complex texts: What are "complex" texts and how can we ensure ELLs/MLLs can access them?* New York State Education Department, Office of Bilingual Education and World Languages. http://www.nysed.gov/common/nysed/files/programs/bilingual-ed/de-mystifying_complex_texts-2.pdf

Brooks, M. (2016, May 16). Does the long-term English learner label hurt the students it was intended to help? [Blog post]. *MANEKA DEANNA BROOKS, PHD*. https://brooksphd.com/blog/2016/5/21/does-the-long-term-english-learn er-label-hurt-the-students-it-was-intended-to-help

Brooks, M. (2020). *Transforming literacy education for long-term English learners: Recognizing brilliance in the undervalued*. Routledge.

Buenrostro, M., & Maxwell-Jolly, J. (2021). Renewing our promise: Research and recommendations to support California's long-term English learners. *Californians Together*. https://californianstogether.org/long-term-english-learners/

Calderón, M. (2007). *Teaching reading to English language learners, Grades 6-12: A framework for improving achievement in the content areas*. Corwin.

Calderón, M., & Minaya-Rowe, L. (2011). *Preventing long-term ELs: Transforming schools to meet core standards*. Corwin.

Calderón, M., Staehr Fenner, D., Honigsfeld, A., Slakk, S., Zacarian, D., Dove, M., Gottlieb, M., Ward Singer, T., & Soto, I. (2020). *Breaking down the wall: Essential shifts for English learners' success*. Corwin.

Carlo, M. S., August, D., McLaughlin, B., Snow, C., Dressler, C., Lippman, D., Lively, T., & White, C. (2004). Closing the gap: Addressing the vocabulary needs of English-language learners in bilingual and mainstream classrooms. *Reading Research Quarterly, 39*(2), 188–215. https://doi.org/10.1598/rrq.39.2.3

Chamot, A., & O'Malley, M. (2001). *The CALLA handbook: Implementing the cognitive academic language learning approach.* Addison-Wesley.

Chiesi, H. L., Spilich, G. J., & Voss, J. F. (1979). Acquisition of domain-related information in relation to high and low domain knowledge. *Journal of Verbal Learning & Verbal Behavior, 18*(3), 257–273. https://doi.org/10.1016/S0022-5371(79)90146-4

Collet, V. (2019). *Collaborative lesson study: Revisioning teacher professional development.* Teachers College Press.

Collier, V., & Thomas, W. (2002). *A national study of school effectiveness for language minority students' long-term academic achievement.* University of California, Berkeley, Center for Research on Education, Diversity, and Excellence.

Collier, V., & Thomas, W. (2018). *Transforming secondary education: Middle and high school dual language programs.* Fuente Press.

Cooper, A. (2020). *And justice for ELs: A leader's guide to creating and sustaining equitable schools.* Corwin.

Covey, S. R. (2014). *The 7 habits of highly effective people: Powerful lessons in personal change.* Simon & Schuster.

Cummins, J. (1981). Age on arrival and immigrant second language learning in Canada: A reassessment. *Applied Linguistics,* 2(2), 132–149. https://doi.org/10.1093/applin/2.2.132

Cummins, J. (2009). *Supporting ESL students in learning the language of Science.* Research Into Practice, Pearson. https://assets.pearsonschool.com/asset_mgr/legacy/200728/SciAut0404585MonoCummins_844_1.pdf

Cummins, J. (2021). *Rethinking the education of multilingual learners: A critical analysis of theoretical concepts.* Multilingual Matters.

Cummins, J., & Early, M. (2015). *Big ideas for expanding minds: Teaching English language learners across the curriculum.* Pearson.

Dare, B., & Polias, J. (2020). *Teaching in English in multilingual classrooms: Language in learning across the curriculum: Participant manual.* Lexis Education.

Darling-Hammond, L., Wei, R., Andree, A., Richardson, N., & Orphanos, S. (2009). *Professional learning in the learning profession: A status report on teacher development in the United States and abroad.* National Staff Development Council. https://learningforward.org/docs/default-source/pdf/nsdcstudytechnicalreport2009.pdf

Derewianka, B., & Jones, P. (2016). *Teaching language in context* (2nd ed.). Oxford University Press.

Dutro, S., & Moran, C. (2002). Rethinking English language instruction: An architectural approach. In G. G. Garcia (Ed.), *English learners: Reaching the highest level of English literacy* (pp. 227–258). International Reading Association.

Echevarria, J. (2016, March 30). Are language frames good for English learners? [Blog post]. *Reflections on Teaching English Learners.* https://www.janaechevarria.com/?p=191

Echevarría, J., Vogt, M., & Short, D. (2017). *Making content comprehensible for English learners: The SIOP model.* Pearson.

EdPod. (2018, May 22). Episode 9. Long term English learners. Separating myth from reality. [Podcast]. *EdPod.* https://edpod.tv/podcast/episode-9-long-term-english-learners-separating-myth-from-reality/

Every Student Succeeds Act. (2015). Public Law 114–95. https://www.congress.gov/114/plaws/publ95/PLAW-114publ95.pdf

Farstrup, A. E., & Samuels, S. (2009). *What research has to say about vocabulary instruction*. International Reading Association.

Fisher, D. (2021, March 23). *Removing labels: Tools and strategies that ensure success in learning*. World Education Summit.

Fleenor, S., & Beene, T. (2019). *Teaching science to English learners*. Seidlitz Education.

Fogarty, R., & Pete, B. M. (2007). *The adult learner: Some things we know*. Corwin.

García, O., Ibarra Johnson, S., & Seltzer, K. (2016). *The translanguaging classroom: Leveraging student bilingualism for learning*. Caslon.

Gay, G. (2018). *Culturally responsive teaching: Theory, research, and practice* (3rd ed.). Teachers College Press.

Gibbons, P. (2015). *Scaffolding language, scaffolding learning: Teaching English language learners in the mainstream classroom* (2nd ed.). Heinemann.

González, N., Moll, L. C., & Amanti, C. (2005). *Funds of knowledge: Theorizing practice in households, communities, and classrooms*. Erlbaum.

Gottlieb, M. (2013). *Essential actions: A handbook for implementing WIDA's framework for English language development standards*. University of Wisconsin System, Board of Regents, WIDA Consortium.

Gottlieb, M. (2016). *Assessing English language learners: Bridges to educational equity: Connecting academic language proficiency to student achievement*. Corwin.

Gottlieb, M. H., & Ernst-Slavit, G. (2014). *Academic language in diverse classrooms: Definitions and contexts*. Corwin.

Gration, E. (2021, November 9). Bilingualism statistics in 2021: US, UK & Global [Blog post]. *Preply*. https://preply.com/en/blog/bilingualism-statistics/

Graves, M. F., August, D., & Mancilla-Martinez, J. (2013). *Teaching vocabulary to English language learners*. Teachers College Press.

Haas, E., & Brown, J. (2019). *Supporting English learners in the classroom: Best practices for distinguishing language acquisition from learning disabilities*. Teachers College Press.

Haas, E., Huang, M., & Tran, L. (2014). *The characteristics of long-term English language learner students and struggling reclassified fluent English proficient students in Arizona*. https://files.eric.ed.gov/fulltext/ED585521.pdf

Halliday, M. A. K. (1993). Towards a language-based theory of learning. *Linguistics and Education*, 5(2), 93–116. https://doi.org/10.1016/0898-5898(93)90026-7

Hammond, Z. (2015). *Culturally responsive teaching and the brain: Promoting authentic engagement and rigor among culturally and linguistically diverse students*. Corwin.

Harmon, J., Wood, K., & Hedrick, W. (2008). Vocabulary instruction in middle and secondary content classrooms: Understandings and direction from research. In A. Farstrup & S. J. Samuels (Eds.), *What research has to say about vocabulary instruction* (pp. 150–181). International Reading Association.

Hattie, J. (2012). *Visible learning for teachers: Maximizing impact on learning*. Routledge.

Hattie, J. (2021, August). [Collective teacher efficacy data]. *Visible Learning Meta^x^*. Corwin. https://www.visiblelearningmetax.com/Influences

Haynes, J., & Zacarian, D. (2010). *Teaching English language learners across the content areas*. ASCD.

Heineke, A. J., & McTighe, J. (2018). *Using understanding by design in the culturally and linguistically diverse classroom*. ASCD.

Honigsfeld, A. (2019). *Growing language & literacy: Strategies for English learners: Grades K-8*. Heinemann.

Honigsfeld, A., & Dove, M. G. (2019). *Collaborating for English learners: A foundational guide to integrated practices*. Corwin.

Honigsfeld, A., Dove, M. G., Cohan, A., & McDermott Goldman, C. (2022). *From equity insights to action: Critical strategies for teaching multilingual learners*. Corwin.

Huynh, T. (2016, September 2). *#3. Making reading visible to MLs—ELL strategies*. TanKHuynh. https://tankhuynh.com/visible-reading/

Huynh, T. (2019, December 6). *#107. Design your tests with MLs in mind*. TanKHuynh. https://tankhuynh.com/design-assessments/

Huynh, T. (2020, July 27). *Five time-saving co-planning strategies* (No. 118) [Video podcast episode]. TanKHuynh. https://tankhuynh.com/5-co-planning-strategies

Huynh, T. (2021a, April 18). *BATS: Co-planning deliverables* (No. 134) [Video podcast episode]. TanKHuynh. https://tankhuynh.com/bats/

Huynh, T. (2021b, November 22). *The collaborative instructional cycle* (No. 140) [Video podcast episode]. TanKHuynh. https://tankhuynh.com/collaborative-instructional-cycle/

Huynh, T. (2023, January 5). *Leading schoolwide changes for LTELs w/ Jen Hanson* (No. 145) [Video podcast episode]. YouTube. https://youtu.be/GyKnGaehHrA

International Baccalaureate. (2019, October 11). *International education*. https://www.ibo.org/

Isola, R. R., & Cummins, J. (2020). *Transforming Sanchez School: Shared leadership, equity, and evidence*. Caslon.

Kibler, A. K., & Valdés, G. (2016). Conceptualizing language learners: Socioinstitutional mechanisms and their consequences. *Modern Language Journal, 100*(Suppl. 1), 96–116. https://doi.org/10.1111/modl.12310

Killion, J. (2015, October). *High-quality collaboration benefits teachers and students*. Learning Forward. https://learningforward.org/journal/october-2015-issue/high-quality-collaboration-benefits-teachers-and-students/

Kim, W. G., & García, S. B. (2014). Long-term English language learners' perceptions of their language and academic learning experiences. *Remedial and Special Education, 35*(5), 300–312. https://doi.org/10.1177/0741932514525047

Knight, J. (2012). *High-impact instruction: A framework for great teaching*. Corwin.

Krashen, S. D. (1982). *Principles and practice in second language acquisition*. Pergamon Press.

Lazarín, M. (2020, June 12). *COVID-19 spotlights the inequities facing English learner students, as nonprofit organizations seek to mitigate challenges*. Migrationpolicy.org. https://www.migrationpolicy.org/news/covid-19-inequities-english-learner-students

Lewis, C. (2022). *What is lesson study?* The Lesson Study Group at Mills College. https://lessonresearch.net/about-lesson-study/what-is-lesson-study-2/

Little, D., Dam, L., & Legenhausen, L. (2017). *Language learner autonomy: Theory, practice and research*. Multilingual Matters.

Macon, J., Bewell, D., & Vogt, M. E. (1991). *Response to literature: Grades K-8*. International Reading Association.

Marley, S. C., & Carbonneau, K. J. (2014). Theoretical perspectives and empirical evidence relevant to classroom instruction with manipulatives. *Educational Psychology Review, 26*(1), 1–7. https://doi.org/10.1007/s10648-014-9257-3

Marzano, R. J., Pickering, D. J., & Pollock, J. E. (2001). *Classroom instruction that works: Research-based strategies for increasing student achievement*. Association for Supervision and Curriculum Development.

McGregor, T. (2018). *Ink and ideas: Sketchnotes for engagement, comprehension, and thinking*. Heinemann.

McLuhan, M. (1964). *Understanding media: The extensions of man*. New American Library.

Menken, K., Kleyn, T., & Chae, N. (2012). Spotlight on "long-term English language learners": Characteristics and prior schooling experiences of an invisible population. *International Multilingual Research Journal, 6*(2), 121–142. https://doi.org/10.1080/19313152.2012.665822

Mercer, N. (1995). *The guided construction of knowledge: Talk amongst teachers and learners.* Multilingual Matters.

Molina, C. (2012). *The problem with math is English: A language-focused approach to helping all students develop a deeper understanding of mathematics.* Jossey-Bass.

Moll, L. C. (2019). Elaborating funds of knowledge: Community-oriented practices in international contexts. *Literacy Research: Theory, Method, and Practice, 68*(1), 130–138. https://doi.org/10.1177/2381336919870805

Motley, N. (2016). *Talk read talk write: A practical routine for learning in all content areas (K-12).* Seidlitz Education.

National Center for Education Statistics. (2021). *English language learners in public schools.* U.S. Department of Education, Institute of Education Sciences. https://nces.ed.gov/programs/coe/indicator/cgf/english-learners

National School Reform Faculty. (2022). *What is Critical Friends Group© work?* https://nsrfharmony.org/whatiscfgwork/

Nguyen, D., & Commins, N. (2020). *Teaching for equity: The CLEAR paradigm* (Working Paper No. 2020-4). University of Wisconsin–Madison, Wisconsin Center for Education Research.

Novak, J. D., & Cañas, A. J. (2006). The origins of the concept mapping tool and the continuing evolution of the tool. *Information Visualization, 5*(3), 175–184. https://doi.org/10.1057/palgrave.ivs.9500126

Novak, K. (2014). *UDL now! A teacher's Monday-morning guide to implementing Common Core Standards using universal design learning.* Cast Professional Publishing.

OELA Podcast Series. (2021). *English learners in secondary schools: Trajectories, transitions, and promising practices* [Podcast]. National Clearinghouse for English Language Acquisition. https://ncela.ed.gov/teacher-resources#ELSecondary1

Okhremtchouk, I., Levine-Smith, J., & Clark, A. (2018). The web of reclassification for English language learners—A cyclical journey waiting to be interrupted: Discussion of realities, challenges, and opportunities. *Educational Leadership Administration: Teaching and Program Development, 29*(1), 1–13.

Olsen, L. (2014, March). *Meeting the unique needs of long term English language learners: A guide for educators.* Californians Together & National Education Association. https://californianstogether.org/meeting-the-unique-needs-of-long-term-english-language-learners/

Ottow, S. B. (2019). *The language lens for content classrooms: A guide for K-12 teachers of English and academic language learners.* Learning Sciences International.

Paris, D., & Alim, H. S. (2017). *Culturally sustaining pedagogies: Teaching and learning for justice in a changing world.* Teachers College Press.

Rafa, A., Erwin, B., Brixey, E., McCann, M., & Perez, Z, Jr. (2020, May 27). *50-State comparison: English learner policies.* Education Commission of the States. https://www.ecs.org/50-state-comparison-english-learner-policies/

Robinson, S. K. (2010). *Teachers are like gardeners* [Video]. YouTube. https://www.youtube.com/watch?v=aT_121H3kLY&t=1s

Rothery, J. (1996). Making changes: Developing an educational linguistics. In G. Williams (Ed.), *Literacy in society* (pp. 86–123). Longman.

Sahakyan, N., & Poole, G. (2022). "Every" student succeeds? Academic trends at the intersection of (long-term) English learner and IEP status. *Journal of Education for Students Placed at Risk (JESPAR)*. https://www.tandfonline.com/doi/full/10.1080/10824669.2022.2123328

Salva, C. (2017). *Boosting achievement*. Canter.

Schleppegrell, M. (2004). *The language of schooling: A functional linguistics perspective*. Routledge.

Shevrin Venet, A. (2021). *Equity-centered trauma-informed education*. Norton.

Snyder, S., & Staehr Fenner, D. (2021). *Culturally responsive teaching for multilingual learners: Tools for equity*. Corwin.

Soto, I. (2021). *Shadowing multilingual learners*. SAGE.

Staehr Fenner, D. (2014). *Advocating for English learners: A guide for educators*. Corwin.

Takanishi, R., & Le Menestrel, S. (Eds.). (2017). *Promoting the educational success of children and youth learning English: Promising futures*. National Academies Press.

Thompson, K. (2015). Questioning the long-term English learner label: How categorization can blind us to students' abilities. *Teachers College Record: The Voice of Scholarship in Education, 117*(12), 1-50.

Thompson, K. D., & Rodriguez-Mojica, C. (2022). Individualized language plans: A potential tool for collaboration to support multilingual students. *Journal of Education for Students Placed at Risk (JESPAR)*, 1-25. https://doi.org/10.1080/10824669.2022.2123330

Tovani, C. (2000). *I read it, but I don't get it: Comprehension strategies for adolescent readers*. Stenhouse.

U.S. Department of Justice & U.S. Department of Education. (2015). *Dear colleague letter: English learner students and limited English proficient parents*. U.S. Department of Justice Civil Rights Division & U.S. Department of Education Office for Civil Rights. https://www2.ed.gov/about/offices/list/ocr/letters/colleague-el-201501.pdf

Uro, G., & Lai, D. (2019). *English language learners in America's great city schools: Demographics, achievement, and staffing*. Council of the Great City Schools. https://files.eric.ed.gov/fulltext/ED597915.pdf

Vygotsky, L. (1978). *Mind in society: The development of higher psychological processes*. Harvard University Press.

Walqui, A., & van Lier, L. (2010). *Scaffolding the academic success of adolescent English language learners: A pedagogy of promise*. WestEd.

WIDA. (2012). *2012 Amplification of the English language development standards: Kindergarten-Grade 12*. University of Wisconsin System, Board of Regents, WIDA Consortium.

WIDA. (2020). *WIDA English language development standards framework, 2020 edition: Kindergarten-Grade 12*. University of Wisconsin System, Board of Regents, WIDA Consortium.

Wiggins, G. P., & McTighe, J. (2005). *Understanding by design* (2nd ed.). Association for Supervision and Curriculum Development.

Yzquierdo, M. (2017). *Pathways to greatness for ELL newcomers: A comprehensive guide for schools and teachers*. Canter.

Zacarian, D., Calderon, M., & Gottlieb, M. (2021). *Beyond crises: Overcoming linguistic and cultural inequities in communities, schools, and classrooms*. Corwin.

Zwiers, J. (2008). *Building academic language: Essential practices for content classrooms, Grades 5-12*. Jossey-Bass.

Zwiers, J., & Crawford, M. (2011). *Academic conversations: Classroom talk that fosters critical thinking and content understandings*. Stenhouse.

Zwiers, J. (2014). *Building academic language: Meeting common core standards across disciplines, Grades 5-12*. Jossey-Bass.

INDEX

Collaborate with us!

Tan Huynh

Tan applies research to his classes and shares streamline approaches that work for busy teachers. He offers interactive and customized professional learning opportunities that show how to implement the research using classroom examples. His workshops can be virtual, in-person, synchronous, or asynchronous to meet the needs of schools. Tan is often requested to provide workshops on topics such as

- Teacher collaboration
- Scaffolding learning in content classes
- Culturally responsive instruction
- Academic language development

Learn more about Tan's work at tankhuynh.com

Beth Skelton

Beth provides customized virtual and on site professional learning, coaching, and consulting services designed to meet the needs of multilingual learners in each unique school or organization. Beth and Tan also offer an on-demand, asynchronous book study course for *Long-Term Success for Experienced Multilinguals*. Frequently requested professional learning topics include

- Teaching academic language through content
- Developing academic vocabulary
- Scaffolding grade-level texts for multilingual learners
- Developing discipline-specific writing

Learn more about Beth's work at bethskelton.com

EQ22204700

CORWIN